Audubon

BIRDFEEDER
HANDBOOK

Audubon

BIRDFEEDER
HANDBOOK

ROBERT BURTON

FOREWORD
Stephen W. Kress

COVENT
GARDEN
BOOKS

Editor Candida Ross-MacDonald
Designer Phil Kay
U.S. Editors Jeanette Mall, Jill Hamilton
Managing Editor Krystyna Mayer
Managing Art Editor Derek Coombes
Production Antony Heller

This American Edition, 2005

Published in the United States by DK Publishing, Inc.,
375 Hudson Street, New York, New York 10014

www.dk.com

Burton, Robert, 1941–
 National Audubon Society North American birdfeeder handbook / by
Robert Burton : introduction by Stephen W. Kress. — 1st American ed.
  p. cm.
 Includes bibliographical references and index
 ISBN 978-0-7566-1722-6
 1. Birds, Attracting of. 2. Birds—North America—Identification. 3. Bird
feeders. I. Title. II. Title: North American birdfeeder handbook.
QL676. 5.B87 1992
598'.0723473—dc20   91–58218
                                                                  CIP

Reproduced by J. Film Process, Singapore
Printed and bound in China by L.Rex Printing Co., Ltd.

CONTENTS

· FOREWORD ·

Feeding and watching birds have become favorite pastimes in the United States and Canada. The U.S. Fish and Wildlife Service recently found that roughly one-third of the population of the United States feed wild birds. Many just toss out scraps, but some 43 percent serve seed, suet, and sugar water. Robert Burton's book provides this growing audience with an excellent guide to the identification, feeding, and observation of backyard birds.

Attracting birds can offer benefits to birds and observers. It is surprising that, despite the fact that over one billion pounds of birdseed are dispensed in the United States each year, relatively little is known about the impact of this feeding. There is a notion that populations would tumble without bird food welfare, but recent studies show that birds eat only a fraction of their food at feeders. Even where choice seeds are put out, seed is not always the preferred food.

Food at feeders does not usually lead to higher bird populations, but when natural supplies fail (in lean beechnut seasons, for example), feeders may be crucial. Severe weather such as heavy snow or ice storms can temporarily remove natural supplies in winter or early spring when food is already scarce. Even though they are well adapted for life in the winter, extended cold periods also stress birds, especially birds that have a small body mass, like chickadees, titmice, creepers, and kinglets. Birds that frequent feeders may also have greater survival rates because they spend less time foraging and can be more alert to approaching predators.

But feeders are not without risks because they expose birds to new threats such as window collisions, predation from cats, and exposure to diseased birds. As researchers look at food needs in different parts of bird ranges and at different seasons, the benefits and problems will become apparent.

Watching birds through a window can be both entertaining and instructive when the behavior patterns of the performers are known. Even the most abundant species, such as house sparrows and starlings, can entertain for hours. This is probably the most important benefit of feeding wild birds. Bird attraction helps close the distance between birds and people. This link often nurtures a life-long interest in wildlife and conservation. The simple act of filling feeders is a behavioral statement that soon aligns attitudes. I hold that one of the best ways to snag a future environmentalist is to recruit a new member to the bird-feeding legion. Those who nurture birds are more likely to become informed about the larger issues of environmental quality and preservation.

Picky eaters
Black-capped chickadees take only about one-quarter of their food from feeders, preferring to eat insects.

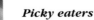

6

This book is an excellent introduction to over 70 of the nearly 800 species that occur on the continent, giving their plumages, voices, and feeding and nesting habits. Where possible, Burton recommends foods and nestboxes. By focusing on this group of common and conspicuous birds, readers will not only close the distance between themselves and the birds, but also come closer to understanding why we should all be concerned about the future of birds.

Yet the book does not stop with bird identification – it shows the reader how birds fly, communicate, nest, and migrate. Here are explanations of behaviors that might be overlooked or misunderstood, such as the body language that birds use and the functions of birdsong in territory defense and mating. Such observation can go a long way toward teaching biology and evolution. Like all vertebrates, birds face challenges such as finding mates, defending territories, avoiding competition, and surviving harsh weather.

Burton also gives guidance on creating the ideal feeding station and yard habitat, with easy-to-build plans and advice on foods, water, and shelter. The best place to start helping wildlife is your own property. From this start, we must move to protecting wild habitats, working with groups such as the National Audubon Society and others.

Well groomed *Preening, sunbathing, and anting all have important functions.*

Each of the 9,000 bird species sharing the Earth with us is an irreplaceable treasure whose songs, colors, and vibrant energy enrich the human experience. Only a knowledgeable and caring public can guarantee a future for all the species we know today.

Stephen W. Kress, Ph.D.

Birds of a feather *Birds form flocks – even of mixed species, as here – for feeding, defense against predators, and migration flights.*

CHAPTER ONE

BIRDS IN THE YARD

AS THE CONTINENT CHANGES and more land is used to house an ever-growing human population, yards, city parks, and derelict land have become important as bird habitats. This chapter presents a bird's-eye view of the yard: it covers the birds that are likely to visit, what features they find attractive in a yard, and how you can improve your yard to tempt more birds to spend time there. Success in attracting birds is less a matter of observing strict rules than of making the most of existing possibilities. Even in an urban area, there are pockets of open spaces that support a surprising amount of wildlife. Peregrine falcons have been introduced to the "canyons" of New York City's skyscrapers. I have seen a bald eagle flying near Boston, Massachusetts, and a snowy owl once perched on the Senate offices in Washington, D.C.

An overgrown garden makes a perfect bird habitat.

· WATCHING GARDEN BIRDS ·

EVEN THE SMALLEST urban backyards attract a wide variety of common birds, which can be just as interesting as the rarer species that live in wild, remote places. Although you can enjoy simply sharing your yard with birds, there are many discoveries to be made in these familiar surroundings if you take some time to watch what your visitors are doing.

PLENTY TO SEE

Across the lawn from my window there is a feeding station for birds. Hopper-type feeders, an open platform, hanging baskets, and other pieces of equipment provide a variety of foods. The trees and bushes, together with vines trained up the walls of the house, provide nesting places for some of the residents of the yard, and there is a selection of nestboxes to attract others. I have tried to make my plot of ground as favorable for birds as possible and have found that attracting birds and observing them in my backyard gives hours of enjoyment for a small investment of time, effort, and money.

I am lucky enough to be surrounded by farmland, but this is an ordinary yard. Most of it is neatly mowed lawn, and the plants were chosen by previous owners for show rather than to provide food and shelter for birds. There is no room for the miniature wilderness of a "wildlife garden."

Most of the birds that visit are common species, but I find them as interesting as the more spectacular and less familiar birds that I have seen elsewhere. This does not mean I am not thrilled when a rarity drops in – like the pileated woodpeckers that I once saw at work in a Florida garden – but I would rather watch a chickadee or a house sparrow doing something interesting than cross the country merely to see and record a rare bird. There is always something new going on in the yard.

A rare visitor The pileated woodpecker's range covers most of North America, but it is only rarely seen in yards.

Backyard favorites
*Chickadees are regular
visitors to backyard feeders; they can become so
bold that they will take food from your hand.*

THE PLEASURE OF WATCHING BIRDS

Many people get pleasure from the birds that come into the yard. Feeders provide the easiest way to obseve wildlife. For people who are confined indoors (and this includes people like me, who sit at a desk all day, as well as those who are truly housebound by age or infirmity), backyard birds are a particular joy. And if your duties take you away from home for most of the day, a few minutes in the backyard in the morning or evening is a perfect way to forget the tensions of the working day.

Close encounters with wild animals are magic experiences that need not involve travel to distant parts of the globe to see the rare and exotic. The thrill that comes from the nearness of nature can be triggered by something as simple as chickadees landing on your hand to snatch seeds boldly, or by a grackle making itself at home on the lawn or stealing crumbs at a picnic. A more unusual and spectacular occurrence, such as a hummingbird buzzing on almost transparent wings at a sugar-water dispenser outside your window, creates a lasting impression.

While we get simple enjoyment from sharing the yard with birds, and even more pleasure from making it attractive for them by putting up feeders and nestboxes, and by organizing our gardening with birds in mind, we can obtain even more pleasure from the birds that visit us if we watch and

understand what they are doing. One of the beauties of birds is that they live almost entirely natural lives next to ours. They give us the opportunity to learn some of the secrets of animal life and the pleasure of discovering things we did not know before. Once we have attracted birds to a place where we can watch them at our leisure, we naturally want to know more about them. The questions of what they do are easily answered by simple observation; the questions of how and why they do it are more difficult.

Not so long ago, some of the simplest, most obvious questions about the behavior of common birds baffled even the experts. Konrad Lorenz, the Austrian naturalist who won a Nobel Prize for his pioneering studies in the field of animal behavior,

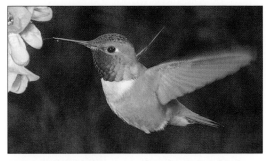

Memorable visitor *A rufous hummingbird hovering as it takes nectar from flowers is a captivating sight in a suburban yard.*

11

commented, "We must remember animals sometimes do things for which there is no reasonable explanation." In the years since he made that remark, studies have shown that there is usually an explanation for the things birds do, although there are still some mysteries waiting to be solved.

Ornithologists, both professional and amateur, have turned their attention to common backyard birds. By banding birds to make them individually recognizable *(see page 213)* and putting in hours of patient observation, they have revealed many surprising secrets in the lives of our most familiar birds.

Unique identification *The movements of this scrub jay can be recorded and studied.*

PRIVATE LIVES

Industrious builders *Barn swallows use mud to build their nests, making dozens of trips to collect enough for each one.*

Bird life is proving to be much more varied and fascinating than we once imagined. Many people have wondered why so many birds make new nests for each clutch of eggs when it must take so much time and effort. Although chickadees and purple martins return to the same nestboxes every year, other birds spend a great deal of time gathering twigs, grasses, and leaves to make two or three nests each year, one for each clutch of eggs.

This behavior pattern was studied at the University of Manitoba, where barn swallows were nesting on the campus buildings. It would seem sensible for the birds to reuse existing nests, rather than build a new one for each clutch. In theory, reusing a nest would save so much time and energy that the swallows could rear more young.

It became apparent from the research that the swallows sometimes reused existing nests and sometimes built new ones. Despite the extra effort, swallows that built new nests reared just as many young as did those that reused old ones. One disadvantage of using a nest a second time is that blood-sucking parasites thrive in the nest lining and attack the nestlings.

The Canadian researcher concluded that, although barn swallows can assess the level of parasites in an old nest, and decide

Weighing it up *Barn swallows must assess both the state of the nest and the availability of food before embarking on a second brood.*

whether or not it is necessary to build a new one, there are other considerations that affect their decisions. When insect food is scarce, for example, the swallows must spend more time feeding, so they have a greater incentive to save the time and effort of building a new nest.

This explains why swallows in some places regularly reuse old nests, while the habit is rarer elsewhere: the birds are so in tune with the environment that they can adapt to local conditions.

The barn swallow's nesting behavior illustrates how scientific research makes our backyard birds much more interesting to watch. Thanks to studies such as this, the experts can now answer many of the difficult questions on bird behavior that once left them baffled. Now that we know why barn swallows behave as they do, we can watch those living around us and understand what they are doing. If you see a pair of barn swallows spending days building a new nest right next to one that they used earlier in the summer, you can speculate that the feathers lining the old nest have too many parasites. New nests take time to build, but the time invested may be worth the effort to reduce the chance of losing chicks to parasites.

PROJECT FEEDERWATCH

Backyard research *The study of birds at feeders like this gives valuable information on feeding, breeding, and migration patterns.*

Once every two weeks, from November to March, about 10,000 backyard birders in the U.S. and Canada watch their feeders and record the highest number of each species seen. The data are recorded on forms and sent to scientists at the Cornell University Laboratory of Ornithology. By noting the number and species of birds, volunteers are helping assess the size and health of wild bird populations.

Project FeederWatch began in 1987 as a joint effort of the Long Point Bird Observatory and the Cornell Laboratory of Ornithology. The project has shown important facts such as: populations of many resident feeder birds have remained remarkably stable; house finches continue to expand their range in the East, but are stable in the West; and dark-eyed juncos are the most common feeder bird in North America. Project FeederWatch has also documented the destructive nature of outdoor house cats to wild birds and the dangers of window collisions.

Project FeederWatch is an independent study, funded by its participants. For a small fee you receive *Birdscope*, which contains updates on the Project. To participate in Project FeederWatch, write to the Cornell University Laboratory of Ornithology or Long Point Bird Observatory (*see page 219*).

· BIRDS AND YARDS ·

OVER THE PAST three decades, yards have become valuable
miniature wildlife reserves, especially for overwintering
birds, because of the loss of natural habitats caused by the dual
demands of intensive agriculture and property development.
For many people, birds and other animals that can be observed
from the window are almost the only wildlife they will see. In
some cases, the interests of homeowner and birds clash, but it
is usually possible to strike a balance between the two.

THE MARCH OF THE SUBURBS

Of the many problems for conservationists, the one closest to home is the changing face of our countryside and its effect on wildlife. Not only are rare plants and animals disappearing altogether, but familiar species that were once taken for granted are becoming uncommon or even rare. The country started to change with the clearing of forests, the draining of swamps and marshes, and the plowing of the grasslands. The rate of change increased with large-scale immigration and the movement of settlers westward. The mechanization of agriculture brought faster and more profound change.

Land is now simply disappearing under concrete and asphalt – partly to house the rising human population, but also because increased affluence and overcrowded cities have tempted people to move into rural areas. By the year 2000, there will be an additional 200 million acres of suburbia across the United States and Canada. Both natural wilderness and semi-natural farmland habitats will be lost.

All this has a profound effect on the birds. While conservationists fight to protect wild places, practical conservation of some birds can be undertaken in new residential areas, especially where the low density of

Natural habitat *Wild countryside like this is increasingly broken up by suburban sprawl.*

Second nature *A wild garden can provide many of the features of a natural habitat.*

housing results in large surrounding yards. These efforts will not save any endangered species from extinction, but they will help maintain our more common animals in a healthy state.

Successful colonist *As a forest-edge bird, the northern mockingbird has adapted easily to suburban habitats.*

The area covered by this new rural civilization can be a haven for the species that can adapt to it. Since Europeans started to settle across the country, birds have adapted to the new, man-made habitats. For example, barn swallows found the settlers' houses and barns suitable for their nests. The main beneficiaries of modern housing areas are birds that prefer the forest edge, such as juncos, mockingbirds, and yellow warblers.

The robin, which likes fruit, is wintering in increasing numbers in New England as berry- and fruit-bearing trees and shrubs are planted in yards. It also appears that the northward spread of mourning doves, evening grosbeaks, and cardinals has been possible because they can exploit suburban habitats. Stranger emigrants are sometimes seen, such as killdeer and nighthawks.

In some yards, however, wildlife is under threat. The well-kept yard can be turned into an ecological desert through the quest to make it as neat and tidy as the inside of the house. Where exotic plants are nurtured at the expense of everything else – plant or animal, weed or insect – it is not surprising that bud-stripping, fruit-eating birds are regarded as pests. Caterpillars, aphids, and other insects are important foods for nestling birds, but enthusiastic gardeners control insects. They also prune hedges and shrubs, keeping the plant neat but denying the birds shelter.

As a result of this kind of gardening, there is often an unintentional destruction of birdlife, especially through the use of chemicals. A study by the National Academy of Sciences in Washington D.C. showed that yards and gardens receive more pesticides per year than does almost any other land in the United States; similar statistics hold true for Canada. These chemicals kill birds, either directly or by poisoning the worms and insects on which they feed. The earthworm pulled up by a robin may be a living cocktail of poisons that will accumulate in the bird's body.

Adapt to survive *Although the yellow warbler will live in suburbs, its future is far from certain.*

DO BIRDFEEDERS HELP BIRDS?

Feeding the birds is a popular pastime. It is estimated that more than 85 million people in North America put food in feeders or plant their yards to attract birds. They do so because the sight of the birds gives them pleasure, but does this extra food, which amounts to many tons a year, really help the birds?

Scientific studies show that several bird species, including nuthatches, titmice, woodpeckers, and chickadees, can benefit from extra food supplies in winter. Black-capped chickadees require 150 sunflower seeds, or the equivalent, each day, and this figure rises to 250 seeds in a severe frost. However, a researcher in Wisconsin found that, in general, chickadees take only a quarter of their food from feeders, so the food we give them is no more than a supplement to their natural diet.

Natural insulation *Just as we use feather quilts to keep us warm in winter, birds fluff out their feathers in cold weather.*

This supplement can, however, be valuable in very cold weather, when temperatures fall below 0°F (-18°C). In these conditions, birds survive by perching quietly, with their feathers fluffed out for extra insulation, as a means of saving energy. They can do this only as long as they have enough body fat to act as fuel. Once this is burned up, they will either starve or freeze. Birds that top up at feeders put on a little more fat and survive longer, so easy meals at a feeder may make the difference between life and death.

Feeding in summer can also be beneficial. Raising a family is a strenuous business; some parent birds make several hundred flights to the nest with food each day. Feeder food is not usually suitable for nestlings, but the feeder is a valuable "fast-food joint" where the parent birds can snatch a nourishing snack for themselves while collecting food for their young.

Winter survival
A black-capped chickadee perches on a cattail, one of its winter foods. When such natural supplies are scarce, feeders can make all the difference.

Family provider
Blue jays have large broods and spend much of their time gathering food for the nestlings. This chore continues even after the young have left the nest, when they perch in trees and beg.

Several kinds of birds, including titmice, cardinals, mockingbirds, mourning doves, and evening grosbeaks, have spread into new areas during the past few decades, nesting or appearing in winter where they were never seen before. It is impossible to be certain what has caused these shifts. Climatic variations are one possibility, changes in land use another. There is some evidence, however, that the popularity of feeders is a factor, especially in movements of wintering ranges.

Whether your backyard is a bird's first or second choice, it is clearly a better place than land given over to intensive agriculture or high-density building. Even if yards seem to compare unfavorably with woodlots, tree-lined streams, and other natural features of the country, there are many ways of making your yard attractive to birds.

Last chance *In late summer, flocks of red-winged blackbirds and common grackles may descend on feeders before leaving the northern parts of their range.*

· WHO'S IN THE YARD? ·

T HE KINDS OF birds that come into a yard depend on its locality. This depends on the surrounding country: forest, farmland, grassland, desert, or mountain. It also depends on whether the neighborhood is built up: a greater variety of birds come to a rural or suburban yard than to one in the heart of a city. The variety of birds also depends on the season, as migrant species come and go.

THE VARIETY OF BIRD LIFE

If you live in a city you may think that the only birds in your neighborhood are rock doves, house sparrows, and starlings – all immigrants from Europe – but there is a good chance of seeing other birds if there is any patch of open ground, even a vacant lot, especially if it contains some trees. In the suburbs, where houses stand in their own yards, the situation becomes more rural, and the possibilities of seeing different birds increase. There may not be many nesting, but there will certainly be some feeding. Opportunities for bird-watching in the yard increase in winter, when birds move over greater distances in search of food.

Avian commuters *Crows do well even in urban surroundings, and a flock flying to the roost at evening is a common sight.*

Local variants *Dark-eyed juncos visit yards across the continent but show plumage variations in different areas.*

The greatest variety comes in spring and fall, when birds are passing on migration. I was once watching juncos feeding on the lawn, outside Burlington, Vermont, when there was a flurry of wings; a northern shrike, a visitor from the Arctic, landed near me with a junco clutched firmly underfoot. Seconds later it flew off with its prey, so it was a chance event that I saw this rare appearance at all.

The kinds of birds that visit your yard depend on where you live. Some species may be seen over much of North America, barring deserts, mountains, and the Arctic. Others are common only in restricted parts of the continent that provide their habitat needs. There is, however, always the possibility of rare birds appearing. This includes accidental visitors knocked off-course by adverse winds when migrating.

Backyard predator *An American kestrel may kill songbirds in the yard, but birds of prey are a fascinating part of the pattern of birdlife.*

COMMON VISITORS

An "average" yard is visited on a regular basis by 15 to 20 bird species, although there will be more calling in on occasional visits, depending on the yard's situation. One family in Minnesota has counted an incredible 191 species in its yard.

Project FeederWatch *(see page 13)* has shown that the dark-eyed junco is the most widespread visitor to feeders, recorded at

83 percent of the feeders in the survey. Across the continent, the most numerous birds are cardinals in the southeast, blue jays in the northeast, black-capped chickadees in the northwest, and house finches in the southwest. Dark-eyed juncos are also the most numerous feeder bird across the whole area covered, averaging 4.3 birds at every site.

Voracious seedeater *Black-capped chickadees eat great quantities of seed and are the most common visitors to feeders in their range.*

Regular visitor *The northern cardinal is abundant across its range and frequently comes to feeders, especially for sunflower seed.*

VISITORS THROUGH THE YEAR

Birds that will visit your garden fall into three categories: winter visitors, summer nesters, and the birds of passage that come through on migration in spring and fall. There is some overlap of these groups, especially between the summer and winter residents, because some chickadees, nuthatches, jays, starlings, woodpeckers, and several others that visited the feeders in winter may stake out territories in your yard and stay to nest. Nevertheless, you should still be able to detect a definite change in the bird life of the yard through the seasons.

At the end of winter, some birds will disappear from the southern part of their range and return to their breeding grounds in the north. These include the snow bunting and the tree sparrow. Other birds, such as

Continental wanderer
Normally a western bird, the Bohemian waxwing ranges more widely during its spring and fall migrations, when it may sometimes even be seen on the eastern side of the continent.

Cool customer *A winter visitor to backyards, the snow bunting returns to the Arctic tundra when warmer weather arrives farther south.*

juncos, chickadees, and jays, will simply leave suburban areas and return to more rural surroundings to nest.

While winter brings a flow of birds into the yard in search of food, territorial behavior limits the numbers that remain to nest in spring and summer, so birds may disappear. This sometimes leads to disappointment, as you can watch the birds

singing, courting, and even collecting nest material, but they will then build their nests and raise their young out of sight in another yard. The consolation is that they may return later in the summer together with their families, and they are replaced in the meantime by summer visitors such as swallows, hummingbirds, house wrens, and kingbirds, who have passed the winter farther south.

Between summer and winter, there are two interesting periods when other birds pass through the neighborhood. In late summer, the birdlife in the yard is supplemented by newly independent young birds wandering around the country in search of homes of their own. Remember that the plumage of some young birds differs greatly from that of their parents, so do not get too excited about an unusual-looking bird before you have checked its identity in a field guide.

In late summer through the fall and again in spring, all sorts of new birds may turn up during migration, and a special watch is worthwhile. In spring, you may see any number of warblers and thrushes feeding on their way to their breeding grounds. They do not stay long because they are in a hurry to start nesting, but the return movement is more leisurely. You may even hear snatches of song in autumn as migrant birds establish a territory while they fatten up before setting out on their long journeys. This is also the time when you are most likely to see unusual birds from the west, such as Bohemian waxwings and western tanagers, turning up in the east.

Disguised *This juvenile American robin is so unlike the adult bird that at first glance it could be taken for a different species.*

RARE VISITORS

Almost every kind of bird has been seen in yards. If escaped cage birds are counted along with exotic visitors, the list includes parrots, waxbills, and canaries. The spring and fall migration seasons provide incredible strangers, which have strayed or been blown far off course.

There is no knowing what may turn up: it could be a parakeet that has escaped from down the road, or it could be the first North American record for an exotic species: the first Xantu's hummingbird recorded in North America was spotted in a California yard. In 1980 birders in Quebec were surprised to spot jackdaws, small members of the crow family native to Europe, which had probably come across the Atlantic on a ship. The authorities removed them, to prevent them from becoming another unpopular immigrant like the starling.

If a strange bird appears in your yard, note the details of its appearance *(see page 62)*, and try to confirm its identity before it disappears. If it is a genuine rarity, prepare to be host to hordes of enthusiasts. I met a crowd of birders patrolling the streets of Lighthouse Point, Connecticut, in search of a tropical kingbird. This species from Central America is a great rarity in New England. The locals must have wondered why their yards had come under such close scrutiny!

Escapees
Budgerigars (often called parakeets) may escape and appear in yards.

· BIRDS IN CITIES ·

Watching Birds in urban yards may be less rewarding than birding in the country, but you can nevertheless widen your birdwatching horizons by stepping outside your home boundaries. Even if you have only a postage-stamp yard, or no yard at all, you will still find plenty of birds in city parks, squares, and empty lots.

CITY SURVIVORS

As cities spread, they engulf the natural habitats of many birds. Some species can adapt, especially where housing remains at low density. Many birds are finding built-up areas to be acceptable living places, and some, such as chimney swifts and nighthawks, seldom nest elsewhere. There are even some advantages to city life: the air temperature is a few degrees warmer than in the country – a great comfort on winter nights – and streetlighting allows birds to feed for longer.

The burrowing owl survives in Cape Coral, Florida. It lives mainly in vacant lots and hunts for insects and lizards around houses. Some people appreciate the owls' presence and dig shelters for them; others regard their strange neighbors as pests that ruin their lawns. But the owls gradually disappear as vacant lots are built on.

Among the more unusual city birds are the merlins that have colonized the Canadian cities of Saskatoon, Regina, Moose Jaw, Calgary, and Edmonton, as well as many small prairie towns. There are about 30 pairs of this open-country falcon in Saskatoon. Urban merlins are successful because they find good nesting places in the ornamental conifer trees planted around cities, and they hunt resident house sparrows to survive the extreme winter weather of the prairie provinces.

Adaptable habits
In its natural habitat, the burrowing owl lives in the abandoned holes of other animals, principally those of prairie dogs and other rodents. In towns and cities, any holes in vacant lots and wilder gardens are seen as possible nest sites.

URBAN BIRDWATCHING

City birds may for the most part be house sparrows, starlings, and rock doves, with few exciting species to be seen, but there is an advantage to watching these birds: they are tolerant of humans, so you can easily approach them to identify them and study their habits.

There has been increasing interest in urban wildlife in recent years, as city-dwellers have become more concerned about their surroundings. Attempts are being made to prevent the urban environment from being totally covered with asphalt and concrete, and to preserve wildlife around workplaces and recreational areas as well as in private yards. Even if some areas are are too densely built-up for the shyer birds, new housing incorporates reservoirs and parks that remain as refuges for wildlife.

Handout *Many city birds, such as these house sparrows, are so used to people that they will come to feed from the hand.*

Desirable property *What is an ugly mass of girders to us is a nest site to this eastern phoebe.*

Some of the best places for watching city birds are the banks of park lakes, reservoirs, flooded gravel pits, rivers, and canals. Moorhens (previously known as common gallinules), mallards, and Canada geese are common, and there may also be herons and gulls. Of greater interest for birders are the birds that visit these stretches of open water in winter. In Boston, I saw flotillas of ducks – canvasbacks, ring-necked ducks, greater and lesser scaup, and green-winged teal – on a reservoir in the middle of the city, and hooded mergansers and ruddy ducks at another on the outskirts. Some of these are unusual and fascinating birds, but few people even realized that they were there.

Aquatic acrobats *It is worth watching hooded mergansers in the mating season, when the males turn somersaults to attract the females' attention.*

BIRDS IN CITIES

CHAPTER TWO

ATTRACTING BIRDS

BIRDS WILL VISIT your yard only if it offers them some of the basic necessities of life. Every bird needs three fundamental things: food, water, and shelter. The presence of these basics both increases the birds' chances of survival and encourages them to make more visits. If these provisions are not naturally available in your yard, there are many ways in which you can introduce them. Food put out in feeders plus nestboxes for nesting and roosting create a bird-friendly environment. This chapter describes various different feeders, the types of food you can put out, and birdbaths and nestboxes that you can make or buy. Guidance on constructing and siting equipment will help you to improve your yard for visiting birds.

A painted bunting takes seeds left out on a tree stump.

· WHAT BIRDS NEED ·

YOUR SUCCESS IN attracting birds depends on how far you can fulfill their basic needs. Even if your yard does not contain a natural wealth of food, a water supply, or large, mature trees, you can create these features by providing food, feeders, birdbaths, and nestboxes. Knocking together pieces of lumber to make nestboxes and feeders is a good way for a novice woodworker to start and provides an outlet for the creative urge. Only a little practice and application are needed, and birds do not mind if construction is less than perfect. Your efforts will not take long and will be quickly appreciated.

FEEDING THE BIRDS

Confident caller *A male red-bellied woodpecker takes a nut from a hopper feeder. These woodpeckers are easily attracted, and many become quite tame.*

"Feeding the birds" ranges from throwing crusts from the kitchen window to supplying commercial quantities of food in feeders. Thirty million tons of seed are put out for birds every year in North America. This can prove a useful supplement in winter or when there are young to feed.

The money and effort you put into feeding birds depend on your interest and the time you can devote to watching them. My feeder array is strategically positioned outside my study window. I check that there is always enough food to keep the birds coming throughout the day, so that they provide a welcome distraction. I am also making some studies of who uses the feeder, so I have every excuse to gaze out the window.

WINTER FOOD

It is often said that once you start putting out food for birds in the winter, you should not stop until winter is over, and that if you cannot guarantee a continuous supply, it is best not to start in the first place. This strikes me as unnecessarily strict, and I was glad to find that my opinion was shared by the assistant director of the Cornell University Laboratory of Ornithology. While food put out in feeders makes life much easier for birds in winter, and is a valuable contribution to their survival in hard

weather, no bird relies entirely on one source of food. In natural circumstances birds have to adapt to changing food sources, and their survival depends on quickly finding new supplies.

There are some situations where birds may become dependent on birdfeeders. In spring, before natural food is readily available, or in unusually hard spells of weather, when it is temporarily unobtainable, well-stocked feeders are lifesavers. These are short-term measures for the birds, however, rather than a lasting dependence. Feeders are also the mainstay for birds in new housing developments, where the yards may be rather bare. Birds do not, however, rely solely on one yard: they make regular rounds of the neighborhood. So if you are away on vacation, the birds will simply bypass the empty feeder until your return.

Where birdfeeders have been maintaining an unnaturally high bird population, a shortage of food could develop if the birds were to be suddenly forced back on to natural food sources – especially at the end of winter, when supplies in the wild are low. I suspect that we simply do not know enough about the winter feeding habits of many birds to make a strict ruling either way, but do not feel guilty if your feeders occasionally remain empty for awhile.

Welcome visitors *Goldfinches are dependent on seeds for most of their diet, and in winter they are frequent visitors to seed feeders.*

SUMMER FEEDING

Many people stop feeding birds at the end of winter, afraid that it will tempt migrants to stay behind when they should fly north. In fact, the birds may need extra food to put on the fat used as fuel for the journey. The same holds for feeding in the fall. In particular, hummingbirds may benefit from a nectar substitute in an early cold spell.

Fast food *Crusts of bread and scraps of high-protein cheese can provide a valuable snack for parent birds collecting food for their young.*

Many of the birds that do not migrate still leave the suburbs and return to the country to nest. Those that do remain in the yard increasingly turn to whatever natural food is available, and ignore feeders, but the yard cannot always be relied upon to be an adequate source of food. If you have coaxed birds to nest in your yard by putting up nestboxes, you should make sure that they have enough to eat.

People are often afraid that nestlings may be fed unsuitable food from a feeder, but in many species the diet of the nestlings differs from that of the adults. The parents can obtain their own requirements quickly and easily at the feeder, while finding the correct natural food for their offspring. Problems may arise when natural food is scarce, and the nestlings are stuffed with dry bread or peanuts, which can choke them. You can stop putting out food during nesting, but do start again when the fledglings appear. They will need the benefit of easy meals, and you may have the pleasure of seeing entire families of small birds together at the feeder.

WATER

A supply of water in a birdbath or pond provides another incentive for birds to visit your yard throughout the year. Birds need fresh water for both drinking and bathing, and it is as important in winter as in summer. Those birds that feed on juicy worms and caterpillars do not need to

Wash and brush *A cinnamon teal, a marsh-dweller that visits ponds, preens and oils its clean, wet feathers after a bath.*

provide in your yard becomes a vital reservoir when frost and snow seal off natural supplies. Fresh drinking water is a valuable resource at these times, the alternative being to eat snow, which costs birds dearly in energy needed to thaw and warm it. Birds also continue to bathe and preen throughout winter. This helps maintain the insulating properties of the plumage, which are vital for the survival of birds in cold weather.

Watering hole *Even the insect-eating eastern bluebird appreciates a cooling drink from a birdbath on a hot summer day.*

drink as much as those that live on a diet of dry seeds, but a supply of water is always welcomed by all birds.

The birdbath is obviously very popular during hot summer weather, when birds need to keep cool, and puddles and small pools have dried up. Birds do not sweat but pant to keep cool, evaporating moisture from their mouths and lungs rather like dogs. It comes as a surprise to many people that birds need a birdbath as much in winter as in summer. The water that you

Drinking fountain *A house sparrow, attracted by the sound of running water, takes a quick drink from a running faucet in a yard.*

NEST SITES

Even in a mature yard that is well planted with trees, dense vines, and shrubs, there is likely to be a shortage of suitable nest sites. This is especially true if large numbers of local birds have been maintained through the winter by food supplies at feeders, or if a zealous gardener has pruned the vegetation.

A few birds will nest in hidden corners and raise families. It is easier to follow the unfolding saga of birds' family lives if you put up well-placed nestboxes. These bring more birds into the garden and provide security so that nesting attempts are less likely to end in disaster. House wrens, chickadees, bluebirds, and other hole-nesting birds eagerly accept nestboxes, but other species, especially most members of the warbler family, do not use them.

A nestbox must be sited at least 6 feet (2 meters) above the ground, and away from the worst effects of the sun and rain, for example, under the shelter of a canopy of branches. It must be secure enough not to fall down, but it does not matter if it wobbles a little.

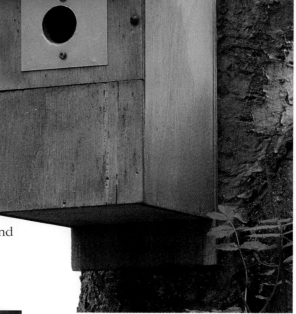

Home security *Fix a metal plate around the entrance hole of a nestbox to prevent predators such as squirrels from enlarging the opening and attacking the eggs and nestlings.*

Natural appearance *Strips of bark nailed to the outside of a nestbox can make it more attractive to some bird species.*

Resist the temptation to visit a nestbox or any other nest. The laying period is a very sensitive time, and some birds desert their nests if disturbed. Visits also make the nest more vulnerable to predators who will follow the trail of your scent, out of curiosity. Research shows that a single visit to a robin or bluebird nest increases the chances of both desertion and predation. If well-grown nestlings are disturbed, they are likely to erupt out of the nest in a panic. If they do, gently place them back into the nestbox and stuff the entrance hole with a handkerchief until they settle down.

· GARDENING FOR BIRDS ·

THE PROVISION OF food and places for birds to nest, drink, and bathe ensures that some birds will visit a yard. More time, money, and commitment are required if you want to make it a favorable habitat for as many birds as possible. It is easy enough to put up a feeder on the lawn and nestboxes in trees; it is another matter to plan, landscape, and plant the yard to encourage birds to visit and nest.

BIRDS AND PLANTS

It is hardly worth creating a bird habitat if your yard is a playground for cats or small children. You may also find it difficult to attract birds if you are a keen gardener devoted to growing the best flowers and vegetables, because a tidy yard does not provide the best food and shelter for birds. It is not usual practice to leave weeds like dandelions and thistles to seed, but that is the best way to attract pine siskins and goldfinches.

Flower feeder *Finches such as this purple finch sometimes strip buds in spring, a habit that looks destructive but does not appear to harm the plant.*

Most gardeners try to destroy as many plant-eating pests as possible. Apart from the danger of birds eating poisoned pests, remember that insects are especially important to birds feeding their young. A profusion of vegetation encourages the insects needed for successful nesting, yet no one pursuing horticultural excellence will grow plants as nurseries for caterpillars.

Unfortunately, you cannot rely on birds to control insects. Birds feed on the foods that are most abundant. When a swarm of aphids, for example, begins to dwindle, the birds search for something else, leaving plenty of aphids to carry on the infestation.

Double attraction *Goldfinches come to thistles not only to feed on the seeds, but also to collect the soft down, which they use in their nests.*

The best plan for any bird yard is to settle on reasonable compromise. Careful choice of plants and a little judicious laziness in weeding and tidying will create an environment that attracts a wide range of birds without making the garden unsightly.

If you have moved into a new house, what can you do to attract birds, apart from erect feeders and nestboxes? The creation of a bird habitat is within everyone's reach, although it takes some time, and may not be worth it unless you plan to stay where you are for awhile. It is largely a matter of letting the garden grow a little wild and choosing the right plants. Local nurseries and wildlife organizations can advise you on the plant varieties, or you can take a look at what is growing wild nearby.

Wild garden *Flowering and fruiting trees, long grass, and hedges allowed to grow wild all combine to create an ideal bird habitat.*

TREES

Trees are the most important feature for attracting many birds and are vital for woodpeckers, nuthatches, tanagers, and creepers. Choose trees that support plenty of insects and provide seeds or fruit. These include birches, maples, hollies, mesquite, mountain ash, palmetto, mulberries, and evergreen oaks. Black alder is fast-growing and good for fall migrants, and sumacs retain their seeds – eaten by pine grosbeaks and robins – through the winter.

Fruit trees provide food for both humans and birds, as well as attractive blossoms in spring. Cedar waxwings will even feed on apple blossoms. If you plant more trees than will provide your own needs and net part of the crop, then you will not mind the birds taking a share.

Trees also provide nest sites and cover from predators and weather. Evergreens on the windward side of a lot shelter the house and provide cover for birds, but even bare branches create a warmer environment in winter *(see pages 168–69)*.

Ideal home *A dead tree can be an asset, because birds such as flickers will nest in the hollow stumps of dead branches.*

The ground under the trees can be planted with smaller, shade-tolerating trees and shrubs, such as dogwood, holly, and serviceberry, and a variety of ground-cover plants. This makes the yard habitat more like a natural grove and enhances its appeal to birds and people.

VINES AND SHRUBS

Trees take years to become established, so quick-growing vines form a useful stopgap and are useful for hiding walls and fences. Try honeysuckle, clematis, Virginia creeper, English ivy, wintercreeper, and grapevine. Some vines, like the trumpet creeper, have flowers that attract hummingbirds, others have edible berries, and all form dense growths that are good for nesting.

Shrubs are similarly useful for shelter and food and, unlike trees, provide these needs within a few years of planting. Good shrubs for attracting birds – especially thrushes, orioles, and vireos – include firethorn (pyracantha), cotoneaster, serviceberry, blackberry, and dewberry.

Be sparing when clipping shrubs. Dense growth provides the best nesting places, so wait until nesting has finished and the berries have been eaten before pruning.

High rise and low level *Varied shrubs and ground cover will attract a wide range of birds that like to nest and feed at different heights.*

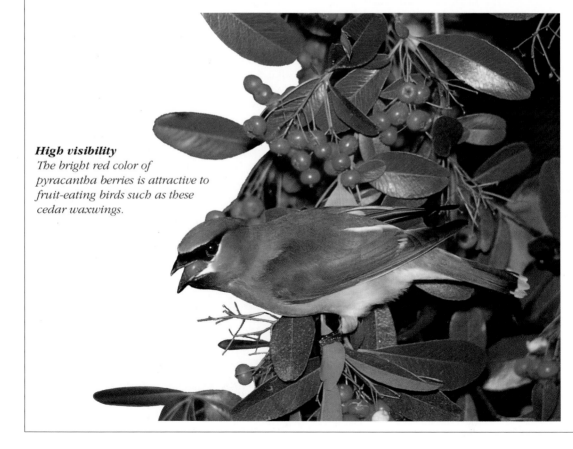

High visibility
The bright red color of pyracantha berries is attractive to fruit-eating birds such as these cedar waxwings.

LAWNS

A lawn is similar to a clearing in the woods. It gives you a clear view to the surrounding trees and shrubs and attracts birds that like to feed in open spaces. Avoid using chemicals on the lawn *(see page 15)*.

If you are serious about attracting birds, weeds in the lawn will be very useful. If the lawn is allowed to grow a little long, the plants will set seed for doves, sparrows, and finches. You can leave the grass long around trees and in odd corners. It also shelters many small animals that other birds will hunt.

Watch the contrasting feeding styles of birds on the lawn. Robins hop and pause stealthily with head cocked to stare into the grass for the slightest movement of a worm or grub. Starlings stride about purposefully, thrusting their bills into the ground and squinting down the holes. Flickers search for ants and other insects with their long tongues. They will be joined by juncos, grackles, red-winged blackbirds, mockingbirds, ring-necked pheasants, rosy finches, horned larks, and meadowlarks, as well as bobwhites in the east and California quail in the west.

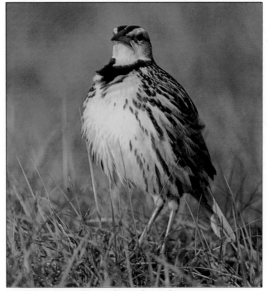

Home ground *Birds such as this eastern meadowlark feed and nest on the ground and will be attracted to longer grass.*

Watering your lawn in dry weather is a great help to the birds because it brings earthworms to the surface. Worms are a boon when there are nestlings to feed.

Soil at the edges of the lawn and around trees and shrubs is useful to seed-eating birds such as doves and gamebirds, which need to swallow grit to assist their stomachs with grinding their hard food – a mourning dove needs 150 grit fragments each day. Bare soil will also be used by all birds for dust-bathing *(see page 165)*.

Happy hunting *Although it is often seen, a robin hunting worms and grubs on a lawn is still a captivating spectacle.*

Earthworm

Wireworm

Caterpillar

Moth chrysalis

Natural supplies *The average lawn can harbor a surprising stock of foodstuffs, if it is left unpoisoned by chemicals.*

· FEEDERS ·

THERE ARE A wide variety of feeder types, suitable for all
tastes and situations. Making your own is much more fun,
and acceptable results can be produced with few tools and
minimal skill. Feeders bring birds up from the grass and out of
the cover of trees and shrubs, providing closer views and
better opportunites for watching their behavior.

SITING YOUR FEEDER

The simplest way of feeding birds is to scatter food on the ground, but most of it will be lost to scavengers or seized by the larger, bolder birds. Food on the ground also quickly becomes messy. For this reason, elevated feeders are needed, but it is worth putting out food on the ground to divert undesirable visitors from the more expensive food that attracts shyer species.

Remember that birds feed at different levels. Feeders at various heights attract more birds and lessen conflicts.

A sheltered southeast exposure gives the best conditions in the morning, when birds prefer to feed. Feeders should be near shrubs and trees where birds can rest and escape if a hawk appears, but should not be immediately next to undergrowth because this gives cover for predators such as cats. A brush pile is useful if your feeders are exposed. Feeders on or near the windowsill are best for watching the birds, but it may take time for birds to become used to coming close to a house.

OPEN PLATFORM FEEDER

Although the old-fashioned platform is seen less often these days, it is worth stocking one with scraps or cheap food to act as a beacon for passing birds.

Platforms can be a source of infection, as a result of trampled food or droppings, and should be cleaned regularly. Scrape out debris, and scrub the feeder with a solution of soapy water and a little household bleach, but rinse thoroughly before putting it out again. The feeder shown is a commercial model, but you can make one using fine mesh or plywood sandwiched between wooden frames. Keep larger birds out by covering the platform with 1-inch (2.5-centimeter) mesh.

Mesh platform
The mesh allows rain to drain away from the food, so that it does not become soggy.

Support
A platform feeder should be mounted on a post at least 6 feet (2 meters) high. The post should be made of metal and may need a baffle against squirrels (see page 41).

HOPPER FEEDER

You can use the base of this feeder alone as an open platform, or you can make a covered platform. The gaps in the edges on the base allow water to drain from the platform. A roof will keep the food dry and provide a place to hang a seed hopper.

MATERIALS
½-inch (12-millimeter) plywood for the tray, ¾-inch (20-millimeter) square wood for the edges and uprights, and ⅜-inch (9-millimeter) plywood for the roof pieces.

Chain and cuphooks

Hanging table Screw four cuphooks through the corners of the roof, into the gables. Hang the table from a branch or line on chains. The table can also be fixed on a post.

9½ in (238 mm)

18 in (458 mm)

← 21 in (533 mm)

← 18 in (458 mm)

8½ in (220 mm)

12 in (300 mm)

ASSEMBLY Screw the uprights to the inside corners of the tray. The uprights should slant outward slightly. Attach the gables to the outer sides of the uprights, and fix the roof ridge between them. Attach the roof pieces, ensuring that the beveled edges meet at the ridge.

Ridge and roof pieces *The ridge is a V-shape, and one side of each roof piece is beveled.*

Tray base and edges

Screws
1¼ in (30 mm)

12 in (300 mm)

Gables
2½ in (60 mm) high at center

Nails
1¼ in (30 mm)

Uprights 13 in (335 mm) with an angle at each end

35

SUET MIXTURE HOLDER

Hole To attach the holder to a tree

If you decide to make a suet mixture *(see page 47)* in an old food can, you can turn the "pudding" out onto a platform feeder, hang it up in a mesh bag or wire basket, or make a simple holder for the can. The holder can be nailed to a post or a tree trunk. It keeps the pudding dry and makes it last longer because it is difficult for birds to break off large chunks of the pudding and carry them away. The small screws in the side supports that hold the can in place are easily removed to release the can for refilling. To ensure that the top edge of the can is not jagged or sharp, use a can opener that leaves a smooth, blunt edge. This feeder holds a 16-ounce (450-gram) can; if you use a can of a different size, adjust the dimensions below accordingly, attaching the brace higher or lower to accommodate the diameter of the can.

3⅝ in (94 mm)

5 in (125 mm)

Side support

Empty can

Brace To fit over the can
5 in (125 mm)

6 in (150 mm)

9 in (225 mm)

Holes Drilled for the screws

Back

3⅝ in (94 mm)

5 in (125 mm)

Side support

Small screws
⅝ in (15 mm)

Oval nails
1¼ in (30 mm)

Rust-proof screws
2½ in (60 mm)

LOG FEEDER

Drill a few ½- to 1½-inch (13- to 38-millimeter) diameter holes in a log, and stuff them with suet. Insert a cup hook at one end and hang the log. You can also coat a pine cone in suet and hang it up.

MATERIALS ¾-inch (20-millimeter) board for all parts.

ASSEMBLY Place the can and side supports on the back, and mark the position of the supports as shown. Drill holes and attach the supports by screwing the four long screws through the back into them. Nail on the brace. Fit the can in position, and make pilot holes for the two small screws. Turn the screws until they hold the can in place.

SCRAP BASKET

Holes
To attach the scrap basket to a tree.

Mesh
5¼ × 7⅞ in
(130 × 200mm)

Kitchen leftovers *(see pages 44–45)* or nuts are appreciated by many different birds. The simplest container is a mesh bag, but this soon becomes messy. It is quite easy to make a refillable basket to keep food dry. Use galvanized or plastic-coated mesh to cover the front and base of the basket – a smaller mesh should be used for food such as nuts. Avoid sharp edges, and never use collapsible mesh that can trap a bird's leg.

MATERIALS ¾-inch (20-millimeter) board for the sides, back, brace, and batten, and ½-inch (12-millimeter) plywood for the lid.

ASSEMBLY Nail the sides to the back and to the front brace. Attach the hinge to the lid and one side with the brass screws, and fix the hook and eye to secure the lid on the other side. Bend the mesh and attach it to the sides and back with staples. Drill two holes in the batten, and fix it to the back with the longer screws.

Brass screws
½ in (12 mm)

Hook and eye

Side view

2½ in (60 mm)

7⅝ in (195 mm)

5½ in (140 mm)

6 in (150 mm)

Lid

Batten

Piano hinge

Nails
1½ in (38 mm)

Screws
1½ in (38 mm)

Staples

4 in (100 mm)

4 in (100 mm) square

4 in (100 mm)

4¾ in (120 mm)

Side

Back

Front brace
4 in (100 mm)

4¾ in (120 mm)

Side

¾ in (20 mm) →

SEED HOPPER

A hopper is the most practical way of providing seed, as it keeps the food dry and prevents it from being blown away by the wind. Other methods tend to be wasteful, although ground-feeding birds prefer their seed scattered on the lawn. This hopper design is simple to make. You can adjust the distance between the mouth of the jar and the tray to regulate the flow of different sizes of seed. To replenish the hopper, fill the jar with seed, invert it while holding a piece of cardboard over the open end, place it back in the hopper, and remove the cardboard. The dimensions given here are for a hopper that will hold a 16-ounce (450-gram) glass jar.

MATERIALS 1-inch (25-millimeter) board for the base, ¾-inch (20-millimeter) square wood for the edges, and ½-inch (12-millimeter) plywood for the back.

Hold firm *The rubber strap allows the jar to be removed and refilled. The pegs hold it steady.*

Long screws

Screws

Nails

2¾ in (70 mm)

← 5 in (125 mm)

2¼ in (57 mm)

2 in → (52 mm)

Back

Base

Dowel pegs
3⅛ in (80 mm)

Glass jar

Adjustable flow *Screw the three screws farther in to restrict the flow of smaller seed.*

7¼ in (185 mm)

← 5¼ in (130 mm)

Edges *(Corners cut at 45°)*

Rubber strap and tacks
12 in (300 mm)

ASSEMBLY Fix the back onto the base using the long screws. Nail the edges to the base, leaving gaps between the mitered corners for drainage. Drill two holes in the base, and wedge the dowel pegs into them. Screw the three small screws partially into the base, where the rim of the jar will rest on them. Secure the rubber strap to the back with the tacks.

BOWL FEEDER

There are many seed feeder models on the market. If you buy a plastic feeder, make sure that it is made from a tough plastic, such as Lexan, which is unbreakable and resistant to chewing by predators. The design shown here is a very successful pattern of feeder, popular with a variety of birds.

The height of the dome above the bowl of the feeder is adjustable; if you want to keep large birds out, simply lower the dome until the gap is too narrow for them to reach the food. The dome also acts as a squirrel guard and can be bought separately to protect other kinds of feeders.

Keeping stock *Consider the size and design of the seed container when buying this type of feeder. A bowl that holds a large amount of seed will not need to be refilled too often. The feeder should be easy to clean and fill, and clear plastic will allow you to see when a refill is necessary.*

Easy access *Birds that cling easily, such as chickadees, nuthatches, and finches, can use the perches to reach the seed that is dispensed to the ports below the feeder bowl. Larger, less agile seed-eating birds, such as cardinals and grosbeaks, land on top of the seed hopper.*

TUBE SEED FEEDER

Tube feeders have become extremely popular in recent years, because they are an efficient way of dispensing seed, and the food is protected both from the weather and from unwanted visitors. A favorite with songbirds, these feeders attract the smaller birds, such as finches, siskins, chickadees, and nuthatches.

To appeal to a range of birds, fill the feeder with a seed mix or a variety of seed types in layers. Staggered perches allow several birds to feed at once, although the seed must be constantly topped up to get the full benefits of this. Cardinals searching for sunflower seed may pull out and discard other types of seed. It can be worth putting out a separate feeder for sunflower seed alone to prevent the feeder from being emptied in this way.

Tube feeders are available with different kinds of ports. The size of the holes in the ports affects the kind of seed that can be used in the feeder: a feeder designed to be filled with thistle seed will have smaller holes than one designed for sunflower seed, to prevent spilling and waste. There are also different kinds of perches. Look for a design like this one, with metal perches and ports with reinforced edges that cannot be enlarged by squirrels chewing them.

Some tube feeder designs include trays below the perches to catch seed dropped by the feeding birds, but these can provide landing platforms for acrobatic squirrels, if the feeder is close to trees. Birds that do not fly up to feeders, such as meadowlarks, California quail, and pheasants, may also be attracted to seed dropped on the ground by birds feeding above.

Most tube feeders can be hung or mounted on a post and fitted with a domed guard above or a baffle below if squirrels or other predators are a problem.

Another kind of seed feeder is the red mesh bag filled with thistle seed. This attracts finches, especially goldfinches, which cling to the mesh. This is a less expensive option but is less convenient and more limited in its appeal.

Squirrel resistant *Metal-reinforced holes and perches limit the damage that can be caused by sharp-toothed squirrels.*

ANTI-SQUIRREL DEVICES

In many areas, feeders are visited by squirrels, raccoons, opossums, and skunks. Although some people like to see these animals in the yard, they not only eat all the food, but also chew the feeders.

A problem with squirrels is that they are extremely acrobatic and resourceful. The most important factor is the positioning of the feeder: it should be at least 10 feet (3 meters) from any branch or building. Post-mounted feeders – on a metal post at least 5 feet (1.5 meters) high – are more squirrel-resistant than are hanging models.

Baffles, or squirrel guards, can be used. If you have hanging feeders, fix a baffle onto the line that holds the feeder. This should prevent squirrels from finding a footing, but it is often ineffective. Baffles can be fixed around the post supporting a feeder. They provide a barrier against squirrels attempting to climb up to the food.

Tantalizing barrier *A cage surround to a feeder, with holes that only allow in small birds, can be effective.*

Overheads *A plastic or metal roof fixed over a hanging feeder will protect the food from both rain and squirrels.*

Baffles can be bought or made from galvanized iron or aluminum sheets. You can construct a cone to fit around a post or line with the open end downward. Empty containers, large coffee cans, or the lids of trash cans will also work as barriers. All surfaces should be slippery and should offer no projections for the squirrels to grip.

An alternative method is to suspend your feeder from a clothesline or wire, and string empty thread or photographic film spools onto the line. These will spin, dislodging any squirrel trying to cling to the line. Old records threaded alternately with 3-inch (8-centimeter) lengths of hose can also be threaded onto the line as a form of baffle.

Slippery slope *This metal disk on a spring tilts when weight is placed on it, dislodging any squirrel that tries to land on it or cling to it.*

• FEEDER FARE •

SOME BIRDS ARE GLUTTONS and will eat anything that you put out, while others can be quite fussy eaters. Some may be difficult, or even impossible, to attract to your feeder, although unusual birds will sometimes appear, especially in severe weather. A variety of foods will attract a wide range of birds to your feeder, and you can dissuade starlings or doves by witholding their favorite foods.

GRAIN AND SEED

Grain and seed provide fats, carbohydrates, oils, minerals, and vitamins. Some birds eat almost any seed, but most are more choosy. It is not possible to predict any bird's taste completely, although sunflower seed is the most popular with the majority. You have to experiment to find what your birds like. Many stores sell seed mixes for wild birds.

You can also make up your own mix or add seed from wild plants in your area to a commercial mix. Serve seeds in a hopper, with a tray under it so that ground-feeding birds can clear up spilled seed.

Seed in hull

Black-oil type hearts

Sunflower seed
This can be bought in the striped hulls or as dehulled hearts. Hearts are more popular, and have the added advantage that there are no hulls to clear up. The most preferred is the black-oil type.

Sunflower head

Dehulled hearts

Cracked corn
This is useful as a source of oil and starch. It can be used to distract large, ground-feeding birds from more expensive seed.

White millet seed
A grass seed with a high starch content, this is a good source of vitamins and minerals. It is especially enjoyed by the small seed-eaters.

Peanuts These have a high fat and protein content, and attract titmice, chickadees, nuthatches, and starlings. You will see birds caching the nuts *(see page 153)*. Thread peanuts in their shells onto a length of thin wire or string, or fill a mesh bag with kernels. Use only raw kernels, never the roasted, salted types. If you put peanuts out in summer, grate them, because they may be fed to nestlings that could be choked by whole kernels.

Commercial wild bird seed mix
Commercially available mixes contain a wide range of seed and grain. Choose one carefully, or buy a recommended mix.

Canary seed mix You can use birdseed sold for pet birds, to attract smaller birds, although it is expensive.

Thistle seed
This small, oil-rich seed is especially popular with goldfinches.

43

KITCHEN SCRAPS

Scraps and leftovers from your kitchen are the cheapest foods available for birds. Their use saves the waste of trashing them and cuts down the use of expensive commercial seed mixes. Scraps are often rich in carbohydrates and fats, which help birds build up the vital reserves of body fat necessary for surviving winter nights, for migration, and for nesting. The main problem with putting out scraps is that they tend to attract rats, raccoons, and other unwanted scavengers. Scraps should be placed on platform feeders and in scrap baskets, where these animals cannot reach them or used as ingredients in suet mixtures *(see page 47)*.

Crusts and crumbs Bread is a cheap, nutritious food for birds. It is not the best choice, but it helps fill empty stomachs. Brown bread is preferable. All bread should be soaked before it is put out. Stale cake, donuts, and broken pieces of cookies are also good, because they are rich in fat. Fine crumbs will mean that some is left for small, shy species.

Broken cookie

Bread crumbs and crusts

Stale cake

Stale cheese

Donut

Stale cheese Cheese that has dried out and become hard is ideal for birds. It makes an excellent addition to suet mixtures, and cheese crumbs sprinkled under bushes are appreciated by shy birds. Mild American cheese is more popular than strongly flavored or blue types.

Baked potato with skin

Starchy foods Leftovers of cooked rice and pasta, and any raw or cooked pastry that remains from your baking, are all rich in starch. They are useful for keeping voracious birds such as crows busy. Potatoes are also a good source of starch. They last well if they have been cooked in their skins because the birds can carry the soft contents only a beakful at a time.

Uncooked pastry dough

Cooked spaghetti

Cooked rice

Fat and meat These should only be put out in cold weather: in warm weather they quickly become rancid. Put suet, bacon rinds, or fat trimmed from meat into a scrap basket *(see page 37)*. Fat or suet can also be melted over a low heat and poured over branches or pine cones or into a log-feeder *(see page 36)*. Hang up cooked meat or bones, making sure that they are out of the reach of pets and scavengers. Leftover hamburger is also popular, but it must be cooked. Cat or dog food is gourmet food for birds: put it on the feeder rather than throwing it away when your pet is not hungry.

Bacon rinds

Catfood

Cooking fat

Meat bone

Marrow bone

FRUIT

Windfall fruit attracts birds as well as insects, and fruit is an important energy provider in the diets of many birds. Windfalls, and store-bought apples and pears that have passed their prime, can be put out on the lawn or impaled on spikes on the feeder during cold spells. Halved oranges attract northern orioles, tanagers, and rose-breasted grosbeaks, especially in summer. Grapes and bananas will also be appreciated. Dried fruit can be used in suet mixtures or put on the feeder after soaking.

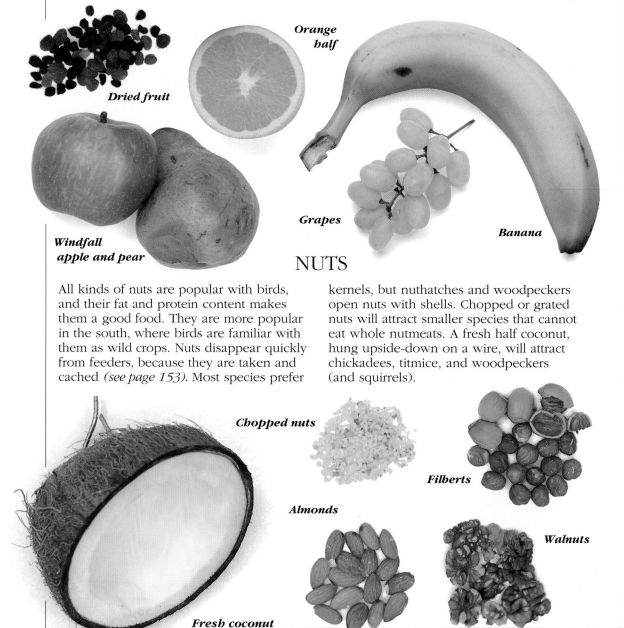

Dried fruit

Orange half

Grapes

Banana

Windfall apple and pear

NUTS

All kinds of nuts are popular with birds, and their fat and protein content makes them a good food. They are more popular in the south, where birds are familiar with them as wild crops. Nuts disappear quickly from feeders, because they are taken and cached *(see page 153)*. Most species prefer kernels, but nuthatches and woodpeckers open nuts with shells. Chopped or grated nuts will attract smaller species that cannot eat whole nutmeats. A fresh half coconut, hung upside-down on a wire, will attract chickadees, titmice, and woodpeckers (and squirrels).

Chopped nuts

Filberts

Almonds

Walnuts

Fresh coconut

MAKING FOOD

These easily prepared foods appeal to people who have the time to make special meals for the birds in their yards. Suet mixtures, which are sometimes called bird cakes or bird puddings, are a collection of all sorts of ingredients set in melted fat.

Many people experiment with making up their own recipes for mixtures, and it is an ideal way of using up kitchen scraps: a mixture of peanut butter and baked beans has been found to be very popular with several species.

Suet mixtures Melt enough suet or fat to bind the ingredients together into a thick pudding. Stir the ingredients into the melted fat, pour the mixture into a can or other container, and leave it to cool and set. You can then turn out the solid mixture, and put it in a suet holder or mesh bag, or you can hang the container as it is or put it in a holder (*see page 36*).

Seed mixture

Nut mixture

Shredded suet

Peanut butter

Suet

Cornmeal

Peanut butter mixture

Fat ball

Suet stick

Peanut butter mixtures The basic mixture is one part fat, one part peanut butter, and six parts cornmeal. You can mix in seeds, nuts, raisins, crumbled stale cheese, crumbled cake or bread, oat groats, or whatever is handy.

· FEEDING HUMMINGBIRDS ·

HUMMINGBIRDS ARE THE jewels of the yard, whether you are visited by the ruby-throated hummingbird in the east or by one of several species found in the west. All the species are attracted by showy flowers in bright colors, particularly red. Flowers provide hummingbirds with nectar, which is their main food. Protein is obtained from insects: hummingbirds either pick these from flowers or hover around a swarm, darting in repeatedly to seize individual insects.

HUMMINGBIRDS AND FLOWERS

Hummingbirds and the flowers on which they feed operate a mutually beneficial partnership. The flowers have bright coloration, often red, to attract the birds, and copious supplies of nectar to nourish them. The nectar is specially formulated for the birds: it is sweetened with glucose, which hummingbirds prefer, while the nectar of flowers pollinated by insects contains fructose. In return, the hummingbird contributes to the survival of the plant, forming a vital link in the pollination process. While a hummingbird is sipping nectar from a flower, its head or breast is dusted with pollen from the long stamens. The pollen is transferred to the next flower that the bird visits, ensuring pollination and a crop of seeds. The best way to attract hummingbirds to your yard is to plant a variety of flowers that will come into bloom in succession from early spring. Success is most likely if the hummingbirds' attention can be caught when they arrive in spring and are looking for somewhere to settle.

Natural attraction *More than 100 flower species are visited by hummingbirds in North America. The best-known varieties for cultivation are trumpet vine, bee balm, columbine, fuchsia, petunia, tiger lily, mimosa, and larkspur.*

ARTIFICIAL FEEDING

If you already have hummingbirds in the neighborhood, you can attract them by putting out feeders. Hummingbirds are often territorial, defending their flowers, so you may get more hummingbirds if you hang up several feeders in different parts of the yard.

Hummingbird feeders of various designs can be bought. They can also be improvised from waterbottles used for pet rodents, or even a jar suspended at an angle. Painting the feeder red may help

Hovering at the bar A broad-billed hummingbird sips from a bottle-type feeder. Initially the red on the glass will have attracted the bird's attention.

Artificial flowers One of the many designs of hummingbird feeder available. The red flower shapes are feeding ports.

attract hummingbirds. Most commercially available models incorporate red in their design in some way.

Make a sugar solution of one part white sugar to four parts water. Boil the solution briefly to sterilize it and dissolve the sugar crystals. There is no need to add red food coloring. Do not mix honey and water since it might nourish a mold that is fatal to hummingbirds. In all cases, feeders must be washed every few days with very hot water and kept scrupulously clean.

OTHER VISITORS

Hummingbirds are not the only birds that will come to sugar-water feeders. Orioles, tanagers, warblers, grosbeaks, woodpeckers, and many other birds will visit a feeder if they can perch at it to drink, but they lack the ability to hover.

There are also less attractive visitors to these feeders. While you may be prepared for other birds to share your bounty, bees and ants can be a pest. You can move the feeder so that the bees lose track of it, or fit a bee guard in the form of a plastic screen. Ants can be kept at bay by greasing their approach to the feeder.

Interloper The Baltimore oriole, its colorful plumage almost as bright as the iridescence of a hummingbird, is just one of the birds that may visit a sugar-water feeder.

· BIRDBATHS AND PONDS ·

T HE BIRDBATH IS useful in any attempt to attract birds to
your yard, because water is as vital to birds as food. It is
particularly important for seed- and fruit-eating birds. Birds will
come to a birdbath throughout the year, both to drink and to
bathe. Bathing helps maintain plumage in good condition and,
in summer, keeps birds cool. Water may bring a greater variety
of birds into the yard than food, especially in drier areas.
Watching the activity at the birdbath is entertaining. Starlings,
sparrows, pigeons and doves, warblers, and many other birds
are keen bathers.

BIRDBATHS

There is a wide range of birdbaths on the
market, but some are more ornamental than
practical. From a bird's point of view, there
are two major considerations in the design
of a birdbath: gently sloping sides to allow
small birds to paddle in and out easily, and
a rough surface to provide safe footing.
Ideally, the bath should also have a deep
end, about 3 inches (7.5 centimeters) deep,
that is big enough for a large bird to soak
itself or for a flock of smaller birds to have
a good splash without emptying all the
water out. A birdbath with a diameter of
about 12 inches (30 centimeters) should be
large enough.

Acceptable birdbaths can be improvised
from shallow receptacles. The upturned lid
of a trash can gives a good sloping surface,
but the metal may be too slippery.

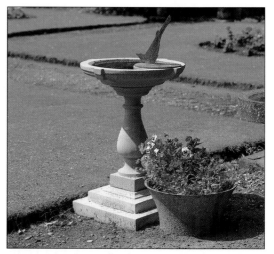

Roman bath *Birdbaths can be bought in all
kinds of designs, but the features that attract
birds have little to do with style.*

Flowerpot saucers and large dishes, such as
pie plates, are also possibilites. If the shape
of the container does not provide both shallow and deep areas, make a submerged
island with a large stone. Alternatively, you
can mold a simple presentable birdbath from
mortar, as shown opposite.

Site your birdbath near trees or bushes,
where the birds can retire to dry and preen
in safety. An ornamental birdbath may well
look attractive as a feature in the center of
the lawn, but it leaves the birds exposed to
predators, especially birds of prey.

Improvised *Flowerpot
saucers make ideal baths.*

Birdbaths that are placed near bushes should be raised off the ground – if they are not, it is possible for predators such as cats to creep up on the birds, using the bushes as cover.

Keep an eye on the water in the birdbath, making sure that it is plentiful and clean. It may be necessary to check on it daily in the height of summer. Birdbaths should be emptied out and cleaned regularly, but do not use chemicals – a thorough scrubbing should be sufficient.

Fit to drink?
Birds use birdbaths for drinking and bathing, so keep the water clean and free of chemicals.

MAKING A SIMPLE BIRDBATH

Cut a strip of sturdy cardboard, about 3 feet (1 meter) long and 6 inches (16 centimeters) wide. Nail the ends to a wooden block to form a girdle. Embed the girdle in sand, and pour in the mortar mix. As the mortar sets, shape it with a piece of cardboard or metal to form a shallow dish.

A good soak A birdbath should have a deep area to allow larger birds, such as this gray catbird, to immerse themselves in the water.

WATER-DRIPS

One of the best ways to attract birds is to install a water-drip. For running or dripping water, you can buy a miniature fountain or a drip-spout, or you can make a hole in the side of a bucket of water suspended over a birdbath. Put a lid on the bucket to prevent debris from falling into the water.

A lawn sprinkler or a nozzle on a hose that creates a fine spray will also attract birds. Hummingbirds, in particular, like to bathe by flying through a mist. Rather than leaving the water on all the time, which is wasteful if it is not recirculated, turn it on for a while at the same time every day.

Bird lure A water spout is at its most useful during migration. The sound and movement of the water bring in an amazing variety of birds as they pass through.

PONDS

A pond is an attractive alternative to a birdbath, but it must follow the same guidelines to be suitable for birds to use. The edges should shelve away gently so that the bird can wade in. A platform of bricks or stones, or a boggy shore planted with marsh plants, will provide an area of shallower water for small birds.

Simple and effective *A pond need not be elaborate to attract birds: a simple pool, with stones for smaller birds to stand on, is enough.*

There are plenty of books that give technical information on the construction and stocking of ponds. These details are not relevant here – suffice it to say that the simplest way to install a pond is to buy one of specially molded fiberglass, and the cheapest way is to dig a hole and line it with thick plastic sheeting. In either case, you will be left with a heap of excavated

Construction materials *Phoebes will come to the edges of ponds to gather the mud that they use in their nests.*

soil that can be piled into a bank behind the pond and planted with waterside plants. You will also find that several birds, such as cliff and barn swallows and phoebes, appreciate water-logged soil as nest-building material.

If you make a larger pond, you will attract birds in other ways. Purple martins and tree swallows, in particular, like to nest near some area of water. Ponds also form an attractive habitat for other wildlife, which in its turn brings in more birds. Small invertebrates and amphibians, for example, are prey for other birds, such as grackles, herons, and egrets. Standing water with plants around it will also become a breeding ground for insects, attracting insect-eating birds that might not otherwise have a reason to visit your yard regularly.

High-density living *Cliff swallows build large colonies of nests from pellets of mud: a plentiful supply of materials will encourage them to nest.*

Rich pickings *The wildlife that establishes itself in and around a pond will attract larger birds such as grackles, which even hunt in water.*

Hunting ground *Swarms of insects gather over water, providing prey for flycatchers, swallows, and this eastern bluebird.*

WATER IN WINTER

It is important to maintain a supply of water for birds during the winter, both for drinking and for maintenance of the feathers. You sometimes see birds eating snow to get water, but this wastes their energy. To obtain water from ice takes 12 times as much energy as to warm water from freezing point to body heat.

Birds also need to bathe in frosty weather because they must maintain their plumage in peak condition to keep warm. If birds cannot find water, both their flight efficiency and their insulation will be impaired, and this will cost them dearly in wasted energy.

To guarantee the birds access to water, keep the bath free of ice. A bath set just off the ground, such as an upturned trash can lid, may be kept free of ice by a slow-burning nightlight candle placed underneath it. You can rush out with boiling water to melt ice as it forms, but this will be a never-ending job in places where frosts are severe. It is easier to install an electric heater and thermostat, concealed under a pile of gravel. You can also buy a thermostatic immersion heater designed for use in a birdbath. With either of these heaters, be sure to use the appropriate exterior cord and plug, and make sure that the equipment has proper waterproof insulation – if in doubt, consult an electrician. Never use antifreeze or salt to prevent water in a birdbath from freezing, because these will harm the birds.

Expensive drink *This pine siskin will have to use valuable energy to thaw and warm the snow that it is eating.*

· NESTBOXES ·

NESTBOXES WILL ENCOURAGE the birds that visit you in winter to stay. They will bring more birds into the yard. It is only worth putting up nestboxes if you know that the appropriate birds live nearby: some birds are frequent tenants of nestboxes, others use them only rarely. You can never predict with absolute certainty who will take advantage of a custom-built nest-site. Nestboxes are also used for roosting – groups of brown creepers, for example, cluster in nestboxes on cold nights.

SITING AND MAINTAINING A NESTBOX

The site of the nestbox is of primary importance in attracting birds to use it. The position must be sheltered from the worst effects of the sun and rain and be out of the reach of predators. Baffles fixed around the supporting post or tree trunk, or a wire mesh around the box that allows only small birds through, will keep predators out.

The size and type of the nestbox and its entrance will determine which birds use it, because different species are attracted to boxes of different dimensions *(see page 59)*.

Some birds also like a lining of fresh wood in a box, especially the woodpeckers and others that do not make a nest.

Clean the nestbox out after the fledglings have left, removing old nest material, addled eggs, and dead nestlings. There may be blood-sucking parasites in the old nest, which would attack next year's brood *(see page 12)* and weaken them. Sprinkling the box with a safe, pyrethrum-based insecticide, such as poultry-dusting powder, is an extra precaution.

BUILDING NESTBOXES

You do not need any carpentry skills to build nestboxes – most birds are not fussy about the appearance of their housing. Some specifications improve the chances of success: neat joints, glued or sealed with silicone, look better and reduce the chance of the nest getting wet in heavy rain. To avoid rusting, you should always use galvanized nails and brass or coated screws, hinges, and catches. If construction is good enough to be watertight, a drain hole in the base of the box is needed.

The plans given here are intended only as a guide. The exact construction depends on your skill, the time that you can devote to carpentry, and the availability of materials. Follow either the U.S. or the metric measurements in the instructions: do not mix the two.

The easiest material to work with is 6-inch floorboard. Thick plywood is effective, but make sure it is of exterior quality. All wood must be treated with a nontoxic wood preservative to prevent it from rotting.

LOG BOX
A natural-looking box can be made from a log with minimal effort. Halve the log, hollow out a chamber in the halves, and drill an entrance hole in one half. Nail the two halves together again, and add a piece of wood for the roof.

ENCLOSED BOX

Small holes, such as the cavities found in old trees, are usually in short supply in the yard. An enclosed box is a good substitute and appeals to a variety of small birds, as well as wood ducks and screech owls.

To hinge the roof, tack on a strip of waterproof material (inner tube or webbing are ideal). If you do not want to inspect the nest, screw the roof down – it is easy to open the box for the annual clean-out. The size of the entrance hole can be crucial in attracting different species (*see page 59*). Make the hole with an adjustable bit, or drill a circle of holes and join them up with a jigsaw. A metal plate around the hole will prevent predators from enlarging it. A perch below the entrance hole is unnecessary, encourages disturbance by sparrows, and gives predators a foothold.

The same basic design can also be used to make an open-fronted nestbox by cutting a panel that covers half of the front. An open box will be used chiefly by robins and flycatchers and also by kestrels if made much larger.

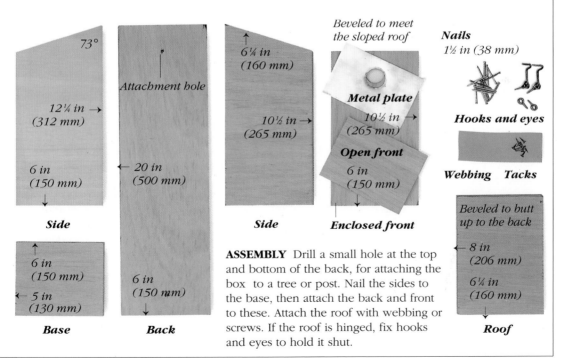

Side
73°
12¼ in → (312 mm)
6 in (150 mm)

Base
6 in (150 mm)
← 5 in (130 mm)

Back
Attachment hole
← 20 in (500 mm)
6 in (150 mm)

Side
6¼ in (160 mm)
10½ in → (265 mm)

Beveled to meet the sloped roof
Metal plate
10½ in → (265 mm)
Open front
6 in (150 mm)
Enclosed front

Nails
1½ in (38 mm)
Hooks and eyes
Webbing   Tacks

Roof
Beveled to butt up to the back
← 8 in (206 mm)
6¼ in (160 mm)

ASSEMBLY Drill a small hole at the top and bottom of the back, for attaching the box to a tree or post. Nail the sides to the base, then attach the back and front to these. Attach the roof with webbing or screws. If the roof is hinged, fix hooks and eyes to hold it shut.

PURPLE MARTIN HOUSE

Unlike many other birds, purple martins prefer to nest in close communities. Condominiums for purple martins are the most popular of the nestboxes put up. The key to success is location. There must be plenty of open space, so a field or a large lawn is essential. A nearby pond will attract martins, and overhead wires provide perches. If you feel that you have a good chance of success, instructions on the construction of these multiple residences are given in the pamphlet "Homes for Birds" Conservation Bulletin no. 14, stock no. 024-010-00524-4, which can be obtained from the office of the Superintendent of Documents, U.S. Government Printing Office, Washington, D.C. 20402.

Humble beginnings *A purple martin colony that starts in one purple martin house can grow to a population in the hundreds.*

Put up the box just before the martins are due to arrive in spring. The males appear first and take up occupation, defending their compartments against other martins. Do not be disappointed if the box stays empty: often the house is first discovered later in the summer, by young birds. If these birds survive the winter, they will return to nest the following spring. Once one or two pairs take up residence, you will have a good chance of a colony building up, and more houses may become necessary.

Starlings and house sparrows are a nuisance, because they take over the nest compartments before the martins arrive. You can take the box down or stop up the entrance holes in winter. Put up the box or unplug the holes when the martins appear, and remove the nests of unwanted birds as soon as they are built.

Old-fashioned *Native Americans used to put gourds out for purple martins to nest in, and the birds still appreciate this kind of "nestbox."*

OPEN-ENDED BOX

This very simple box has been used successfully for owls, which nest and roost in large cavities. It is wired or nailed to a branch at an angle, to imitate the cavity that forms in the stump of a branch. When you put the nestbox up, spread a thick layer of sawdust or peat in the bottom of the box to absorb the foulings of nestlings.

You may tempt screech-owls and other birds. The disadvantage of this box is that, being large and open, it needs protection from raccoons and other nest predators.

MATERIALS ½-inch (12-millimeter) plywood for the roof and base, and ¾-inch (20-millimeter) timber for the sides, end, and batten.

Box placement
Nail the batten to the side of a tree branch, so that the box is at an angle of more than 45° to the horizontal. The projecting roof over the opening helps keep the box dry.

↑
10½ in
(265 mm)

Galvanized nails
2 in
(52 mm)

9 in
(225 mm)
square

End

↑
10½ in
(265 mm)

Batten
27½ in × 2¾ in
(700 mm × 70 mm)

ASSEMBLY Drill several small drainage holes in the end. Drill three holes in the batten to attach it to the box, and one at each end to fix it to the tree. Hold the batten in position on one of the box sides, mark the three holes on the side, and make pilot holes in these positions with an awl. Nail the sides to the end, then nail the base and the roof to these. Finally, attach the batten to the side of the box with screws, making sure that these do not penetrate the side into the interior of the box.

← 30 in
(760 mm)

9 in
(225 mm)

← 36 in
(915 mm)

Base

←
30 in
(760 mm)

Roof

Sides

BIRD SHELF

The bird shelf, which is similar to the open-fronted version of the standard enclosed nestbox (*see page 55*), provides a solid foundation for the nests of robins, barn and cliff swallows, and phoebes. The size and shape of the shelf are not critical, so it is cheap and easy to make.

Nails 1½ in (38 mm)

Long nails

← 6 in (150 mm)

5¼ in (130 mm) ↓

Roof

Mirror plate

Screws ½ in (12 mm)

Side 100°

6¼ in (160 mm) →

← 2 in (52 mm)

Back 6¼ in (160 mm) 4 in (100 mm) ↓

Side 4⅛ in (105 mm) ↑ 5¼ in (130 mm)

4 in (100 mm) square

Base

Front ← 1¼ in (30 mm)

Retaining wall *The front wall is just high enough to keep the nest in place.*

MATERIAL Scraps of timber can be used. For the shelf shown here, ⅝-inch (15-millimeter) plywood was used.

ASSEMBLY Nail the front and the back to the base, then attach the sides. Attach the roof so that it overhangs the box at the front. Finally, fix the mirror plate to the back with the screws.

BOWL NEST

Cliff swallows build nests of mud beneath gutters or eaves. They usually nest at traditional sites, but you can encourage birds to adopt a new house by putting up artificial nests. Construct nests from plaster-of-paris or quick-drying cement, using a 5-inch (12.5-centimeter) diameter beach ball as a mold. If you leave the bowl open at the top, it will attract barn swallows.

CONSTRUCTION Chalk the outline of the nest on the ball, marking out an entrance hole 2½ inches (60 millimeters) across and 1 inch (25 millimeters) deep. Mold the wet material over the ball to a thickness of ⅜ inches (9 millimeters), and embed a bracket in each side. Nail two boards together to form a simple, right-angled support. When the bowl is dry screw the two brackets into the support.

Options *The top may be closed or left open.*

Molding the nest *Smooth the material with an old, flat knife as it dries. When it is dry, file the edges to fit the frame neatly.*

Bracket *Set brass right-angled brackets into the material.*

DIMENSIONS GUIDE

The measurements are internal, so add the thickness of the boards as necessary. With enclosed boxes, the diameter of the entrance is crucial for keeping house sparrows and starlings out. Even the largest birds need entrance holes small enough to keep out cats and raccoons. Allow 2 inches (5 centimeters) between the entrance hole and the roof.

ENCLOSED NESTBOXES

	Floor area	Entrance hole	Height to hole	Comments
Chickadees	4 × 4 in 100 × 100 mm	1⅛ in 30 mm	7 in 180 mm	Line with woodchips
Titmice	4 × 4 in 100 × 100 mm	1¼ in 33 mm	7 in 180 mm	Line with woodchips
Nuthatches	4 × 4 in 100 × 100 mm	1⅜ in 35 mm	7 in 180 mm	Line with woodchips
House wren	4 × 4 in 100 × 100 mm	1⅛ in 30 mm	7 in 180 mm	
Bluebirds	4 × 4 in 100 × 100 mm	1½ in 38 mm	8 in 205 mm	Place near the ground
Tree swallow	5 × 5 in 130 × 130 mm	1½ in 38 mm	5 in 130 mm	
Downy woodpecker	4 × 4 in 100 × 100 mm	1⅜ in 35 mm	7 in 180 mm	Line with woodchips
Hairy and red-headed woodpeckers	6 × 6 in 150 × 150 mm	2 in 52 mm	10 in 255 mm	Place 12–20 ft (4–6 m) up, and line with woodchips
Northern flicker	7 × 7 in 180 × 180 mm	2½ in 64 mm	15 in 382 mm	Line with woodchips

OPEN-FRONTED NESTBOXES AND BIRD SHELVES

	Floor area	Height	Height of front	Height above ground
Mourning dove (box)	12 × 20 in 300 × 510 mm	12 in 300 mm	6 in 150 mm	8–12 ft 2.5–4 m
American robin (shelf)	6 x 8 in 150 x 205 mm	6 in 150 mm	2 in 52 mm	6–15 ft 2–5 m
Barn swallow (shelf)	6 x 6 in 150 x 150 mm	7⅞ in 200 mm	1 in 26 mm	8–12 ft 2.5–4 m
Phoebes (shelf)	6 × 6 in 150 × 150 mm	4 in 100 mm	1 in 26 mm	8–12 ft 2.5–4 m

SPECIAL NESTBOXES

	Floor area	Height	Height of front	Height above ground
Cliff swallow	Bowl nest			
Barn swallow				Place 10–30 ft (3–9 m) up, and line with woodchips
Screech-owls				Place 10–30 ft (3–9 m) up, and line with woodchips
American kestrel	8 x 8 in 200 x 200 mm	15 in 382 mm	12 in 300 mm	3 in (76 mm) hole

BIRD PROFILES

Birds can be enjoyed simply for their color, movement, and song, but anyone with a little curiosity wants to know which birds are visiting the yard. Confident identification is essential, for instance, if the Behavior Guide is to prove useful. The directory of profiles is a means of identifying many species that visit yards or parks, and it describes their typical feeding and nesting habits. Guidance is given wherever possible on distinguishing sexes and age groups. It is more interesting to watch birds if you know why they act as they do. For example, it is useful to know that the hairy woodpecker with a red crown that is being chased up a tree by an adult male, with red on the back of its head, is a young male rather than a female, because it explains the intent of the male that is giving chase.

Markings tell us a woodpecker's species, sex, and age.

· WHAT BIRD IS THAT? ·

The purpose of this chapter is to introduce a selection of common birds that may be seen in yards, parks, and city environs, and to describe their habits so that they become familiar. This reference guide is not a substitute for one of the many bird identification guides available, but it will help readers with little birdwatching experience who want to play host to birds in their yards and learn more about them.

POSITIVE IDENTIFICATION

To identify a bird, you can either use a field guide or ask a birder. Both work only if you observe and note the bird's features carefully. Otherwise the book will present an array of birds almost, but not quite, like the one you saw, and the birder will not be able to match your description with known birds. Note the bird's physical features and details of its voice, flight, posture, how it walks or hops, and where you saw it.

Size, length of wings, tail, and bill, and habitat (fields, woods, near water) identify the type of bird. You can then determine the species by its voice and plumage. It takes time to develop an eye for the significant details. Bold features are easy to remember but they may be shared by more than one species. Tiny but vital details are often easy to miss. You may find it helpful to make notes or drawings.

THE PARTS OF A BIRD'S BODY

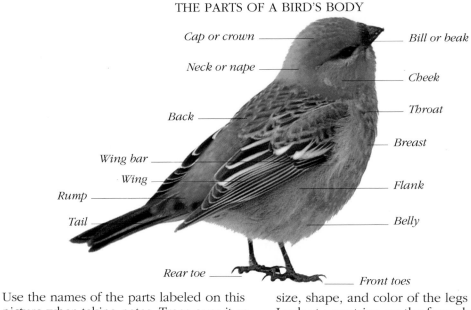

Cap or crown — Bill or beak

Neck or nape — Cheek

Back — Throat

Breast

Wing bar — Flank

Wing —

Rump — Belly

Tail —

Rear toe — Front toes

Use the names of the parts labeled on this picture when taking notes. Trace over it so that you have an outline on which you can quickly fill in the detals of a mystery bird. Note the colors of the plumage, and the

size, shape, and color of the legs and bill. Look at any stripe on the face: does it run through the eye or above it? Judge the size of the bird by comparing it with well-known birds, or a leaf or a brick.

THE BIRD PROFILES

Seventy-eight North American bird species are presented on the following pages. They are listed in their family groups in the order of the American Ornithologists' Union classification (*see pages 215–17*). It might seem that it would be easier to find them if they were listed in alphabetical order, but common names can vary from place to place. Also, the scientific classification groups bird species according to their natural relationships, from the least to the most evolved species, so you will find birds of similar appearance and behavior grouped together.

IDENTIFICATION
The family group, the common and the scientific names of the species, and the bird's length from bill to tail

PLUMAGE *Colors, patterns, whether female and juvenile differ, and changes occurring at molting*

VOICE *Any typical calls or songs*

FEEDING *The diet and feeding method* ✿ *feeder foods*

Nesting season
The usual period in which there are eggs or young present

Finch family (FRINGILLIDAE)
AMERICAN GOLDFINCH
Carduelis tristis
Length: 5 inches (13 centimeters)

The yellow plumage is molted after nesting

THE AMERICAN goldfinch is closely related to the less colorful pine siskin (*see opposite*), and the two species are very alike in their general behavior. This may lead to competition, and it is unusual to see both birds at the feeder at the same time. One remarkable trait of the goldfinch is that it molts its feathers twice a year: in fall after nesting is completed and again in spring. This results in a great difference in the appearance of the males between summer and winter.

PLUMAGE The winter plumage of both sexes is a brownish gray, but the male has yellow on the throat and face. In spring, the male becomes brilliant yellow, with a black cap, wings, and tail, and white at the base of the tail. The female acquires a yellow tinge but is still quite drab.

VOICE The calls include a *per-chick-o-ree* and, in flight, a *see-me, see-me*. The song is a medley of trills and *swee* notes.

FEEDING Tree seeds, thistles, dandelions, evening primrose, sunflowers, goldenrod, lettuce, and other plants that have gone to seed are the main foods. Berries and insects make up a small part of the diet. ✿ Feeders with seeds, especially thistle and sunflower, are popular.

NESTING Loose colonies nest in bushes or trees. The cup nests are sometimes so tightly woven that they can hold water. Nesting is connected with thistles, because the nest is often lined with thistledown.

Solid food *Partly digested thistle seeds are fed to the nestlings.*

Nesting information June through September • 1 brood • 4 or 5 pale blue eggs • 12 to 14 days incubation by the female • 10 to 16 days fledging

141

RANGE MAPS
The areas in which the species is usually found at different times of year: yellow indicates its summer range, blue its winter range, and green the areas in which it is resident throughout the year

NESTING
The construction and usual location of the nest, and details of the breeding habits ❚ *suitable nestboxes*

Broods *The usual number of broods that are raised by a pair within one nesting season*

Incubation *The average number of days that a bird spends brooding the eggs, and which sex broods*

Fledging *The average number of days until a young bird is able to leave the nest*

Egg details *The average number of eggs that are laid in one clutch, and their colors and markings*

The figures that are given in the nesting information panel for the nesting season, the number of broods and eggs, and the incubation and fledging times are all approximate. They are likely to vary with circumstances (*see page 184*). For example, egg-laying tends to start earlier in southern parts of the range, and first-time breeders tend to lay fewer eggs than older, more experienced birds. The availability of food is another important factor influencing the numbers of eggs in a clutch.

Duck family (ANATIDAE)

CANADA GOOSE

Branta canadensis

Length: 25–45 inches (64–114 centimeters)

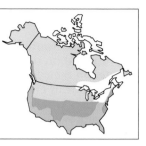

THE CANADA GOOSE is the most familiar and widespread of North American waterfowl. Canada geese migrate by day, flying in V-formation. Goslings remain with their parents until the next breeding season. Flocks of Canada geese have become a common sight in city parks and suburban office complexes, and around reservoirs. They have benefited from islands, where they can nest in safety, and extensive lawns for grazing.

The legs are far enough forward on the body to make it easy for the bird to walk

PLUMAGE The body is dark gray-brown, the head and neck black with white cheeks. The tail is white at its base and black at the tip. There are 11 races that have similar plumage but that vary in size, such as the mallard-sized cackling Canada goose and the giant Canada goose.

VOICE Canada geese use a large number of calls. The most common is the musical *ah-honk* uttered when flying in formation. Smaller races have higher, cackling calls.

FEEDING "Honkers" eat mainly grasses (sprouting grain crops and lawn grasses) and other vegetation, plus mollusks and crustaceans on shores and estuaries.

NESTING The nest is a large pile of vegetation gathered by the female, usually near water and often close to other Canada geese. After the goslings have hatched, they are led to water by their parents. Sometimes one pair will adopt the goslings of other pairs, so large familes may be seen. Canada geese do not start breeding until their third spring. They mate for life, but they will remate if the partner dies.

Communal living *Like many geese, Canada geese live and migrate in flocks.*

Nesting information *March through June • 1 brood • 4 to 6 white eggs • 25 to 28 days incubation by the female • 42 days fledging*

Duck family (ANATIDAE)

MALLARD

Anas platyrhynchos
Length: 23 inches
(58 centimeters)

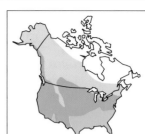

ONE OF THE best known of all birds, the mallard is the ancestor of almost all domestic ducks. It is native to western areas of North America; eastern populations have been introduced. Mallards are often seen on lakes and reservoirs, and they will come into yards that have a pond or that are near a lake or river. Mallards might nest in large yards if there is plenty of cover. The female could need your assistance in leading her ducklings across roads to water.

Unlike most other birds, ducks molt all their flight feathers at once

PLUMAGE The male has a bottle-green head, separated from his brown breast by a white ring. The female is mottled brown and black. Both have a patch on the wing, of brilliant purplish blue edged with black and white, called the speculum. After courtship, the male molts into the "eclipse" plumage, which is similar to the female's coloring. After breeding season he molts back into the familiar brilliant coloring.

VOICE Mallards have a variety of quacks. Loud, harsh quacks come from the female, and quiet, nasal ones from the male.

FEEDING Mallards eat a wide variety of animal and plant food. They graze, eat acorns, and hunt in shallow water for water snails, insects, frogs, and fish.
🏵 Mallards take bread and grain in parks and yards and can become tame enough to take food straight from the hand.

NESTING A nest of leaves and grasses, lined with down, is built under dense vegetation, sometimes in a tree. The female, who rears the family alone, covers

Vegetable strainer *Mallards "dabble" for food, sifting plant fragments out of the water.*

the nest with down when she leaves to feed. The ducklings leave the nest before they are a day old. Although their mother is aggressive towards intruders, many ducklings are killed by predators.

Nesting information *March through July • 1 brood • 8 or 10 white or light green eggs 26 to 30 days incubation by the female • 50 to 60 days fledging*

Hawk family (ACCIPITRIDAE)

SHARP-SHINNED HAWK

Accipiter striatus

Length: 10–14 inches (25–36 centimeters)

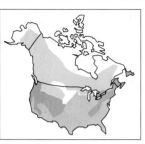

Wings are short and rounded for maneuverability in woodland

TWO TYPES OF hawk may be seen in cities and suburbs. The accipiters are woodland hawks with short wings and long tails, while the buteos are open-country, soaring hawks with long wings and short tails. Many species are observed during migration, but the "sharpie" is the one most likely to be seen coming into yards to prey on small birds. It darts through trees, across lawns and paths, seizes an unwary bird in its talons, and speeds on.

PLUMAGE Adult birds are blue-gray above, and white cross-barred with reddish brown below, with a narrow white strip on the tip of the tail. Juveniles are brown above and darker underneath. Similar species include Cooper's hawk (*Accipiter cooperii*), which is bigger, with a longer tail, larger head, and a contrasting dark crown, and the red-tailed hawk (*Buteo jamaicensis*), which has a noticeable red tail and frequently perches on utility poles.

VOICE The call is a repeated *kek-kek-kek* when disturbed on the nest.

FEEDING Prey consists mainly of small birds up to the size of pigeons but occasionally includes frogs and lizards, small mammals, and large insects.

NESTING The nest is built of twigs and lined with bark strips and is often sited in a conifer tree. Occasionally an abandoned crow or squirrel nest is used. The parents may strike humans who come too close.

Natural cull *Hawks may prey on birds at feeders, picking off weak and sick individuals.*

Nesting information *March through July • 1 brood • 4 or 5 white eggs blotched with brown 34 to 35 days incubation by both parents • 23 to 24 days fledging*

Falcon family (FALCONIDAE)

AMERICAN KESTREL

Falco sparverius

Length: 10½ inches (27 centimeters)

Once called the sparrow hawk, the American kestrel is the most common member of the falcon family in North America. Kestrels are recognized by their hunting methods. They hover, searching for small animals on the ground below, then drop to the grass or fly on and hover again if their search reveals no prey. They prefer to hover when there is a strong breeze to provide lift, and much of their hunting is done from a perch on wires or bare branches.

Often raises and lowers the tail when perched

PLUMAGE The kestrel has a rust-colored back and tail, pointed wings, and white underparts with dark spots. There is a vertical black stripe below the eye. The underparts are more streaked in the female, and the male has blue-gray wings.

VOICE The call is a shrill *klee-klee-klee.*

FEEDING Kestrels eat mainly large insects, rodents, small reptiles, and frogs, but they also take small birds. Surplus food is cached *(see page 153).*

NESTING Like all members of the falcon family, the kestrel does not build a nest but uses old woodpecker holes or other cavities, including niches on buildings. The female incubates the eggs and is called off the nest by the male when he brings her food.

🗂 Kestrels may come to an open-fronted nestbox *(see page 55).*

Split family *The male will care for the first brood while the female incubates the second.*

Nesting information *March through May or June • 1 or 2 broods • 4 or 5 white, brown-blotched eggs • 29 to 30 days incubation by the female • 30 to 31 days fledging*

Pheasant family (PHASIANIDAE)

RING-NECKED PHEASANT

Phasianus colchicus

Length: Male 33 inches (84 centimeters)
Female 21 inches (53 centimeters)

T HE RING-NECKED PHEASANT was brought from Asia to Europe by the Romans, and from Europe to America in the late nineteenth century. It is now a popular gamebird. Pheasants enter yards in autumn and winter, especially in hard weather. The male usually has a harem of several female birds.

Tail is carried vertically when running

FEEDING

Pheasants clamber in trees for buds and fruit and scratch on the ground for a wide range of foods, especially grain and seeds. Animal food includes insects, snails, worms, and occasionally small mammals and lizards. Grass, leaves, and roots are eaten in winter.
🔔 Grain, bread, and kitchen leftovers will attract pheasants.

PLUMAGE The male is red-brown above with brown, black, and white markings and has an iridescent green or purple head with red wattles and cheeks, a double crest and ear tufts, and a white collar. The female is mottled light and dark brown.

VOICE The cock's song is a loud *KORK-kok,* accompanied by rapid beating of the wings. There is a loud *kut-ok, kut-ok* of alarm. The hen has a variety of calls, one of which sends her brood into hiding.

NESTING The nest is a shallow depression under a hedge or in long grass. The hen pheasant blends into her surroundings perfectly; as with other species in which the female is duller in color than the male, she is wholly responsible for raising the family. The chicks leave the nest shortly after hatching.

Nesting information April through July • 1 brood • 10 to 12 olive brown eggs • 23 to 28 days incubation by the female • 7 days fledging

Pheasant family (PHASIANIDAE)

NORTHERN BOBWHITE
Colinus virginianus
Length: 9¾ inches (25 centimeters)

THIS QUAIL TAKES its name from the loud call of the male. Bobwhites are lively birds, always on the move, and if possible will run to safety rather than flying when they are threatened. If they are disturbed suddenly, however, they burst into the air and fly away rapidly. Bobwhite flocks, called coveys, will come into parks and yards in winter if there is dense cover near the lawns. When roosting, a covey of 10 to 15 birds form a circle facing outward, for safety. If they are disturbed, the birds will rise up and scatter with a loud roar of wingbeats, regrouping later in the night.

White outer tail feathers may show in flight

PLUMAGE Bobwhites are a reddish brown, with an eyestripe and throat patch that are white in the male and buff in the female.

VOICE The male gives a rising *bob-WHITE*. The most common of the varied calls is a whistled *hoy*.

FEEDING The diet is made up mainly of the seeds of weeds and grasses. These are supplemented with the new leaves of green plants in the spring, with bugs and insects in summer, and with fruit and acorns in autumn.
🌼 Cracked corn and grain sorghum scattered on the ground attract bobwhites.

NESTING A shallow scrape is dug in undergrowth by either partner. It is lined and domed with grasses and has a small opening in the side.

Safety in numbers *At night, a group of roosting bobwhites forms a circle.*

Nesting information *March through September • 2 broods • 14 to 16 white or cream eggs 23 to 24 days incubation by both parents • 6 to 7 days fledging*

Pheasant family (PHASIANIDAE)
CALIFORNIA QUAIL
Callipepla californica
Length: 9½–11 inches (24–28 centimeters)

Scaly belly helps distinguish it from Gambel's quail

THIS LIVELY BIRD is common in western states, with an introduced population in Utah. Its main home is in scrubby country, where clearings provide plenty of weed seeds, conditions that are often provided in suburbs. The other main requirement of the California quail is water, and the birds are attracted by ponds and birdbaths. Outside the nesting season, California quail live in flocks, or coveys.

PLUMAGE California quail are gray or brownish gray above. The breast is blue-gray, the belly scaly in appearance, and the flanks brownish gray with broad white streaks. The head is dark brown, with a short black plume, and the male has a white eyestripe and a black throat bordered with white.

Just visiting *Flocks of California quail are often seen in barnyards.*

VOICE The call is a rising *chi-ca-go*, which is used to bring the flock back together after a disturbance.

FEEDING California quail have regular feeding habits, visiting favorite places in the morning and evening. The main foods are leaves, seeds, and fruit, but some insects, spiders, and snails are also eaten. ✿ A variety of seeds, from cracked corn to millet, will bring in this quail if there is cover nearby.

NESTING The eggs are laid in a grass-lined hollow under a bush, among weeds or beside a log. Yards and roadside verges are commonly used. Female California quail sometimes lay their eggs in the nests other quail, or even of other species, such as roadrunners *(see page 202)*.

Nesting information January through October • 1 brood • 12 to 16 cream or buff eggs with brownish gray markings • 21 to 23 days incubation by the female • 10 days fledging

Plover family (CHARADRIIDAE)

KILLDEER
Charadrius vociferus
Length: 10½ inches (27 centimeters)

PLOVERS ARE SHOREBIRDS, but many live inland, and the killdeer is found all over North America. Its normal nesting place is in open country, but it will lay eggs on gravel roads and drives, railroad tracks, and graveled and tarred roofs. If chicks hatch on a rooftop, they will jump down and follow their parents to a feeding ground. The black and white stripes actually camouflage the birds on the nest. If disturbed, they leave the eggs and draw intruders away, spreading their tails and flapping their wings to make themselves conspicuous.

Long legs are typical of shorebirds

PLUMAGE Brown above and white below, with a reddish rump. There are two black bands on the breast, and one below the eyes. Juveniles have only one breast band.

Start as you mean to go on *Like adult birds, eggs and chicks are almost invisible on pebbles.*

VOICE The call is a shrill *killdee, killdee*, which has led to the alternative names of chattering plover and noisy plover.

FEEDING When feeding, the killdeer runs rapidly forward for several feet, then stops abruptly and scans the ground for insects, spiders, snails, and worms.

NESTING The female makes a shallow scrape in the ground, and her eggs match their surroundings so well that the nest is hard to find. The chicks, which are also well camouflaged, leave the nest soon after hatching but are frequently brooded under their parents to keep them warm.

Nesting information *March through July • 1 brood (occasionally 2) • 4 buff eggs blotched with black and brown • 24 days incubation by both parents • 2 days fledging*

Pigeon family (COLUMBIDAE)

ROCK DOVE
Columba livia
Length: 13 inches (33 centimeters)

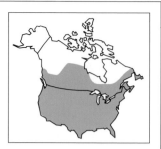

THIS INHABITANT OF towns and cities is a descendant of the rock dove domesticated and bred for the table centuries ago in Europe. One variety, often called the homing pigeon because it can find its way home over long distances, was used for carrying messages and is still kept for racing in competitions. The rock dove, or domestic pigeon, was brought to North America in 1606. Native to coastal cliffs, the pigeon has found the urban "cliffs" of buildings ideal homes. Easily procured food allows sick and injured pigeons to survive much longer in cities than they would in natural conditions. As a result, you often see rock doves with deformed legs and damaged bills.

The neck of the male is usually thicker than that of the female

PLUMAGE The rock dove is very varied in appearance. The usual coloring is gray-blue, often marked with white, but it can range from white to black or brown. The rump is often white.

Solar heating *Rock doves basking in the sun are a common sight in city parks.*

VOICE The low, cooing *ooor-ooor* or *o-roo-coo* is a familiar sound in cities.

FEEDING Rock doves eat spilled grain, bread, and any other edible litter.

NESTING The nest of twigs is built by the female on a ledge or in a hole, with the assistance of the male. Nestlings are not fed on solid food until they are ten days old (*see page 73*).
🏠 Rock doves will use dovecotes.

COURTSHIP The male bows and circles, puffing out his neck and fanning his tail, then high-steps with head held erect.

Nesting information *Any time of year but mainly March through November • 2 or 3 broods 1 or 2 white eggs • 17 to 18 days incubation by both parents • about 26 days fledging*

Pigeon family (COLUMBIDAE)

MOURNING DOVE

Zenaida macroura

Length: 12 inches (30 centimeters)

NAMED FOR THEIR sad cooing, mourning doves are birds of farmland, open woods, and semi-deserts, and they have adapted well to suburban areas. The recent increase in numbers is probably due to the crops of weed seeds on suburban wasteland and food at feeders. Mourning doves nest at almost any time of the year because, like all members of the pigeon family, they feed their young "pigeon's milk," a protein-rich secretion from the throat.

The white edges of the tail show in flight

PLUMAGE The long, tapering tail has white edges. The wings have black spots and are pink below. There is a black spot on the neck. Juveniles have more heavily spotted wings and lack the neck spot.

VOICE The song is a soft *ooh-ah-woo-woo-woo.*

FEEDING The diet is almost entirely seeds. Insects and snails are also eaten, and grit for grinding seeds is important. ✿ A common visitor to ground feeders or seed spilled from hanging feeders.

NESTING The nest of twigs is so thin that the eggs can be seen through it. The male incubates the eggs by day, the female by night. Both parents brood and feed the nestlings.

Good site *Cacti are favored nest sites, but trees, such as this palm, and buildings are also used.*

Nesting information *January through December (April through August in north) • up to 5 broods • 2 white eggs • 14 to 15 days incubation by both parents • 14 to 15 days fledging*

Owl family (STRIGIDAE)
EASTERN SCREECH-OWL
Otus asio
Length: 8½ inches (22 centimeters)

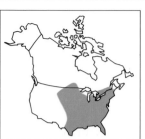

UNTIL RECENTLY IT was believed that there was only one species of screech-owl, but ornithologists have now decided that there are two. The western screech-owl (*Otus kennicottii*) is very similar to the gray variety of the eastern species. The screech-owl is common in rural areas but is one of the most nocturnal owls, more often heard than seen. You may be able to attract it by imitating its calls or by making mouselike squeaks. The presence of a roosting owl is often given away when it is harassed by noisy jays and crows, or by the pellets of fur and bones that gather under a favored roost.

The ear tufts can be raised or laid flat at will

PLUMAGE Barred and streaked overall. There are two varieties: gray, seen mainly in the north, and red, mainly in the south.

VOICE A quavering whistle that descends in pitch, and an even-pitched trill. The western screech-owl's calls – an accelerating series of whistles and two trills, one short followed by one long – are the most reliable means of differentiating between these two similar species.

FEEDING Eats small mammals and large insects, but also birds and other animals.

Wide eyed *Although nocturnal, the screech owl can see quite well in daylight.*

NESTING The eggs are laid on the floors of natural tree holes, or in abandoned woodpecker holes.
◼ The screech owl will use a flicker-sized nestbox (*see page 59*).

Nesting information *March through July • 1 brood • 5 or 6 white eggs • 26 to 28 days incubation by the female • 27 to 34 days fledging*

Owl family (STRIGIDAE)

GREAT HORNED OWL
Bubo virginianus
Length: 18–25 inches (46–62 centimeters)

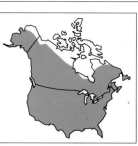

The edges of the wing feathers are softened, for silent flight

THE GREAT HORNED owl is one of the most powerful and fearless North American birds. Its habitat ranges from the Arctic forests to city parks and suburbs to the Strait of Magellan. As with other owls, the young disperse from their parents' territory at the end of the summer, and this is the time when they are most likely to be seen in built-up areas. The presence of owls is given away by their deep hooting calls and by the flocks of small birds that gather to mob them at their roosts *(see page 201).*

PLUMAGE Great horned owls are brown spotted with darker brown above and are barred light and dark below. The ear tufts that give the bird its name are orange, as is the area around the eye, and the throat feathers are white. The great horned owl's color varies regionally, tending to be paler in the south. There is also a very pale Arctic form.

VOICE The call is *whoo! whoo-whoo-whoo! whoo! whoo!* Young owls following their parents on the wing utter blood-curdling hunger screams.

FEEDING Great horned owls usually hunt by night. Their prey consists of other birds, small mammals ranging from shrews to large hares, and occasionally fish.

NESTING The old nests of other large birds are preferred.
◪ Great horned owls may use platforms at least 15 feet (5 meters) from the ground.

Nesting information *January through June • 1 brood • 1 to 3 white eggs • 26 to 30 days incubation by both parents • 35 days fledging*

Swift family (APODIDAE)

CHIMNEY SWIFT

Chaetura pelagica

Length: 5¼ inches (13 centimeters)

Swifts fly with quick, batlike flutters of the wings

SWIFTS SPEND MORE TIME airborne than any other bird. They feed and mate, gather their nesting material, and even sleep in the air. Because their legs are short and all their toes face forward, they are clumsy on the ground, and usually land on a vertical surface, using the tail as a prop. Chimney swifts are often seen in cities and over yards. Flocks use chimneys for roosting. They gather about an hour before sunset, then descend in a mass.

PLUMAGE Swifts are a sooty gray color overall. The chimney swift is found on the eastern side of the continent. Vaux's swift *(Chaetura vauxi)* and the black swift *(Cypseloides niger)* have more restricted ranges in the west. Vaux's swift is paler underneath, and the black swift is darker and has a slightly forked tail. Swifts look rather like swallows but are more streamlined, with long, slender wings and a short, blunt tail.

VOICE Calls are loud, twittering notes.

FEEDING Swifts feed entirely on the wing. They catch mainly small insects, such as wasps and flies, as well as small spiders floating on gossamer.

NESTING Chimney swifts originally nested inside hollow trees, but they started to nest in chimneys and ventilation shafts as soon as settlers built houses. Lighting fires or starting the central heating in a late cold spell can be fatal to swifts. The nest is a cup of twigs, glued together and fastened to the wall with thick saliva.

Nesting information May through July • 1 brood • 4 or 5 white eggs • 19 to 21 days incubation by both parents • 20 days fledging

Hummingbird family (TROCHILIDAE)
RUBY-THROATED HUMMINGBIRD

Archilochus colubris

Length: 3¾ inches (10 centimeters)

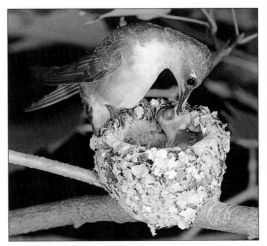

Hummingbirds' wings beat up to 80 times per second

Almost all of the hummingbirds that nest in North America are found in the west. Only one, the ruby-throated hummingbird, lives in the eastern half of the continent, although others sometimes wander up the east coast. The birds' dependence on nectar means that, unless there is a plentiful supply of flowers throughout the year, they have to migrate to Central America for the winter.

PLUMAGE Shimmering green above, whitish underneath. The male has a brilliant red throat patch (called a gorget), a black chin, and green flanks. The juvenile has a speckled throat. A similar species is the black-chinned hummingbird (*Archilochus alexandri*): the male has a black gorget with a violet band, but the female and juvenile forms are similar to those of the ruby-throated hummingbird.

VOICE Hummingbirds squeal when they are chasing each other, and use soft *chew* call notes.

FEEDING Hummingbirds take nectar from a variety of showy flowers and feed on sap oozing from sapsucker holes (*see page 81*). They also pluck insects and spiders from vegetation.

🕭 Hummingbirds regularly come to sugar-water dispensers (*see page 49*).

NESTING The nest is a tiny cup of soft plant material, bound with cobwebs and decorated with lichen and insect cocoons.

Intrepid parent *The female, who rears the family alone, will swoop even at large intruders.*

Nesting information *March through July • 2 or 3 broods • 2 white eggs • 16 days incubation by the female • 20 to 22 days fledging*

Hummingbird family (TROCHILIDAE)

ANNA'S HUMMINGBIRD

Calypte anna

Length: 3½–4 inches (9–10 centimeters)

Recognizable by the red crown

A RESIDENT OF THE Pacific seaboard, Anna's hummingbird is the only hummingbird to winter in North America. It is the first Californian bird to start nesting: eggs are sometimes laid in late December. Males have a spectacular courtship display, plunging at high speed toward a perched female, then flying away vertically.

PLUMAGE The male is bright metallic green above and mostly green below, with an iridescent red crown and gorget. The female is grayish below with a heavily spotted throat, which sometimes has a few red feathers.

VOICE Anna's hummingbird is the only west coast hummingbird to sing from a perch. The song is a medley of squeaks and rasps. The call is a *chit*.

FEEDING Anna's hummingbird feeds more on insects and spiders than other North American hummingbirds, but the diet is largely made up of the nectar of fuchsia, tobacco plant, and century plant flowers. A single bird requires the nectar of about 1,000 blossoms each day. Sap from sapsucker holes is also taken *(see page 81)*.

🐦 Like all hummingbirds, Anna's hummingbirds will come to sugar-water feeders *(see page 49)* and suitable flowers planted in the yard.

NESTING A tiny lichen-covered cup is built by the female in a bush or small tree, usually in semi-shade near water. The female may begin to lay her eggs when the nest is no more than a platform, adding the walls afterward.

One of the crowd *The female resembles other West Coast hummingbird females, but is larger.*

Nesting information *December through August • 2 broods • 2 white eggs • 14 to 18 days incubation by the female • 18 to 21 days fledging*

Hummingbird family (TROCHILIDAE)

RUFOUS HUMMINGBIRD

Selasphorus rufous

Length: 3¾ inches (10 centimeters)

Long tongue for probing flowers

THE RUFOUS hummingbird nests farther north than any other hummingbird, traveling up as far as the southern Yukon and Alaska. In spring, the birds follow a low-altitude route up the Pacific coast along the warmer western side of the Rockies. The return to their winter home in Mexico is made by a higher route further inland, along the Rockies and Sierras, where the later-blooming flowers in the mountain meadows provide nectar.

PLUMAGE The male rufous hummingbird has reddish brown upperparts from the base of the crown to the tail, and rust below, with a white breast and a brilliant red gorget. The female is metallic green above and white below, with rust-colored sides. Allen's hummingbird *(Selasphorus sasin)* is similar: the male can usually be distinguished by his green back, but the female is almost indistinguishable from the female rufous hummingbird.

VOICE The call is a soft *chewp, chewp.*

FEEDING The rufous hummingbird is especially attracted to red flowers, such as columbines, penstemons, and tiger lilies. Running tree sap is also taken from sapsucker holes *(see page 81)*.
✿ Rufous hummingbirds will come to sugar-water dispensers, especially those that have red parts.

NESTING The cup of plant down, moss, and lichen is usually built on a drooping branch of a conifer. Electrical cables and hanging ropes are also used. Rufous hummingbirds sometimes build a new nest on top of the previous year's nest.

Lookalike *Females, with some rusty coloring, are identical to female Allen's hummingbirds.*

Nesting information *May through July • 2 broods • 2 white eggs • 12 to 14 days incubation, usually by the female • 20 days fledging*

Kingfisher family (ALCEDINIDAE)
BELTED KINGFISHER
Ceryle alcyon
Length: 13 inches (33 centimeters)

THIS AGGRESSIVELY independent species is an interesting addition to the birdlife found along any stretch of water. It keeps watch for possible prey from a perch in a low tree or while hovering over open water. On sighting fish, it plunges headfirst into the water in a spectacular vertical dive. The catch is carried back to a perch and beaten senseless against it, then tossed into the air, neatly caught, and swallowed head first. Indigestible parts are cast up as pellets *(see page 154).*

Distinctive ragged double crest helps identify this bird

Prize pickings *A female with her prey. Belted kingfishers can hover before diving for fish.*

PLUMAGE Both sexes are blue-gray above and white below, with a white collar, a gray band across the breast, and a ragged crest. The female has red flanks and a chestnut band across the belly.

VOICE The call is a loud, rattling *rickety, crick, crick, crick.*

FEEDING The diet is mainly small fish, but includes insects, tadpoles, amphibians, small reptiles, mammals, and birds.
🏠 Shallow ponds or wetlands with fish will attract kingfishers.

NESTING Both sexes excavate a burrow in a bank of a river or lake or a gravel quarry. It may be some distance from water. The eggs are laid in a chamber at the end of a tunnel.

Nesting information *April through July • 1 brood • 6 or 7 white eggs • 23 to 24 days incubation by female • 23 days fledging*

Woodpecker family (PICIDAE)

YELLOW-BELLIED SAPSUCKER

Sphyrapicus varius

Length: 8–9 inches (20–23 centimeters)

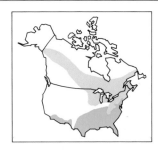

THE YELLOW-BELLIED SAPSUCKER is, in many ways, a typical woodpecker. Its distinction is, as the name suggests, its feeding specialization. While other woodpeckers occasionally take sap from the holes they drill in search of insects, sap is the major food source for the sapsucker. Other birds are attracted to sap left oozing out of bark where sapsuckers have been feeding, as are other animals, including squirrels and insects. There is no evidence that the holes harm the trees.

All forms have the distinctive white wing patch

PLUMAGE Upperparts are barred black-and-white, with a white wing patch and rump. The male has a scarlet forehead and white stripes over the eyes and at the bill. He is yellow below, with a red throat and a black bib. The female is light and dark brown below, with a white throat. Immature birds are brown.

VOICE Calls include a *che-err* of alarm, and a *hoih-hoih*.

FEEDING Sapsuckers drill holes in soft wood just under bark and lap up the sap with brush-tipped tongues. Insects, fruit and buds, and inner bark are also eaten, and the young are fed sap and insects. ✿ Sapsuckers are attracted by nut meats, suet, and fruit.

NESTING Both birds, but principally the male, excavate the nesthole in a tree, and line it with chips of wood.

Feeding sign *Over 250 species of tree, shrub, and vine are used in this way by sapsuckers.*

Nesting information *April through June • 1 brood • 5 or 6 white eggs • 12 to 14 days incubation by both parents, the male at night • 25 to 29 days fledging*

Woodpecker family (PICIDAE)

DOWNY WOODPECKER

Picoides pubescens
Length: 6¾ inches (17 centimeters)

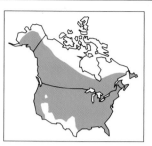

THE "DOWNY," the hairy woodpecker *(see opposite),* and the red-bellied woodpecker *(Melanerpes carolinus)* of the southeast are the most likely of North America's 21 woodpeckers to visit yards and feeders. The downy woodpecker is a confident bird, and you can often see one working through the trees with chickadees. The stiff tail is used as a prop as it works its way up a tree, and the unusual arrangement of the toes – two facing forward and two backward – gives it a good grip when climbing or chiseling the wood in search of insects.

Bristles around the bill protect the nostrils from sawdust

Feeling peckish *Downies will come to feeders, especially when insects die off in winter.*

PLUMAGE Both sexes are black above, with a white back and white spots on the wings, and white underneath. The male has a red nape. Juvenile males and some juvenile females have red crowns. The downy is smaller and has a shorter bill than the hairy woodpecker.

VOICE The call is a *chick;* also a horse-like whinny that slurs downward in pitch.

FEEDING The main food is insects found in rotten wood, but large quantities of fruit and tree seeds are eaten in winter.
🏠 Sunflower seed, corn, cornbread, peanut butter, and suet attract downies.

NESTING Both sexes excavate a cavity in a tree trunk or branch stump. A few chips are left on the floor as a lining.
🏠 May use a nestbox *(see page 59).*

Nesting information *April through June • 1 brood (2 in southern areas) • 4 or 5 white eggs 12 days incubation by both parents • 21 to 24 days fledging*

Woodpecker family (PICIDAE)

HAIRY WOODPECKER

Picoides villosus

Length: 7½ inches (24 centimeters)

The toes are specially adapted for climbing

ALTHOUGH IT IS shyer than the similar downy woodpecker, the hairy woodpecker is the noisier and more active of the two birds. From November onward, the male and the female can both be heard drumming on trees and posts. This is the start of the long courtship ritual, which also includes flights in which the wings are beaten against the flanks to produce a clapping sound. During nesting, the male and female change shifts on the eggs with a short ritual, one arriving and perching nearby to call the other from the nest. Once settled, hairy woodpeckers tend to remain in one territorial range throughout their lives.

PLUMAGE Hairy woodpeckers have white backs, black tails, and black-and-white wings. The head is striped black-and-white, with a red nape. The hairy woodpecker can be distinguished from the downy woodpecker *(see opposite)* by its larger size and longer, heavier bill.

VOICE The calls are a loud, sharp *peek!* and *hueet*. There is also a slurred, descending, kingfisher-like rattle.

FEEDING The diet consists mainly of insects, but some fruit is also eaten, and sap is taken from sapsucker holes *(see page 81)*.
🐦 Hairy woodpeckers come to sunflower seeds, meat scraps, nuts, cheese, apples, bananas, suet, and peanut butter.

NESTING Both sexes excavate a cavity in a tree branch.
🐦 Will use enclosed boxes *(see page 59)*.

Home building *Excavating the nesting cavity is a task that can take up to three weeks.*

Nesting information *March through June • 1 brood (2 in southern areas) • 3 to 6 white eggs 14 days incubation by both parents, the male at night • 28 to 30 days fledging*

Woodpecker family (PICIDAE)

NORTHERN FLICKER

Colaptes auratus

Length: 12½ inches (32 centimeters)

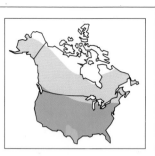

The shafts of the feathers show the race of the bird – this is a red-shafted flicker

FLICKERS ARE COMMON across North America, although in Canada and the most northern parts of the United States, they are summer visitors only. The presence of flickers is given away by their ringing calls. Like all woodpeckers, the males drum loudly on trees, utility poles, and houses to advertise their territories (*see page 172*). Flickers are easily recognized by their distinctive white rumps, which can be seen as they fly up swiftly from a lawn. Unlike other woodpeckers, they regularly come to the ground to feed on ants, which they pull out of the ants' nests with their long tongues.

PLUMAGE The northern flicker is brown with a white rump, and spotted with black underneath, with a black V-mark on the breast. The male has a red "mustache." There are two races, showing variations in color under the wings and tail. The red-shafted, west of the Rockies, has red feather shafts. The yellow-shafted, east of the Rockies, has yellow, with red on the back of the head, and a black mustache.

VOICE The call is a rapid, repeated *wick-wick-wick* and a single *kee-yer.*

FEEDING Flickers feed mostly on insects but also eat seeds and berries.
🐦 Suet, peanut butter, sunflower seeds, fruit, meat, and bread attract them. Suet holders and hanging logs are preferred.

NESTING The pair excavate a hole in a branch of a dead tree, a large cactus, or a fence post. In suburban areas, they are often driven out by starlings.
🐦 Flickers will use a nestbox *(see page 59)* fixed to a pole among shrubs.

True colors *A male yellow-shafted flicker fans his tail out in a display.*

Nesting information *March through June • 1 brood • 5 to 10 white eggs • 11 to 12 days incubation by both parents, the male at night • 23 days fledging*

84

Tyrant flycatcher family (TYRANNIDAE)

BLACK PHOEBE
Sayornis nigricans
Length: 6¼ inches (16 centimeters)

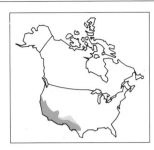

Rarely straying far from water, the black phoebe lives around reservoirs or marshy areas, or along streams or canals, and is attracted to yards by ponds and other water features. A stealthy hunter, it waits on a low tree branch, often slowly raising and lowering its tail, and then swoops out to snatch insects. The black phoebe's flight is almost silent, but insects are snapped up with a loud click.

This is the only black-breasted flycatcher

PLUMAGE The black phoebe has black upperparts, head, and breast, and a white belly. This pattern makes it similar to a junco *(see page 128)*, but it is distinguished by its thin bill and erect posture.

VOICE The call is a short *tsip,* or a longer *chee.* The song is a repeated *ti-wee,* which first rises and then falls.

FEEDING The black phoebe's diet consists mainly of insects, but it has also been known to catch small fish. It often feeds just above water. Indigestible parts of insects are regurgitated as pellets.

NESTING The nest is made of mud and fibrous plants such as mosses. It is built and anchored very strongly on the side of a tree or building, or over a doorway.

Firm foundations *The nest will break before being dislodged from its site.*

Nesting information *March through August • 2 broods • 3 to 6 white eggs, may be heavily blotched with red • 15 to 17 days incubation by the female • 20 to 21 days fledging*

Tyrant flycatcher family (TYRANNIDAE)

EASTERN PHOEBE

Sayornis phoebe

Length: 7 inches (18 centimeters)

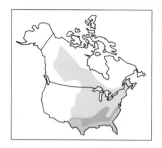

BIRDS OF THE tyrant flycatcher family, as the name suggests, hunt flying insects. Eastern phoebes perch upright on a twig, then sally out to snap up a passing insect (often with a loud click of the bill), and return to the perch. The eastern phoebe adapts well to urban life, finding plenty of nest sites in sheltered niches on buildings.

At rest, eastern phoebes bob their tails up and down repeatedly

FEEDING The phoebe feeds mainly on flying insects, from ants, bugs, and flies to dragonflies and wasps. It eats some ground insects and berries in winter.

NESTING Phoebes often nest near water, in tree cavities, on cliffs, and on buildings or bridges. The nest is a cup of moss and mud, lined with feathers and grass. New nests may be built on top of old ones. ▪ Phoebes will use a nest shelf *(see page 59)* under eaves or in a porch or deck.

PLUMAGE The eastern phoebe is brownish gray above, and white with a faint olive tinge (yellowish in the fall) underneath. An all-black bill, and the absence of both the wing bars and the eye ring, distinguish it from similar flycatchers. The black phoebe *(see page 85),* and Say's phoebe *(Sayornis saya),* which is a uniformly grayish brown, replace the eastern phoebe in western North America.

VOICE The call is a rapid *fee-bee.*

Snapped up *Eastern phoebes often feed above water, hunting insects such as dragonflies.*

Nesting information *April through June • 2 or 3 broods • 5 or 6 white eggs • 14 to 17 days incubation by both parents • 15 to 16 days fledging*

Tyrant flycatcher family (TYRANNIDAE)

EASTERN KINGBIRD

Tyrannus tyrannus
Length: 8½ inches (22 centimeters)

As THE SCIENTIFIC name *Tyrannus tyrannus* indicates, the eastern kingbird was the first of the tyrant flycatcher family to be identified and named. It is named for its aggressive nature. Kingbirds will harass harmless birds for no apparent reason. They also fearlessly attack larger birds such as crows and hawks, sometimes landing on their backs to peck at their heads. A kingbird has even been known to attack a slow, low-flying airplane.

Kingbirds fly with quick wingbeats. When hovering, the bird's wings appear to quiver

PLUMAGE The plumage of both male and female adults is slate-gray above, with a white tip to the tail. The head is black. It has an orange crown, although this is not always easy to see. The underparts are white, and the breast has a faint gray color. The juvenile is brownish-gray above with a darker breast.

VOICE The eastern kingbird is a noisy bird, calling often when it is perched, with loud, chattering notes.

FEEDING The diet consists mainly of flying insects. The kingbird has a particular fondness for bees and may nest near wild bee colonies. Insects are usually caught in the air, as the kingbird flies out from a treetop perch, but they may sometimes be taken from the ground or from water. Kingbirds will also pluck berries and seeds from trees and shrubs while hovering.

NESTING Kingbirds usually nest in a tree or shrub, but they may choose a fence post or a rain gutter as a site instead. The nest is a bulky cup of grass and other plant material, lined with fine grasses and roots.

Riverside residence *The eastern kingbird often chooses to build its nest close to water.*

Nesting information *May through July • 1 brood • 3 to 5 white eggs marked with small brown blotches • 12 to 13 days incubation by the female • 13 to 14 days fledging*

Swallow family (HIRUNDINIDAE)

PURPLE MARTIN

Progne subis

Length: 7¼ inches (18 centimeters)

Purple martins often spread their tails in flight

THE ORIGINAL NEST sites of purple martins were cavities in trees and saguaro cacti, old woodpecker holes, and crevices in cliffs, but they have long been accustomed to human habitation. Centuries ago, Native Americans hung up gourds for them to nest in, and today elaborate multiple nestboxes are put out in yards. Purple martins nest in colonies, usually of six or eight pairs but sometimes comprising up to 300 birds. Recent research has shown that they are polygamous.

PLUMAGE The male purple martin is a glossy blue-black overall. The female and juvenile forms are grayish white underneath.

VOICE The song is a loud chirruping.

FEEDING Flocks of purple martins chase flying insects with a typical circling flight, alternating flapping and gliding. Wasps and flying ants are often eaten, as are beetles, flies, and bugs, and occasionally dragonflies and butterflies. Sometimes martins will land and snatch insects from the ground.

NESTING The female gathers mud and sticks for a platform and lines it with straw, feathers, and paper. The male gathers green leaves for inclusion, which may help control parasites *(see page 201).*

Nowadays, most purple martin populations on.the eastern side of the continent nest in fabricated martin houses *(see page 56).* They suffer from competition with more aggressive birds that take over the nesting apartments.

Traditionalists *Western populations still use the original nesting sites.*

Nesting information *March through July • 1 brood • 4 or 5 white eggs • 15 to 16 days incubation by the female • 28 to 31 days fledging*

Swallow family (HIRUNDINIDAE)

TREE SWALLOW

Tachycineta bicolor

Length: 5¾ inches (15 centimeters)

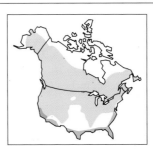

This is the only swallow with clear white underparts

THE TREE SWALLOW is the first of the swallow family to arrive in spring. Other species may be driven back or face starvation if there is a cold snap, but tree swallows can survive on berries and seeds even when there is snow on the ground. The tree swallow is also the only swallow species to overwinter in North America, staying in the southern United States.

The violet-green swallow (*Tachycineta thalassina*) has white around the eyes. The bank swallow (*Riparia riparia*) has a brown back and breast band.

VOICE The song is a liquid chattering, and the contact note is a repeated *siyip*.

FEEDING During the nesting season, tree swallows feed mainly on insects caught in flight. In winter and early spring, as much as one-third of the diet is berries, such as bayberry and dogwood, and the seeds of sedges, bulrushes, and bayweed.

PLUMAGE Dark greenish blue above, becoming more green in fall, and white below. Juveniles are gray-brown above and may have a gray band on the breast.

Fall departure *Like other swallows, tree swallows make their migration flights in flocks.*

NESTING Tree swallows nest near water in tree cavities and old woodpecker holes. The female builds a nest of grasses, lined with feathers. For some reason, white feathers are especially favored. Parent birds will swoop at intruders.

▪ Tree swallows frequently settle in buildings or use enclosed nestboxes *(see page 59).*

Nesting information *April through June • 1 brood • 4 to 6 white eggs • 13 to 16 days incubation by the female • 16 to 24 days fledging*

Swallow family (HIRUNDINIDAE)

BARN SWALLOW

Hirundo rustica

Length: 6¾ inches (17 centimeters)

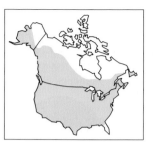

T HE BARN SWALLOW is seen as the herald of spring, although the tree swallow *(see page 89)* actually arrives earlier. The barn swallow flies north as the air warms and flying insects appear, and the time of arrival varies from year to year. The first swallows are most likely to be seen over lakes and reservoirs where there are abundant early insects. Swallows are also among the first birds to leave in fall as the insects dwindle. You can see them gathered on utility wires.

Deeply forked tail gives great maneuverability in flight

PLUMAGE Barn swallows are blue-black above and buff underneath, with a red-brown throat. The forked tail has white spots. The juvenile has a shorter tail, and is paler underneath. Other swallows have less forked tails. The bank swallow (*Riparia riparia*) has a white throat and a dark band across the breast.

Feathering the nest *A cup of mud and grass, lined with feathers, is built on a ledge or beam.*

VOICE The song is a pleasant, quiet twittering. The call is a repeated *swit-swit-swit.*

FEEDING Flying insects are hunted in swoops or circling glides alternating with sharp turns. The swift's flight *(see page 76)* is more direct. If flying insects are scarce, insects are taken from leaves or the ground. Large flies are preferred, but butterflies, moths, and other large insects are also caught. Tiny bugs are hunted in cold weather.

NESTING Buildings and bridges have all but replaced natural sites. Nests are usually grouped in small colonies, and eggs may be laid in neighbors' nests *(see page 202).* ▧ Barn swallows may use half a coconut or a bowl fixed to a wall in a shed or barn, or a shelf or nail that gives a foundation.

Nesting information *April through July • 1 or 2 broods • 4 or 5 white eggs spotted with red 13 to 17 days incubation mainly by the female • 18 to 23 days fledging*

Crow family (CORVIDAE)

STELLER'S JAY

Cyanocitta stelleri
Length: 12 inches (30 centimeters)

STELLER'S JAY IS a permanent resident of the pine forests of the west. It interbreeds with the blue jay *(see page 92),* where their ranges meet in the Rockies. It can often be seen around campsites and parking lots. In winter it moves into more open country and also becomes a regular visitor to feeders. The scrub jay *(Aphelocoma coerulescens),* another western jay (with a separate population in Florida), may nest in yards. Farther north, the gray jay *(Perisoreus canadensis)* can become very tame at forest campsites.

Dark foreparts help identify this bird

PLUMAGE The crest and the front part of the body are black, and the rest of the body is cobalt blue or purplish in color. The wings and tail are barred with black.

VOICE Calls include a harsh *waah, waah, shaak, shaak, shaak,* and a mellow *klook, klook, klook.* The song is similar to that of a robin, and the scream of a red-tailed hawk is sometimes imitated.

FEEDING Acorns, pine seeds, insects, and fruit are eaten, and small birds' nests and acorn woodpeckers' caches are raided.
✿ Nuts, scraps, and suet attract these jays.

NESTING The nest is of sticks and mud lined with roots and pine needles. Steller's jays become very secretive during nesting.

The hand that feeds *At campsites, Steller's jays can become almost tame around people.*

Nesting information *April through July • 1 brood • 3 to 5 pale blue or greenish blue eggs lightly spotted with brown • 16 days incubation by the female • 18 to 21 days fledging*

Crow family (CORVIDAE)

BLUE JAY

Cyanocitta cristata

Length: 11 inches (28 centimeters)

Blue jays' crests can be raised or lowered

QUIET AND UNASSUMING during the nesting season, blue jays form noisy, inquisitive parties from the late summer on. The species is spreading westward, and its success is partly due to its intelligence and the way that it investigates every possible source of food. Blue jays attack cats and other prowlers, but they are not friends of other birds, because they will sometimes also take eggs and young from nests.

PLUMAGE The blue jay is bright blue above and white below. It has a crest and a black "necklace," and black and white on the wings and tail. The scrub jay *(Aphelocoma coerulescens)* of the south is bluish gray above and gray below, with a bluish breast band, and no crest.

Life cycle *Uneaten seeds from a buried cache may sprout, helping renew forest areas.*

VOICE Common calls are a harsh *jay-jay,* and shrieks when confronting a predator. There are a variety of notes and mimicry of many other species, including hawks.

FEEDING Jays eat almost anything but prefer vegetable food, especially tree seeds, which are often buried for later consumption *(see page 153).* Insects are eaten, especially in summer, as well as the eggs and nestlings of other birds.
✿ Peanuts, sunflower seeds, corn, suet, and bread will be taken on the ground or on platform feeders.

NESTING A cup of sticks, broken from branches with the bill, is built in a tree, bush, or vine. It is lined with grasses, moss, and leaves. The parents are aggressive toward intruders, including humans, and dive-bomb them.

Nesting information *March through July • 1 brood • 4 or 5 green or buff eggs, spotted with brown • 17 to 18 days incubation by both parents • 17 to 21 days fledging*

Crow family (CORVIDAE)

BLACK-BILLED MAGPIE

Pica pica

Length: 19 inches (48 centimeters)

WHEN THE LEWIS AND CLARK expedition first encountered this species, the birds were bold enough to steal food from their plates. Normally, however, the magpie is very wary around human habitation. It will often come down to food put out on lawns, but it does not like to feed under trees. This is not surprising because it has often been persecuted as a thief and a nest robber.

Magpies use their feet when feeding

PLUMAGE The black-billed magpie has unmistakable black and white (pied) plumage and a very long tail. There is a greenish gloss to the black feathers. The yellow-billed magpie *(Pica nuttalli)* of central California is identical, except for the color of its bill.

Table manners *A magpie dunks dry bread in water to make it easier to swallow.*

VOICE The calls are a harsh *kyack* or a *shak-shak-shak* of alarm.

FEEDING Like most members of the crow family, the magpie eats almost anything – especially insects, ticks from the backs of large animals, carrion, eggs and nestlings, and some fruit.
♙ Meat and bread scraps attract magpies.

NESTING The nest is a substantial structure of sticks and twigs, lined with mud and plant material. It is usually built in a tree or tall shrub, although in some areas magpies nest on buildings or telephone poles. The family stays near the nest for several days after fledging, and the young remain in a loose flock.

Nesting information *March through June • 1 or 2 broods • 6 to 8 greenish gray eggs marked with brown • 22 days incubation by the female • 22 to 27 days fledging*

93

Crow family (CORVIDAE)

AMERICAN CROW

Corvus brachyrhynchos
Length: 17½ inches (45 centimeters)

A LSO CALLED the common crow, this is the most widespread member of the crow family. In the south and east, it overlaps with the fish crow *(Corvus ossifragus)*. American crows frequent cities, where they feed on garbage, and in some areas they are treated as vermin. Crows are wary, but they come into yards if they are not disturbed, and may become tame. Outside the nesting season, flocks commuting from feeding grounds to roosts are a familiar sight.

Wide, blunt tail distinguishes the crow from the raven

PLUMAGE A large, all-black bird with a fan-shaped tail. The raven *(Corvus corax)*, which may at first seem similar, is much larger, with a heavier bill and a wedge-shaped tail.

VOICE The repeated *caw-caw-caw* has many variations. The fish crow has a higher, single or double *cah*, similar to a young American crow's begging call. The northwestern crow *(Corvus caurinus)* has a hoarser and lower-pitched note.

FEEDING Virtually anything edible is taken, including insects, worms, snails, and other invertebrates, carrion, eggs and nestlings, small reptiles, grain, and fruit.

Carrion meal *The crow's large, strong bill allows it to eat a wide variety of food, including flesh torn from dead animals.*

🏠 Crows are attracted to bread, scraps, and corn on the ground and to suet and other food if they can reach feeders.

NESTING Crows are very wary when nesting. The bulky bowl of twigs lined with leaves, moss, and other material is usually hidden in the fork of a tree, but it may sometimes be built on a utility pole or on the ground. Young crows stay with their parents for up to four years.

Nesting information *February through June • 1 brood • 4 to 6 greenish eggs spotted with brown • 16 to 18 days incubation mainly by the female • 28 to 35 days fledging*

Titmouse family (PARIDAE)
BLACK-CAPPED CHICKADEE
Parus atricapillus
Length: 5¼ inches (13 centimeters)

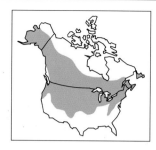

A CHEERFUL AND FREQUENT visitor to feeders, the black-capped chickadee is a woodland bird. A woodlot in winter may seem silent and empty, but then a small flock of chickadees will appear, working their way through the trees and keeping in touch with each other by a variety of calls. The acrobatic skills used for finding insects are also employed for clinging to feeders. Seeds are carried away to a perch and held under one foot while they are pecked open.

Flight is fast and agile

PLUMAGE The distinctive black cap and bib contrast with white cheeks. The body is gray-brown above and yellowish below, and the wings and tail are black. White edges to the wing feathers distinguish it from the Carolina chickadee *(Parus carolinensis)*. The boreal chickadee *(Parus hudsonicus)*, which has a brown cap and back, may come south in winter.

VOICE The song is a whistling *fee-bee,* the first note higher. Calls include a soft *tseet,* to keep the flock together, and the familiar *chick-a-dee-dee-dee,* often given by a bird separated from its flock.

FEEDING The diet is mainly small insects found among twigs and foliage. Beetles, caterpillars, insect eggs, aphids, ants, spiders, and snails are popular. In winter, berries and tree seeds are eaten.

🌰 Seeds (especially sunflower seeds and peanuts), donuts and bakery scraps, suet, and bones are popular in feeders.

NESTING A hole is excavated in rotten wood, or an old woodpecker hole is filled with leaves, hair, moss, plant down, and feathers. When disturbed, an incubating bird may hiss like a snake.
🏠 The chickadee is a frequent user of enclosed nestboxes *(see page 59)*.

Nesting information April through July • 1 brood • 6 to 8 white, brown-spotted eggs • 11 to 13 days incubation by both parents • 14 to 18 days fledging

Titmouse family (PARIDAE)

TUFTED TITMOUSE

Parus bicolor

Length: 6½ inches (17 centimeters)

The crest may not always be raised

WITH ITS POINTED topknot of feathers and large eyes, the tufted titmouse is a very appealing visitor to the yard. The crest is raised when a titmouse is feeling aggressive, for instance when it is about to drive another bird from the feeder. Like the chickadees, to which it is related, the tufted titmouse is a woodland bird that gathers in small flocks during winter.

PLUMAGE The tufted titmouse is a gray bird, paler underneath, with a pointed crest. In southern Texas, it has a black crest. The plain titmouse *(Parus inornatus)* of the southwest is gray-brown and has a smaller crest.

VOICE The song is a whistling *peter-peter-peter*. A high *tseep* keeps the flock in contact and a harsh *jay-jay-jay* is given when disturbed.

FEEDING Titmice feed on small insects, caterpillars, and moth pupae. They also take small snails and spiders. In winter, they eat seeds and fruit, including acorns, sumac, beechnuts, and cherries. Food is often cached *(see page 153)*.
🔩 Seeds (especially sunflower seeds), suet, and bread will be taken from feeders. Titmice prefer hanging feeders.

NESTING A cavity in a tree or an old woodpecker hole is lined with leaves, moss, bark, and hair. Titmice will even pull hair from animals. When a pair raises

two families in a summer, the young of the first brood help feed the second brood.
🔩 Titmice use nestboxes *(see page 59)*.

Settling in *If tempted into a nestbox, titmice may continue to use it throughout their lives.*

Nesting information *March through May • 1 or 2 broods • 5 or 6 white, brown-spotted eggs 13 to 14 days incubation by the female • 17 to 18 days fledging*

Bushtit family (AEGITHALIDAE)
BUSHTIT
Psaltriparus minimus
Length: 4½ inches (11 centimeters)

Females are born with dark eyes that later turn creamy

THIS TITMOUSE-LIKE bird is resident through the year. For much of the year, bushtits live in noisy, acrobatic flocks, splitting up when courtship starts in January and February. They are most likely to appear in the yard in winter, and they nest where there are shrubs and groves of trees. Bushtits like to bathe, so water is also a great attraction.

PLUMAGE The bushtit is a gray-brown bird with a long tail and a very short bill. It has no prominent markings. The eyes of the males and newly hatched young are dark, while those of the adult females are cream. The males of populations in the southwest have black masks and were once regarded as a separate species, the black-eared bushtit.

VOICE Bushtits utter a high, twittering *tsit-tsit-tsit* as they feed but have no song.

FEEDING Bushtits feed in flocks, moving through trees rather like chickadees, picking insects, spiders, and caterpillars and pupae from foliage. Some seeds and fruit are also eaten.
✿ Bushtits may come to feeders for breadcrumbs, sunflower seeds, and birdseed mixtures.

NESTING The nest is a woven, gourd-shaped pocket, hanging from and supported by twigs, and is usually built in plain view. Both birds work on the nest, which may take several weeks to complete. It is constructed from twigs, mosses, rootlets, lichens, oak leaves, and flowers, bound together with spider webs. The birds are extremely sensitive during the nesting period. If they are disturbed they will often desert both nest and mate to remate and embark on a new nest and clutch elsewhere.

Front ball *A tunnel leads from the entrance hole to the chamber, where the eggs are laid.*

Nesting information *April through July • 2 broods • 5 to 13 white eggs • 12 days incubation by both parents • 14 to 15 days fledging.*

Nuthatch family (SITTIDAE)

WHITE-BREASTED NUTHATCH

Sitta carolinensis
Length: 5¾ inches (15 centimeters)

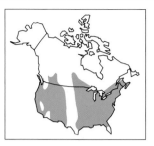

NUTHATCHES ARE DELIGHTFUL, acrobatic birds that often join flocks of downy woodpeckers and chickadees in winter. Unlike woodpeckers and creepers, nuthatches hop down treetrunks as well as up. They usually feed high in the tree canopy, and their whistled song and repetitive calls can be heard throughout the year.

The beak is long and thin, for probing under bark

PLUMAGE Gray above, with a black cap. The face and underside are white, with rusty red under the tail. In the northeast, the females have a dark gray cap. The red-breasted nuthatch *(Sitta canadensis)* is rust red below and has a black eye stripe.

VOICE The call is a rapid *yank-yank-yank*, the song a series of whistles.

FEEDING Bark and foliage are probed for insects and spiders. From fall, tree seeds are the main food. These are wedged into crevices and hammered open with the bill. Surplus nuts are cached *(see page 153)*.
✿ Peanuts, sunflower seeds, and suet are popular. Hanging feeders are preferred.

In a flap Clinging to the bark, a nuthatch flaps to deter an intruder from its nesthole.

NESTING A nest of feathers and wool is made in a hole in a tree. Nuthatches only occasionally excavate their own holes.
❏ Covering a nestbox with strips of bark makes it more acceptable to nuthatches.

Nesting information *March through June • 1 brood • 7 or 8 white eggs with brown, red, and gray markings • 12 days incubation by both parents • 14 days fledging*

Creeper family (CERTHIIDAE)

BROWN CREEPER
Certhia americana
Length: 5¼ inches (13 centimeters)

On bark, the mottled plumage gives near-perfect camouflage

THE BROWN CREEPER is fittingly named, because it can look like a mouse scuttling up the trunk of a tree. Creepers always climb upward, beginning each journey at the base of a tree, and flying down from the top of it to the base of the next tree. Brown creepers prefer mature trees, where they are often hard to spot until they come around to the side of the trunk and stand out against the background. Sometimes they are seen on utility poles and the sides of houses.

PLUMAGE The brown creeper is mottled brown above and pale below. The stiff tail is used as a prop when climbing. The bill is slender and curves slightly downward.

VOICE The song is a thin, whistling series of notes, the call a faint *see* note.

FEEDING Crevices in bark are probed for small insects and spiders, as well as their eggs and cocoons.
✿ Suet and other fatty food, and occasionally peanut fragments, smeared into crevices, attract brown creepers.

NESTING A nest of twigs, leaves, and moss, lined with feathers, is built under loose bark on a mature tree, or sometimes in a natural tree cavity or an old woodpecker hole.

Favored feeder *Creepers prefer to cling onto feeders vertically, as they do to trees.*

Nesting information *March through July • 1 brood • 5 or 6 white, brown-spotted eggs 14 to 15 days incubation by the female • 13 to 14 days fledging*

Wren family (TROGLODYTIDAE)

HOUSE WREN

Troglodytes aedon

Length: 4¾ inches (12 centimeters)

The tail is typically cocked

I T IS AMAZING that such small birds as wrens are able to migrate over long distances, but the house wren and the similar winter wren *(Troglodytes troglodytes)* travel hundreds of miles in spring and fall. However, the larger Carolina wren *(Thryothorus ludovicianus)* does not migrate. Both male and female house wrens sometimes have more than one mate. Males build several nests and try to entice passing females to enter them, but only a few males get more than one mate. Once the brood hatches, some females leave and seek out a second mate.

PLUMAGE Wrens are small, brown birds with cocked tails. The smaller winter wren has a shorter tail, a line through the eye, and barred flanks. The Carolina wren is paler underneath, with a white throat and white eyestripe.

VOICE In the medley of bubbling, whistling notes, the pitch rises and falls.

FEEDING Wrens eat insects, spiders, and other tiny animals.
🔲 Wrens may come to take suet or bread crumbs from a feeder.

NESTING A ball of grasses, moss, and other plant material is constructed in any one of a variety of natural and man-made cavities. The male builds the nest, and the female then lines it and carries out all the nesting duties.
🔲 Nestboxes, empty coconut shells and plant pots are readily used *(see page 59).*

Single parent *Care of the young may be left to the male, while the female seeks a second mate.*

Nesting information *April through July • 2 or 3 broods • 6 to 8 white, brown-speckled eggs 13 to 15 days incubation by the female • 12 to 18 days fledging*

Thrush family (MUSCICAPIDAE)

GOLDEN-CROWNED KINGLET

Regulus satrapa

Length: 4 inches (10 centimeters)

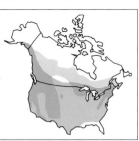

THE GOLDEN-CROWNED kinglet shows surprisingly little fear of people. It will come into open cabins and sometimes even allows itself to be stroked or picked up. Like the ruby-crowned kinglet, it has the habit of nervously flicking its wings when hopping from twig to twig. Its habitat is coniferous forests; fluctuations in the populations of golden-crowned kinglets are directly linked to shifts in conifer plantations.

The wings are often flicked as the bird hops around

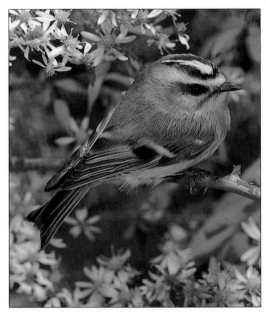

Winter home *The kinglet nests in coniferous forests, spreading into deciduous areas in fall.*

PLUMAGE Golden-crowned kinglets are olive above and pale buff below, with two whitish wing bars. The distinctive crown is orange in the male and yellow in the female, and bordered with yellow and black.

VOICE The call is three lisping notes. The song, seldom heard outside the northern breeding grounds, sounds similar to the call at the start and ends with louder, harsh, staccato descending notes: *zee, zee, zee, zee, zee, why do you shilly shally?*

FEEDING The diet is almost entirely insects, but tree sap is also drunk.
🔔 Suet and peanut butter in log or suet feeders may be visited in severe weather.

NESTING The hanging nest is usually built in a conifer, from mosses and lichens lined with soft bark, rootlets, and feathers.

Nesting information *April through July • 2 broods • 5 to 10 cream eggs spotted or blotched with gray or brown • 14 days incubation by the female • 14 to 19 days fledging*

Thrush family (MUSCICAPIDAE)
RUBY-CROWNED KINGLET
Regulus calendula
Length: 4 inches (10 centimeters)

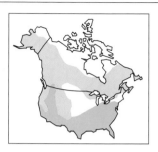

Wings are flicked frequently

THE KINGLETS ARE as small as the largest hummingbirds, and they sometimes hover near foliage while they pick tiny insects from the leaves. This and their habit of flicking their wings as they forage in the trees distinguish them from warblers. Their summer home is in dark, coniferous woods. They are most likely to be seen in yards in winter, when they join flocks of chickadees and other small birds, or when on migration.

PLUMAGE Ruby-crowned kinglets are dull olive above and whitish below, with a white eye ring. It is possible to mistake them for warblers at first glance, because the male's bright red crown patch is not usually visible, being held erect during the courtship display or at other times when the bird is excited.

VOICE The calls are a wrenlike *cack* and a lisping *zhi-dit,* and the song is a varied warble, rendered as *liberty, liberty, liberty.*

FEEDING Insects and spiders are picked from the foliage and twigs of trees while perched or hovering, or they are snatched in flight. Fruit, weed seeds, and tree sap from sapsucker holes *(see page 81)* are also eaten.

🔔 Ruby-crowned kinglets will occasionally come to take suet mixtures and chopped nuts from feeders.

NESTING The hanging nest of mosses and lichens lined with soft bark, rootlets, and feathers is usually built in a conifer.

Uncrowned *Even if the crown cannot be seen the bird's habit of bobbing its tail is distinctive.*

Nesting information *May to July • 1 brood • 5 to 11 cream eggs spotted or blotched with gray and brown • 12 days incubation by the female • 12 days fledging*

Thrush family (MUSCICAPIDAE)

EASTERN BLUEBIRD

Sialia sialis

Length: 7 inches (18 centimeters)

Bluebirds can appear round-shouldered when perched

THE REAPPEARANCE OF the eastern bluebird in the northern part of its range is a welcome sign of spring. Its preferred habitat is one of open fields with scattered trees, so it has benefited from the spread of agriculture and settlement. There has, however, been a general decrease in both suitable farmland and natural nesting cavities, and the problem has been made worse by the usurping of nestholes by foreign invaders such as starlings and house sparrows. Nestbox projects have dramatically reversed the decline of the bluebird in many places.

PLUMAGE The male is a striking blue above and chestnut underneath, with a white belly. The female is grayer above, and the juvenile is darker above with a spotted breast. The western bluebird (*Sialia mexicana*) has a blue throat and gray belly.

VOICE The call is a rising *churr-wee* or *tru-ally*, repeated in the song.

FEEDING The eastern bluebird's main food is insects, which the bird catches by dropping to the ground from a post or utility wire or the limb of a tree. Small fruits and berries are also eaten, especially in winter.

☐ Peanut kernels, raisins, and suet are popular with bluebirds, especially in hard winter weather.

NESTING Old woodpecker holes or holes in dead branches are the natural nest sites. The duties of building the nest and defending the nesthole are carried out by the female. The nest is constructed from grasses and twigs and lined with grass, hair, and feathers. The fledged young from the first brood will sometimes return to help feed the nestlings of the second brood *(see page 191)*.

☐ Bluebirds will use enclosed nestboxes *(see page 59)*. Secluded but open sites are preferred and precautions must be taken against competition from sparrows and starlings and predation by raccoons *(see page 54)*.

Nesting information *March through July • 2 broods • 4 or 5 pale blue eggs • 13 to 16 days incubation by the female • 15 to 20 days fledging*

Thrush family (MUSCICAPIDAE)

MOUNTAIN BLUEBIRD

Sialia currucoides

Length: 7 inches (18 centimeters)

Only the belly of this bird lacks the striking turquoise color

THE WARBLING song of the mountain bluebird resembles a robin's caroling and is heard in the early hours of the morning between first light and shortly after sunrise. The future of this bird is a matter of concern to conservationists, like that of the eastern and western bluebirds. Aggressive introduced birds, such as starlings and house sparrows, drive mountain bluebirds out of nest sites, and they are becoming ever rarer.

PLUMAGE The male mountain bluebird is bright turquoise-blue, paler below, with a whitish belly. The female is brown with blue on the wings and tail, lacking the rust-colored breast of the female eastern or western bluebirds *(see page 103).*

VOICE The calls are a low *chur* and *phew,* and the song is a clear, short warble. The mountain bluebird starts singing before dawn, then stops abruptly when the sun has risen.

FEEDING Through most of the year the mountain bluebird lives on a diet of insects, but this diet is supplemented by fruit when it is in season.
🌸 Bluebirds are attracted by dried fruit.

NESTING A nest of stems, rootlets, grasses, and pine needles, lined with hair and feathers, is built mostly by the male.

The usual nest site is a natural cavity such as a fissure in a cliff face or an old woodpecker hole in a tree.
🐦 Mountain bluebirds use the same nestboxes as eastern bluebirds *(see page 59).*

Quiet colors *The female, who carries out the nesting duties, is drab compared with the male.*

Nesting information April through July • 2 broods • 4 to 8 pale blue or occasionally white eggs • 14 days incubation by both parents • 12 to 14 days fledging

Thrush family (MUSCICAPIDAE)

WOOD THRUSH

Hylocichla mustelina

Length: 7¾ inches (20 centimeters)

The heavily spotted breast identifies this bird

T HE WOOD THRUSH is a migrant that arrives in spring, making its presence known by singing from the tops of trees. Later, it sings from lower down, even on the ground, but is usually inconspicuous because it spends its time in thick undergrowth. It is a welcome addition because its song is, to some people, the most beautiful of any bird's.

PLUMAGE The wood thrush is rich brown above, and reddish on the head, with a white eye ring. The underparts are white with large brown spots. The similar veery (*Catharus fuscescens*) is a more cinnamon color above, with gray flanks and less spotting on the breast. The hermit thrush (*Catharus guttatus*) has a buff breast with inconspicuous spots. Thrashers have longer tails, streaked underparts, and yellow eyes.

VOICE The call is a rapid *pit-pit-pit*. The song is made up of loud, liquid phrases of three to five bell-like notes.

FEEDING Insects and other small animals are plucked from leaves or snatched from the ground. Before migration the wood thrush turns to eating berries.

NESTING The nest is a compact cup of dead leaves and moss, lined with mud and an inner layer of rootlets. White paper or

rags are often used in the outer layer of the nest. It is built by the female in a crotch of a tree or large shrub. The wood

Persistent The young may continue to beg for almost three weeks after leaving the nest.

thrush has recently adapted to nesting in gardens and city parks, where dense shrubs have been planted and where there is water nearby.

Nesting information April through July • 2 broods • 3 or 4 blue or blue-green eggs • 13 to 14 days incubation by the female • 12 to 13 days fledging

105

Thrush family (MUSCICAPIDAE)

AMERICAN ROBIN
Turdus migratorius
Length: 10 inches (25 centimeters)

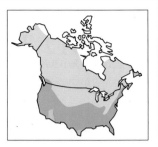

THIS IS ONE of the most widespread and best known of North American birds. Populations from Canada, the Great Lakes, and the plains regions of the United States migrate for the winter to join the resident populations farther south. The American robin is famous for its tame, friendly nature, although robins are aggressive toward each other. The robin has adapted well to human settlement and colonized the prairies when they were plowed up. Where its natural nesting places in trees are in short supply, it readily takes to fences and buildings.

Robins have touches of white under the tail, and the outer feathers are tipped with white

PLUMAGE The robin is gray-brown above, darker on the head and tail, and brick-red underneath, with some white under the chin and tail. There is a white ring around the eye. The female is duller, and the juvenile is heavily spotted below.

VOICE The calls include a *tut-tut*, and the song is a loud *cheerily-cheerily*.

FEEDING Robins eat large quantities of fruit – mulberry, sumac, and cherry are popular – and may sometimes become pests, but large quantities of insects, especially plant-eating caterpillars, are also taken. A robin hunting earthworms on the lawn *(see page 33)* is a common sight.
✿ Apples, sunflower seeds, and bread will attract robins to feeders.

Shared duties *The male cares for the fledged first brood while the female incubates a second.*

NESTING The cup of mud and grass is built in a crotch of a tree. Similar sites are used on man-made structures.
✿ Robins will use a platform placed on a tree or building *(see page 59)*.

Nesting information *April through July • 1 to 3 broods • 4 blue eggs • 12 to 14 days incubation by the female • 14 to 16 days fledging*

Mimic thrush family (Mimidae)

GRAY CATBIRD

Dumetella carolinensis

Length: 8½ inches (22 centimeters)

THE CATBIRD IS more often heard than seen, because it skulks in undergrowth and scrub but has a powerful voice. It can become tame, however, and some catbirds become persistent but popular visitors to feeders. It is one of the forest-edge birds that have benefited from settlement *(see page 14).*

The chestnut tail coverts are usually visible

PLUMAGE This plain gray bird has a black cap and tail. The long tail is usually cocked up, showing chestnut underneath.

VOICE The call is a nasal, catlike mew, for which the species is named. The song includes mewing notes among a selection of squeaks and more tuneful sounds. The catbird also mimics the songs of a variety of other birds.

FEEDING The catbird's diet is divided between plant and animal food. Insects are eaten in the warmer months, and berries and other fruits are important through the winter months.
🐦 Fruit-bearing bushes and vines attract catbirds. Peanuts and peanut butter, chopped fresh fruit, cooked potatoes, suet, cheese, and dried fruit such as raisins will bring them to a feeder. Some individuals even take milk and cornflakes.

Bright berries *Holly, bittersweet, elderberry, and honeysuckle will attract catbirds.*

NESTING The nest is a mass of twigs and leaves lined with skeleton leaves, pine needles, fine rootlets, and bark, and it is placed in dense cover near the ground. Most of the construction is undertaken by the female, with the male bringing material for her to work into the nest.

Nesting information *May through August • 1 or 2 broods • 4 glossy, greenish blue eggs 12 to 15 days incubation by the female • 10 to 15 days fledging*

Mimic thrush family (MIMIDAE)

NORTHERN MOCKINGBIRD

Mimus polyglottos

Length: 10 inches (25 centimeters)

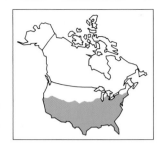

White patches can be seen in flight

IT SEEMS ODD that the state bird of five southern states is known as the northern mockingbird. It is so called because its range reaches quite far north in comparison with other related species – as far as Canada. This spread may have been aided by an increase in multiflora roses, the fruit of which is a favorite food.

PLUMAGE The northern mockingbird is gray with white wing patches, and white edges to the tail, which are seen in flight. Juveniles are light brown with a speckled breast. The similar northern and loggerhead shrikes *(Lanius excubitor* and *Lanius ludovicianus)* show more contrast in their plumage and have a black eye stripe, or mask.

VOICE The call is a sharp *chack* or *chair*. Mockingbirds often sing at night, mostly under a full moon. They imitate other birds, toads croaking, dogs barking, and mechanical sounds such as pianos tinkling.

FEEDING Insects and small animals are hunted on lawns, where the bird's habit of raising its wings may flush out prey. Berries are also important.

🐦 Raisins, apples, suet, peanut butter, and donuts attract mockingbirds.

NESTING A large cup of twigs, leaves, and grass, lined with rootlets, is built low in a shrub or thicket. Males are sometimes polygamous. Mockingbirds defend their nests by harassing cats, dogs, and people, pecking or flapping at them. No damage is done and the attacks cease after the young have flown.

Berry treasure *Northern mockingbirds are great fruit eaters, especially in winter.*

Nesting information *March through August • 2 or 3 broods • 4 or 5 blue or green eggs with red speckles • 12 days incubation by the female • 10 to 12 days fledging*

Mimic thrush family (MIMIDAE)

BROWN THRASHER

Toxostoma rufum

Length: 10½–12 inches (27–30 centimeters)

Yellow eyes easily distinguish this thrasher from thrushes

THE BROWN THRASHER'S most preferred natural habitat of thickets and woodland edges often brings it into suburban yards. It forages on the ground, tossing leaves into the air with its bill to expose insects beneath them. Although easily approached, this secretive bird rarely comes into the open, except to sing from the top of a tree. It is not often seen at the feeder.

PLUMAGE The brown thrasher is reddish brown above with two white wing bars, and pale buff to white with heavy dark streaks below. The eyes are yellow in adult birds, and gray to yellowish gray in juveniles. The eyes, the long tail, and the streaked breast distinguish thrashers from the similar wood thrush *(see page 105).*

VOICE Like others in the mockingbird family, the brown thrasher has a varied song, typically repeating the phrases twice. The call is a sharp *smack.* The brown thrasher mimics other birds, but less often than most members of its family.

FEEDING The diet consists mainly of insects and other small animals found among dead leaves. Seeds and fallen fruit are also eaten, and berries of many kinds are important in winter.

✿ The brown thrasher is an occasional visitor for scratch feed, corn, suet, breadcrumbs, and dried fruit scattered on the ground.

NESTING The nest often consists of several "baskets" or layers. It is built out of twigs, leaves, thin bark, and grasses, lined with rootlets, and positioned in a low bush or sometimes on the ground.

Messy eater *Thrashers are named for their habit of flinging leaves up in search of food.*

Nesting information *March through July • 1 or 2 broods • 3 to 6 pale blue to white eggs, finely spotted with brown • 12 to 14 days incubation by both parents • 9 to 13 days fledging*

Waxwing family (BOMBYCILLIDAE)

CEDAR WAXWING

Bombycilla cedrorum

Length: 7¼ inches (18 centimeters)

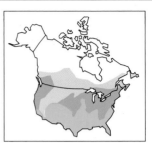

The function of the waxy feather tips is not known

T HIS BIRD IS NAMED for the bright red tips of the wing feathers, which look like blobs of old-fashioned sealing wax. Waxwings may descend on a yard to feed on the berries of pyracantha, mountainash, and cotoneaster. Sometimes they become intoxicated on overripe berries and can be picked up in the hand. Provided that they are not taken by predators, the birds soon recover. Birdbaths are very attractive to waxwings, and in summer they may gather to feed on insects swarming over water.

PLUMAGE Adults are gray-brown above, with red spots on the wings and a yellow tip to the tail, and pale yellow below. The head is brown, with a black eye stripe and pointed crest. The juvenile is streaked. The Bohemian waxwing *(Bombycilla garrulus)* has gray underparts, and white and yellow spots on the wing.

VOICE The call is a high-pitched trill.

FEEDING Waxwings feed mostly on berries, but sometimes they also take maple sap. Insects are caught in summer and are the main food for young nestlings.
✿ Waxwings feeding on fruit in the yard may come to raisins or chopped apples.

NESTING Waxwings nest in small colonies wherever there is a good supply of berries. Breeding starts late, so that by the time the new generation is launched, the berries will be ripe. The nests, constructed from twigs, leaves, moss, and hair, are placed fairly close together in trees and shrubs.
✿ Waxwings will take lengths of wool and string, even from the hand, to weave into their nests.

Get-together *Outside the breeding season, waxwings live in flocks.*

Nesting information *June through September • 1 or 2 broods • 3 to 5 gray, black-spotted eggs • 12 to 16 days incubation by the female • 14 to 18 days fledging*

Starling family (STURNIDAE)
EUROPEAN STARLING
Sturnus vulgaris
Length: 8½ inches (22 centimeters)

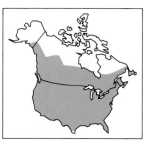

EUROPEAN STARLINGS were released in New York's Central Park in 1890, and they have since spread throughout the continent. They are often unpopular, because they take the food put out for native birds and usurp the nest sites of other birds such as bluebirds. Yet the lively behavior of starlings makes them interesting birds to watch, and there is plenty of action when a flock descends in a yard or park or a pair takes up residence in a nestbox.

The pale tips of the feathers wear away through the winter and spring

PLUMAGE The glossy, black feathers are shot with blue, purple, and green. Pale tips on new feathers in fall give a spangled appearance. By spring much of the spotting is lost, because the tips of the feathers have worn away. The bill is yellow in spring and summer, turning brown in winter.

VOICE The song is a medley of rattles, squeaks, and whistles, especially a rising *phee-oooo*, and often also includes mimicry of other birds and imitations of barking dogs. The calls include an aggressive *chacker-chacker* and a harsh, screaming distress call.

FEEDING Starlings have a varied diet. Their main foods are seed and grain, and earthworms, insects, and other creatures found near grass roots. They stride forward inspecting the ground with rapid thrusts of the bill, which is forced open with each probe.

✿ Bread, scraps, hanging bones, and peanuts will all attract starlings.

NESTING The male builds a nest of grass, sometimes using green leaves *(see page 201),* which is lined by the female, in a hole in a tree or a building. To collect a meal for nestlings, a starling has to drop one item before probing for the next. Fledglings follow their parents, and are fed on the lawn.

🏠 Starlings will use large, enclosed nestboxes *(see page 59).*

Nesting information April through July • 2 or 3 broods • 4 to 6 pale greenish blue eggs
12 days incubation by the female • 21 days fledging

Vireo family (VIREONIDAE)

WHITE-EYED VIREO

Vireo griseus

Length: 5 inches (13 centimeters)

VIREOS ARE insect-eating birds that fly south for the winter, but some white-eyed vireos stay behind in the southernmost states. Vireos live in woods; the white-eyed vireo, like Bell's vireo *(Vireo bellii)* in the west, prefers dense thickets. It comes into yards that have shrubs and tangles of blackberries and multiflora roses. Vireos are active birds: only Hutton's vireo *(Vireo huttoni),* of the west coast, is sedentary.

The white eyes may not be obvious from a distance

PLUMAGE The white-eyed vireo is gray-green above and white underneath, with green flanks and white wing bars. There are yellow "spectacles" around the eyes. The white eyes can be seen close to.

VOICE The song has five to seven variable notes, which usually include a sharp *chick.* Other birds are also mimicked. The call is a softer, short *tick.*

FEEDING Vireos eat mainly insects, snails, and sometimes small lizards plucked from foliage near the ground. Berries are eaten in the fall.

NESTING The nest is a deep cup of woven fibers, grasses, and rootlets, bound with spider webs, and suspended from slender twigs at the end of a branch. It is lined with fine grasses and decorated on the outside with mosses, lichens, and pieces of paper.

Shared duties *Both parents raise the young, and are fearless around the nest.*

Nesting information *March through July • 1 or 2 broods • 4 white, brown-spotted eggs 12 to 15 days incubation by both parents • 20 to 30 days fledging*

Vireo family (VIREONIDAE)

RED-EYED VIREO

Vireo olivaceus
Length: 6 inches (15 centimeters)

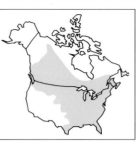

This is one of the largest vireos without wing bars

T HE RED-EYED VIREO is most notable for its enthusiastic singing: a record of more than 22,000 songs in a single day has been noted in one individual. Recent years have seen a fall in the population of the red-eyed vireo in areas where it was once common. Deforestation, the use of pesticides, and the increase in nest parasites such as the brown-headed cowbird, which appears to target this bird especially as a host for its eggs *(see page 202),* have all played a part in this decline.

PLUMAGE Olive green above, and white below, the red-eyed vireo is distinguished by the markings on its head. The cap is gray edged with black, and there is a white stripe above the eye and a black stripe through it. The red iris may not be visible at a distance, and immature birds have brown eyes. The similar warbling vireo *(Vireo gilvus)* lacks the red eyes and striped head.

VOICE The alarm call is a nasal *tschay!* and the song is varied, some of the characteristic phrases being *cherry-o-wit, cheree, sissy-o-wit,* and *tee-oo.* Red-eyed vireos sometimes sing at night.

FEEDING Red-eyed vireos forage in trees for insects and also eat apples, downy serviceberry, and common sassafras fruit.

NESTING The nest is a thin-walled cup of grasses, rootlets, and bark, bound with spiders' webs and decorated with lichen.

Easy victims *Red-eyed vireos are common cowbird hosts and only rarely reject the eggs.*

Nesting information *May through August • 1 or 2 broods • 3 to 5 white eggs, lightly dotted with brown and black • 11 to 14 days incubation by the female • 10 to 12 days fledging*

Warbler family (EMBERIZIDAE)

YELLOW WARBLER

Dendroica petechia

Length: 5 inches (13 centimeters)

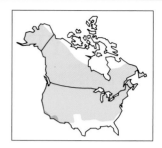

The wings are spotted with different shades of yellow

MOST YELLOW WARBLERS migrate to Mexico and farther south for the winter, but a few overwinter in southern California and Arizona. They are commonly seen in yards during the migration periods, and they may stay to nest, especially if running water is available. Their cheery song is often heard through the day, and you may see the male perched in a tree, guarding his mate while she feeds below.

PLUMAGE Male yellow warblers are bright yellow, with reddish streaks underneath. Females are paler, with tinges of green. Many other warblers have yellow in their plumage, but none of them is so yellow overall.

VOICE The song is rendered as *sweet-sweet-sweet-I'm-so-sweet.*

FEEDING Although yellow warblers may eat some berries in late summer, their diet is made up almost exclusively of insects. Caterpillars, especially those that defoliate trees and shrubs, are consumed in large numbers, so yellow warblers are useful birds to have in a garden.

NESTING Yellow warblers nest in back yards if there is are dense shrubs. The birds are quite tame when building their nests, so they can be watched at work. The nest is built by the female from plant fibers, grasses, wool, and moss, and lined with hair and cotton. Yellow warblers are among the birds whose nests are most frequently used by cowbirds *(see page 202)* for their own eggs.

Self-defense *Warblers may build a false floor over cowbird eggs and raise a new clutch.*

Nesting information *April through July • 1 brood • 4 or 5 gray-green eggs with spots of brown or olive at the blunt end • 11 days incubation by the female • 9 to 12 days fledging*

Warbler family (EMBERIZIDAE)

YELLOW-BREASTED CHAT

Icteria virens

Length: 7 inches (18 centimeters)

A SECRETIVE AND elusive bird that spends most of its time in undergrowth, the yellow-breasted chat is more likely to be heard than seen. It may sometimes be seen flying awkwardly from bush to bush while singing. Its common name comes from its tendency to chatter, the song being an extraordinary medley of sounds.

The tail is unusually long for a warbler

PLUMAGE As its name suggests, the yellow-breasted chat is a clear yellow on its breast, with a white belly and green upperparts. The head is green with a white stripe and eye ring, and a black area below the eye.

VOICE The song may often be heard at night and includes a wide range of sounds, resembling those of other birds, catcalls, and whistles.

FEEDING The yellow-breasted chat feeds mainly on insects but is also fond of berries in season.
❁ Brambles, hedges, and fruit-bearing shrubs attract yellow-breasted chats.

NESTING The female builds a large cup of dead leaves, grass, and bark, well concealed in dense shrubs or on the ground. Several pairs may sometimes nest in a loose colony, but the males will still defend their individual territories.

Shy performer *The yellow-breasted chat prefers to remain out of sight in foliage.*

Nesting information April through August • 1 brood • 3 to 6 white or light cream eggs speckled with rust or violet • 8 days incubation by the female • 8 to 11 days fledging

Tanager family (EMBERIZIDAE)

SCARLET TANAGER
Piranga olivacea
Length: 7 inches (18 centimeters)

THE VISIT OF a scarlet tanager to your feeder is a special occasion. This shy forest bird migrates from South America for the summer and usually lives in the treetops. If it does come into the yard, it is easily driven away by aggressive birds such as mockingbirds. Scarlet tanagers are replaced in the southern states by the summer tanager *(Piranga rubra),* which is less shy and more likely to become a regular visitor.

The black wings distinguish this bird from other red birds

PLUMAGE The male is bright red, with black wings and tail. The plumage is molted to yellow-green in the fall, and the red reappears in spring. The female is yellow-olive throughout the year. The summer tanager is red all over, without the black wings and tail. The northern cardinal

(see page 118), may at first glance appear similar to the summer tanager but has a pronounced crest.

VOICE The song is a robin-like *querit, queer, query, querit, queer.* The female sometimes sings before egg-laying. The call is *CHIP-churr.*

FEEDING The scarlet tanager forages for insects and fruit.
✿ Tanagers occasionally visit feeders for fruit, and more rarely for suet and bread.

NESTING If scarlet tanagers do breed in or near your yard, you may see the male displaying from a low perch. He sings to entice a female to fly over the spot and then spreads his wings so that the black back is shown off to the female overhead. The shallow nest of grass, twigs, and roots is built by the male near the end of a branch, usually at a considerable height.

Harlequin plumage *Male scarlet tanagers can look very odd during the fall molt.*

Nesting information *May through August • 1 brood • 4 pale blue or green eggs with brown spots • 13 to 14 days incubation by the female • 9 to 11 days fledging*

Tanager family (EMBERIZIDAE)

WESTERN TANAGER

Piranga ludoviciana

Length: 7 inches (18 centimeters)

O NE OF THE most colorful birds of the Rockies, the western tanager will sometimes appear at elevations as high as 10,000 feet (3,048 meters). A woodland bird, its preferred habitat is conifer forest. It is a quiet bird with a somewhat shrill whistle, but its bright plumage makes it a welcome visitor to yards. It is attracted by the sound of running water.

This is the only tanager with wing bars

PLUMAGE The male's plumage is mainly yellow. The head is red during the breeding season, but this disappears in the fall and winter. The tail, shoulders, and wings are black, and there are two yellow bars on the wings. The female is dull olive-brown above, with yellow and white bars on the wings, and yellow underneath. She resembles a female oriole *(see page 134)* but has a less pointed bill.

VOICE The call is *pit-ic,* sometimes followed by *chert-it.* The song is described as robin-like but is hoarser and lower in pitch than that of a robin.

FEEDING The diet is made up of insects, berries, and other fruit. Buds are occasionally eaten.

🔸 Western tanagers will come to feeders for dried fruit or halved oranges and will also take sugar-water from hummingbird feeders with perches.

NESTING The nest of twigs, roots, and moss, lined with hair and rootlets, is built in a fork close to the end of a high branch. Conifers are much preferred as nest sites and deciduous trees used only rarely. The female is reluctant to leave the nest when incubating, even if disturbed.

Staple food *Insects hunted in trees and on the ground make up most of the diet.*

> **Nesting information** *May through July • 1 brood • 3 to 5 pale blue eggs blotched with brown • 13 days incubation by the female • 13 to 15 days fledging*

Cardinal family (EMBERIZIDAE)

NORTHERN CARDINAL

Cardinalis cardinalis

Length: 8¾ inches (22 centimeters)

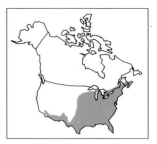

Stout bill for cracking seeds

NO ONE CAN miss the brilliant scarlet of the male cardinal. If your yard has berry-producing shrubs, vines, and trees, and if there is water for bathing, you may get a pair of cardinals nesting, and after nesting, they will bring their families to the feeder. One of the first signs of spring is the cardinal's cheerful song, which may be uttered by the male or female. At this time, the males begin to offer food to the females instead of dominating them at the feeder.

PLUMAGE The male is red, with a black face and a pointed crest. The female is dull brown with a reddish tinge. The juvenile male is less red, and the juvenile female entirely brown.

VOICE The call is a *chink*. The song is a medley of whistles, such as *what cheer, whit whit, pretty pretty,* and many other phrases. The combinations vary, so cardinals in one area sound different from those in another.

FEEDING The cardinal's diet includes fruit, seeds, and many kinds of insects and small animals.
✿ Cardinals will come to cracked corn, nuts, and sunflower seeds on the ground or on platforms.

NESTING The female cardinal builds her nest of weeds, grasses, and twigs in dense shrubs and vines. She incubates the eggs, and the male cares for the first brood of nestlings while she lays and incubates a second clutch.

Drab *Like many females that incubate alone, the female cardinal is duller than the male.*

Nesting information March through August • 2 or 3 broods • 3 or 4 gray to greenish eggs with brown or purple marks • 12 to 13 days incubation by the female • 10 to 11 days fledging

Cardinal family (EMBERIZIDAE)

ROSE-BREASTED GROSBEAK
Pheucticus ludovicianus
Length: 7½ inches (18-21 centimeters)

Rosy underwings show in flight

GROSBEAKS USE THEIR bills for cracking all kinds of seeds, even cherry pits. They also descend upon cherry blossoms, pecking out the developing seeds. Rose-breasted grosbeaks frequently feed and nest in yards and parks, but they often go unnoticed because they live in the treetops. The attractive song resembles that of a robin. The similar black-headed grosbeak *(Pheucticus melanocephalus)* replaces the rose-breasted grosbeak in the west, and the two sometimes interbreed where they overlap on the Great Plains.

PLUMAGE The male is black above, with white patches on the wings, and very white underparts, with a black throat. There is a triangle of rose red on the breast, and rosy underwings. The female is a dark buff above, with two broad white wing bars, and streaked below, with pale yellow underwings.

VOICE The courtship song of the male is a long, liquid carol. The female's song is similar, but softer and shorter. The male sings even while on the nest.

FEEDING Seeds, blossoms, buds, insects and bugs are preferred, and some fruit and grain are taken.
✿ Grosbeaks will come to a platform feeder for sunflower seeds.

NESTING An insubstantial nest of loosely woven sticks, twigs, and straw, lined with grasses and rootlets, is built in thickets or low trees by both birds.

Smartening up *The young males lack the well-defined coloring of the adults.*

Nesting information *May through July • 1 brood • 3 to 5 greenish blue eggs, speckled and blotched with brown • 12 to 13 days incubation by both parents • 9 to 12 days fledging*

BIRD PROFILES

ROSE-BREASTED GROSBEAK

119

Cardinal family (EMBERIZIDAE)

BLUE GROSBEAK

Guiraca caerulea

Length: 6¾ inches (17 centimeters)

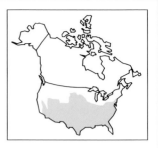

T HE NATURAL FOREST edge and hedgerow habitat preferred by the blue grosbeak brings it into the suburban yard, where it will nest if there is plenty of cover. After breeding, flocks gather and feed on grain crops before heading south to Central America for the winter. Returning flocks of males arrive ahead of the females in spring to establish territories. Usually a quiet, peaceable bird, a blue grosbeak will defend its nesting territory vigorously against competition.

The wing bars help distinguish this from the indigo bunting

Home decor *The female may work snake skins, bark, or strips of plastic into the nest.*

PLUMAGE The male is deep blue with two rust-colored wing bars. The blue color is iridescence; the birds appear black in poor light. The female is brown with two rust-colored wing bars.

VOICE The male sings a sweet melodious song, similar to that of a purple finch *(see page 136)* or an indigo bunting *(see opposite),* from a utility wire or the top of a tree or bush.

FEEDING Insects, weed seeds, and wild fruit are picked from the ground.
✿ Seed on the ground attracts these birds.

NESTING Built low in trees, shrubs, or vines, the nest is a cup of grasses, rootlets, weeds, and leaves.

Nesting information *May through August • 1 or 2 broods • 2 to 5 light blue eggs • 11 days incubation by the female • 13 days fledging*

Cardinal family (EMBERIZIDAE)
INDIGO BUNTING
Passerina cyanea
Length: 5½ inches (14 centimeters)

D URING THEIR MIGRATIONS, small flocks of these birds, sometimes made up of colorful males, invade the yard. If they arrive with evening grosbeaks *(see page 142)*, cardinals *(see page 118)*, and painted buntings *(see page 122)*, you will be treated to a display of color that rivals any flowerbed. Recently some indigo buntings have stopped migrating to South America. Flocks now spend the winter in Florida, and they are increasingly being seen in northern states.

The plumage may appear black in poor light

PLUMAGE The male is deep iridescent blue, appearing black in poor light, with a small black area around the base of the bill. The female and juvenile forms are dull brown, darker on the back and streaked underneath. The similar blue grosbeak *(see opposite)* is larger and has wing bars.

VOICE The call is a sharp *tsick*. The song is a series of double notes that has been described as *sweet-sweet, where-where, here-here, see-it, see-it*. In some areas, it includes elements of the song of the lazuli buntings *(Passerina amoena)*. Indigo buntings sing throughout the day and continue singing into late summer, after other birds have become silent.

FEEDING The indigo bunting eats a variety of insects and seeds, as well as berries in the fall.
✿ Buntings are attracted to peanuts, millet, and seeds. `

NESTING Indigo buntings live in low, dense growth such as overgrown orchards, or where vegetation is regularly cut under utility cables, and in dense shrubs. The female builds the nest of grasses, leaves, and hair near the ground.

Absent fathers *Male parental care varies, but usually all the work is left to the female.*

Nesting information *May through August • 2 broods • 3 or 4 bluish white eggs • 12 to 13 days incubation by the female • 8 to 10 days fledging*

Cardinal family (EMBERIZIDAE)

PAINTED BUNTING

Passerina ciris

Length: 5½ inches (14 centimeters)

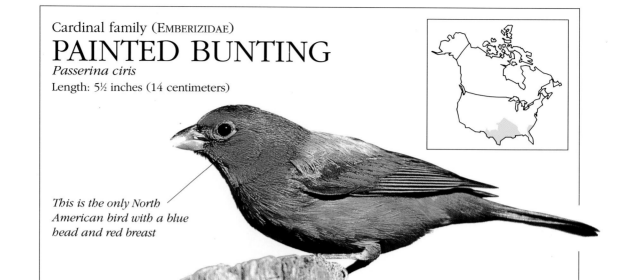

This is the only North American bird with a blue head and red breast

PERHAPS THE MOST COLORFUL of North American birds, the painted bunting is shy and apt to flit off at the first sign of an intrusion. A yard must provide plenty of cover to entice painted buntings into it. Only during the mating season will the male lose this characteristic caution, singing from a perch in the open. In spite of this apparent reticence, painted buntings are formidable fighters: unlike most birds, whose combats are largely bluff *(see page 175)*, they will fight fiercely, and sometimes to the death, in territorial disputes.

PLUMAGE The male has a green back, reddish wings, and bright red underparts. The head is blue with a red eye ring. Rather than coming from any pigment in the feathers, the blue color is an effect caused by the way that the light is reflected from them, with the result that the head may appear black in poor light. The female is green above and yellowish green below.

VOICE Quiet twittering or chipping notes may be heard, and the male sings a sweet, thin, tinkling song in courtship.

FEEDING The diet consists mainly of seeds, but insects, spiders, and caterpillars are also favored.
☘ Painted buntings will come to feeders for sunflower seed and seed mixes.

NESTING The nest is a cup of grasses, weed stalks, and leaves, usually built low in dense cover.

Verdant bird *The female painted bunting is the most uniformly green small finch.*

Nesting information *March through July • 2 to 4 broods • 3 to 5 pale blue eggs spotted with brown • 11 to 12 days incubation by female • 12 to 14 days fledging*

Sparrow family (EMBERIZIDAE)
RUFOUS-SIDED TOWHEE
Pipilo erythrophthalmus
Length: 8½ inches (22 centimeters)

The white flashes that all forms have on the tail can be seen in flight

The female has the same color pattern as the male but is brown rather than black

THE RUFOUS-SIDED towhee is a bird of dense undergrowth, more often heard than seen and identified by its distinctive call. Towhees come into yards with bushes and brush piles, and can be heard scratching for food on bare ground under cover. Their usual method of feeding is to rake with their feet to reveal seeds and insects. The towhee's range is gradually extending northwards.

PLUMAGE The male is black above and white below, with a black breast and red sides. The female is brown above, and the juvenile has scaly plumage. All have white patches on the wings and tail. Western birds, once called spotted towhees, have white wing bars and white flecks above.

VOICE Calls are the *to-WHEE* that gives the bird its name, *chee-WINK*, and *jor-eee*. The song is rendered as *DRINK-your-tea*.

FEEDING Beetles, ants, spiders, snails, and other small animals are the main part of the diet. Berries and the seeds of weeds and grasses are also important.
✿ Scattered sunflower seed, cracked corn, and peanut kernels will tempt towhees.

NESTING The nest of grasses, rootlets, twigs, and leaves, lined with hair and grass, is built by the female on the ground or sometimes in low shrubs or vines.

Home ground *A towhee nest among young trees on the woodland floor, its natural habitat.*

Nesting information April through August • 2 broods • 3 or 4 gray or cream eggs with brown speckles • 12 to 13 days incubation by the female • 10 to 12 days fledging

Sparrow family (EMBERIZIDAE)

AMERICAN TREE SPARROW

Spizella arborea

Length: 6 inches (15 centimeters)

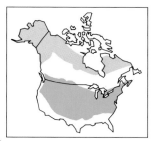

The upper part of the bill is dark, the lower part yellow

The characteristic blotch on the breast makes it easy to identify the tree sparrow

ALTHOUGH THE scientific and the common names suggest woods as their home, few birds spend less time in trees than tree sparrows. In winter, they come south in flocks of 30 to 40 birds, which are seen around hedges, fields, and marshes. The breeding grounds are open plains just south of the Arctic tundra, and even here the birds nest on or near the ground.

PLUMAGE The chestnut back has white and black streaks, and the underparts are gray, with a brown blotch on the breast. The head is white with a chestnut cap and streak through the eye.

VOICE Birds in a flock converse in musical *teedle eet, teedle eet* notes. The courtship song of the male is one or two high, sweet notes, followed by warbling.

FEEDING Tree sparrows forage on the ground for weed and grass seeds, which they eat in great numbers. They also eat insects and some fruit.
✿ Wild bird seed mixes will attract tree sparrows, and white millet is also a favorite food.

NESTING The nest is constructed of grasses, moss, and bark, sometimes lined with ptarmigan feathers, hair, and fur. It is built by the female in a tussock or in a shallow depression in the ground.

Winter survivors *Tree sparrows can survive bitter cold as long as they can find food.*

Nesting information *May through July • 1 brood • 3 to 6 brown-speckled, pale blue or green eggs • 12 to 13 days incubation by the female • Young leave nest at 10 days, unable to fly*

Sparrow family (EMBERIZIDAE)

CHIPPING SPARROW

Spizella passerina

Length: 5–5¾ inches (13–15 centimeters)

The bill is black during breeding, and then turns brown

THE CHIPPING SPARROW is one of the most familiar sparrows because it is a common yard species, often feeding on lawns and uncultivated ground and nesting in evergreens and shrubs near houses. It is not shy of human presence and with time will learn to take food from the hand. Family groups wander after breeding and before migration, and in winter, small flocks of up to 50 birds forage together.

PLUMAGE Chipping sparrows are light brown or drab streaked with rust-brown above, with a bright chestnut cap. There is a black streak through the eye and a broad white line above it. In winter the cap and the black eye stripe become duller and less noticeable. The underparts are unmarked gray.

VOICE The *chip* call notes and song give this bird its name. The song may sometimes be heard at night.

FEEDING The diet consists of seeds and insects. Chipping sparrows also peck at salt blocks.
✿ The chipping sparrow will come to a variety of seeds and crumbs. Food should be scattered widely on the ground, to reduce competition with other, more aggressive species.

NESTING The female builds a nest of grasses, weeds, and rootlets, lined with hair, in a tree, shrub, or tangled vine, or near the foundation of a building.

Unusual site *This chipping sparrow finds a tangle of game traps a suitable nest foundation.*

Nesting information *March through August • 2 broods • 3 to 5 pale blue-green eggs, marked with blue, brown, and black • 11 to 14 days incubation by the female • 8 to 12 days fledging*

Sparrow family (EMBERIZIDAE)

SONG SPARROW

Melospiza melodia

Length: 5½–7 inches (14–18 centimeters)

The tail is pumped up and down in flight

THE SONG SPARROW is one of the best known of the many different North American sparrows, although its plumage lacks the bright patches of color worn by many other sparrows. Found everywhere but the most northern parts of the continent it is a common inhabitant of yards, and makes good use of feeders in the winter and birdbaths throughout the year. The bird's pleasant song may be heard at any time of the year.

PLUMAGE The song sparrow's appearance varies through its range. Generally, it has streaked brown upperparts and is whitish underneath, with dark streaks that meet in a spot in the center of the breast. There is a gray stripe above the eye.

VOICE The song sparrow has 21 different calls and songs. The main call is a nasal *chimp*. The song was rendered by Henry Thoreau as *Maids! Maids! Maids! Hang-up-your-teakettle-ettle-ettle!*, but it is variable enough for some individuals to be recognized by their song.

FEEDING The song sparrow scratches for insects and other small animals and for seeds. It also eats berries. After snowfall, song sparrows scratch away the snow to reveal the fallen seeds.

☘ Sunflower seeds and other seeds, bread crumbs, and millet are taken from platforms or the ground under feeders.

Home lover *Resident birds stay on or near their territory even through severe weather.*

NESTING Nesting starts early, and the first nests of the season are built on the ground, under clumps of grass or thick weeds. Later, when the new leaves of deciduous bushes provide cover, nests are built above the ground in the foliage.

Nesting information *February through August • 2 or 3 broods • 3 to 6 pale green eggs with reddish brown spots • 12 to 13 days incubation by the female • 10 days fledging*

Sparrow family (EMBERIZIDAE)

WHITE-THROATED SPARROW

Zonotrichia albicollis

Length: 6¾ inches (17 centimeters)

MOST WHITE-THROATED sparrows breed in Canada and migrate to the southern United States in the colder months, but increasing numbers are overwintering in the northeastern states. In these areas they have become the most common of the many sparrow species to visit yards and feeders. It is possible that the increasing popularity of feeding birds has helped these "white-throats" survive the hardship of the northern winters.

The breast may be dull or streaked in juveniles

Winter split *As with many other species, the dominant adult males tend to winter farther north than do females and immatures.*

PLUMAGE White-throats have rust-brown upperparts and grayish underparts. The white throat is conspicuous. There are broad black-and-white stripes through the eye and over the crown, and a small patch of yellow in front of the eye. The juvenile has streaked light and dark underparts and a grayish throat.

VOICE Calls include a *pink* and a *seet*. The whistling song is rendered as *Old Sam Peabody, Peabody, Peabody* or *Pure sweet Canada, Canada, Canada*.

FEEDING The white-throat forages for weed seeds, scratching the ground with each foot in turn. Insects are also eaten. 🐦 Millet, sunflower seed, and cracked grain and other seeds are taken from the ground or from platforms.

NESTING The nest of twigs and grasses is built by the female. It is usually placed on the ground, well concealed under the cover of a bush or brush pile, but is sometimes built just above the ground in thick vegetation.

Nesting information *May through August • 1 brood • 4 to 6 bluish or greenish white eggs with brown speckles • 12 to 14 days incubation by the female • 7 to 12 days fledging*

Sparrow family (EMBERIZIDAE)

DARK-EYED JUNCO

Junco hyemalis

Length: 6¼ inches (16 centimeters)

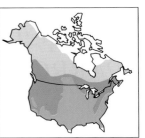

ISTINCTIVE AND POPULAR in yards and at feeders, dark-eyed juncos are birds of forest edges and glades, which makes leafy suburban neighborhoods excellent habitats for them. They breed in Canada and the northern United States and migrate to southern areas for the winter, where they are called snowbirds. Juncos live in flocks, so 20 or more juncos may suddenly appear at a feeder.

White outer tail feathers may be visible in flight

All juncos are pale below

PLUMAGE There are four races of dark-eyed junco, which were once thought of as separate species. All have pink bills and white outer tail feathers, but the males show variations to the color of the upper body. The widespread "slate-colored" junco is dark gray above. The western "Oregon" junco has a black head and neck and brown back and sides, but there is also a "pink-sided" variety in the central Rockies with a gray head and neck and pinkish sides. The "gray-headed" juncos of the southern Rockies are largely gray, with brown backs, and the "white-winged" juncos found in the Black Hills of South Dakota and Wyoming are pale gray above, with two white wingbars. Females of all races are more brown overall, and juveniles are striped like house sparrows *(see page 143)*.

VOICE The song is a long, jingling trill, and the calls are a pebble-tapping *clink* note and a *tack-tack* when disturbed.

FEEDING Juncos search on the ground for insects in summer and seeds in winter. ♫ Juncos sometimes perch on feeders with a ledge but mostly take seeds spilled onto the ground. They appear in yards at the start of winter and depart in spring.

NESTING The female, with the male helping to gather material, builds the nest of grasses, rootlets, and bark on the ground under roots, overhanging banks, and brush piles, or occasionally in bushes.

Variation on a theme *Oregon juncos have the typical dark and light plumage pattern.*

Nesting information *April through August • 2 broods • 4 or 5 gray, brown-speckled eggs 11 to 12 days incubation by the female • 12 to 13 days fledging*

Blackbird family (EMBERIZIDAE)

BOBOLINK
Dolichonyx oryzivorus
Length: 6 inches (15 centimeters)

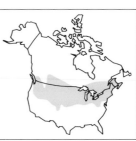

THE STRIKING PLUMAGE OF the male bobolink during its spring migration is so completely different from its appearance on the fall migration that for a long time it was thought that they were two separate birds. During the nineteenth and early twentieth centuries, bobolinks fed in rice fields along the fall migration route. They were called rice birds and were shot by the thousand. So many bobolinks were killed that the population has never fully recovered, although the bird is now protected by law. Currently, hay-mowing in June seriously impairs the breeding success of the species.

The tail has stiff, spiny feathers, like a woodpecker's, and is dragged along the ground in courtship displays

True identity *Spring and fall bobolinks were once thought of as two different birds.*

PLUMAGE After the summer molt, both sexes are streaked light and dark brown on top and light brown below, with a broad stripe above the eye and a narrow stripe through it. During winter the feather tips wear away, and the male's breeding plumage appears: black-and-white above with a white rump and a yellow nape, and black wings, tail, head, and underparts.

VOICE The call is a metallic *pink*. The song is rendered in various ways including *bobolink, bobolink, spink, spank, spink.*

FEEDING In summer, the diet is insects, but in autumn seeds and grain are eaten. ✿ Bobolinks may be attracted to grain scattered on the ground.

NESTING A flimsy nest of coarse grass and weed stems is built in dense grass.

Nesting information *May through July • 1 brood • 5 or 6 pale gray to brown eggs, blotched with brown, purple, and lavender • 13 days incubation by the female • 10 to 14 days fledging*

Blackbird family (EMBERIZIDAE)

RED-WINGED BLACKBIRD

Agelaius phoeniceus
Length: 8¾ inches
(22 centimeters)

The epaulets are displayed in courtship

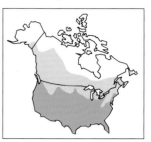

F ROM FALL UNTIL nesting begins, red-winged blackbirds live in large flocks. They spend the night in a communal roost and fly out together in search of food. A visit from a flock can devestate the contents of a feeder. The main habitats are marshes and pastures, but "redwings" are common in parks and suburban areas, especially as they learn to come to feeders. This is also the probable reason for more redwings remaining in northern states through the winter.

PLUMAGE The male is black with yellow-edged red epaulets, which may be hidden when perched. The female is streaked brown, with a faint red tinge on the shoulders and sometimes a pink throat. The epaulets of the Californian form lack the yellow edges, and those of the tricolored blackbird *(Agelaius tricolor)* are white-edged.

VOICE The most common calls are loud *chack* notes, given especially when disturbed or flying in flocks. The song is a repeated, liquid *onk-la-reee* or *o-ka-leee*.

FEEDING Redwings search the ground for seeds and insects. More insects are eaten in the summer.
♧ The redwing visits feeders for bread, cracked corn, and seeds.

NESTING Redwings are among the first birds to fly north. The males arrive early, and will attack passing hawks and crows. The nest is a loosely woven cup bound to the stems of cattails, rushes, or other plants, often in marshes and over water.

Gregarious bird *In winter, flocks mix with other birds to feed on weed seeds and grain.*

Nesting information *March through July • 2 broods • 4 blue-green eggs spotted with black and brown • 11 to 12 days incubation by the female • 10 to 12 days fledging*

Blackbird family (EMBERIZIDAE)

WESTERN MEADOWLARK

Sturnella neglecta

Length: 9 inches (23 centimeters)

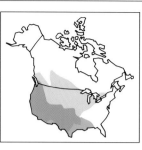

In flight, bursts of flapping alternate with short glides

BOTH THE WESTERN meadowlark and its cousin the eastern meadowlark *(Sturnella magna)* live in open grasslands, but they are adapting to yards. The western meadowlark prefers a drier habitat than the eastern species, but this does not keep them apart, and when they live in the same area interbreeding sometimes occurs. There are some slight differences in plumage, but the best way to tell the species apart is by their songs.

PLUMAGE Slightly paler than its eastern counterpart, the western meadowlark is streaked light and dark brown above, with white outer tail feathers that flash when the bird takes off. The breast is clear yellow marked with a broad black V.

Dependent young *Unlike many ground nesters, meadowlarks hatch naked and helpless.*

VOICE The western meadowlark's song is flutelike and gurgling, while that of the eastern species is a plaintive whistle that sounds like *spring is here.*

FEEDING The main diet is insects, especially locusts, and grain.
🌱 Meadowlarks are attracted to scattered grain, especially in bad weather, and some will come to elevated feeders.

NESTING The female constructs a dome of grass with a side entrance over a scrape in the ground.

Nesting information *April through August • 2 broods • 3 to 7 eggs of white or pink, speckled with brown and lavender • 13 to 14 days incubation by the female • 11 to 12 days fledging*

Blackbird family (EMBERIZIDAE)

COMMON GRACKLE

Quiscalus quiscula

Length: 12½ inches (32 centimeters)

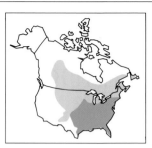

The back may reflect bronze, purple, or green highlights

THESE GREGARIOUS birds nest in loose colonies and roost in thousands, often with starlings *(see page 111)*, red-winged blackbirds *(see page 130),* and other birds. Common grackles are spreading northward, as are boat-tailed and great-tailed grackles *(Quiscalus major* and *Quiscalus mexicanus).* There are also an increasing number of spring sightings of the common grackle on the west coast.

PLUMAGE The male has all black plumage, with a glossy sheen of purple or bronze, which can be seen in bright light or at close quarters. The purple color is seen over most of the bird's range, north and west of the Appalachian chain, and the bronze is found in the southeast of the United States. The female is duller and has a shorter tail than the male, and the juvenile is dark brown. The eyes of all forms are yellow. Both the boat-tailed and the great-tailed grackles are much larger than the common grackle, with longer tails, and females are lighter brown.

VOICE The call is a loud *chuck.* The song is a harsh squeak, like a rusty hinge.

FEEDING Grackles eat a remarkably wide variety of plant and animal food, gleaned both on open land and in woodlands. They feed on acorns, seeds, and fruit, and can be a pest in grain crops. They take

any insects that they can find, probe the ground for earthworms, wade into water to hunt fish and frogs, raid other birds' nests, and even catch bats and birds in the air.

Migrating grackles will descend on feeders in flocks. Grackles become unpopular at feeders because they oust weaker birds. They avidly feed on sunflower seeds and soon finish the supplies. Crusts of bread and kitchen scraps can be used to divert them.

NESTING Grackles nest in loose colonies wherever possible. The nest is a bulky mass of twigs, grass, and mud, lined with more grass, feathers, rags, and string. It is usually built in a coniferous tree or shrub, or sometimes in a building or the bulk of an old osprey nest. Grackles have adapted well to the conditions of human settlement, moving from their original marshy woodland habitats into urban and suburban areas.

Nesting information March through June • 1 brood • 5 or 6 light green or brown eggs with dark-brown blotches • 13 to 14 days incubation by the female • 18 to 20 days fledging

Blackbird family (EMBERIZIDAE)

BROWN-HEADED COWBIRD

Molothrus ater

Length: 7½ inches (19 centimeters)

Cowbirds are named for their habit of following cattle to catch the insects that the mammals stir up from the grass. The birds originally followed bison but switched to cows when herds of cattle replaced bison on the plains. Many people do not welcome cowbirds into their yards, because they arrive in flocks and quickly devour food put out for smaller, more colorful birds. Cowbirds are also disliked because of their parasitic nesting habits.

The beak is conical

PLUMAGE The male is glossy black with a brown head. The female is gray-brown above, and paler below. Juveniles are streaked below and scaly above. In the fall, juvenile males are a patchwork of black and brown.

VOICE The calls are a range of rattles and whistles, the song a bubbling gurgle.

FEEDING The main food is seeds, with some fruit. Many insects are also eaten. ✿ Bread, cracked corn, and sunflower seeds are taken in the yard.

NESTING Cowbirds are nest parasites: they do not build nests but lay their eggs in other birds' nests. The cowbird finds a nest where the parent bird is laying and slips in an egg of her own. Often the foster parent ejects the strange egg or abandons her clutch to start a new one. If the cowbird egg is accepted, it hatches sooner than the others, and the cowbird nestling outgrows its nestmates.

Prospecting *A cowbird sizes up a cardinal's nest as a possible foster home for her eggs.*

Nesting information *10 to 12 white-brown speckled eggs (usually 1 per host nest) • 11 to 12 days incubation by host species*

Blackbird family (EMBERIZIDAE)
BULLOCK'S ORIOLE
Icterus bullockii
Length: 8¾ inches (22 centimeters)

The orange cheeks show that this is a Bullock's oriole

T HE BULLOCK'S and Baltimore orioles are closely related species whose ranges overlap on the Great Plains. They sometimes interbreed in areas where the Bullock's oriole (shaded range) and the Baltimore oriole both occur, producing hybrids with intermediate coloration. This interbreeding causes much debate regarding their relationship, but present concensus is that they are distinct species. Both migrate to tropical America for the winter, but a few birds may remain behind.

PLUMAGE Males are black above and orange below, with orange on the rump and tail, a white patch on the wing, and orange cheeks. Females are olive above and pale yellow below. The male Baltimore oriole has a black hood; the female is brownish olive above and pale orange below.

VOICE The common call is a sharp *skip.* Its song is a musical series of *hew-li,* similar to that of the Baltimore oriole.

FEEDING The main food is insects, but fruit and nectar are also eaten.
✿ In winter, orioles are attracted to oranges, apples, and jelly. In summer, they visit sugar-water feeders that have perches.

NESTING A pouch of plant fibers, hair, and plant down bound with spider webs is hung from the tips of twigs of large trees.

🔖 Putting out short lengths of horsehair and odd pieces of yarn may entice orioles to nest nearby.

Hanging around *A female Baltimore oriole at the nest, which may take two weeks to build.*

Nesting information May through June • 1 brood • 4 streaked and blotched, gray-white eggs 12 to 14 days incubation by the female • 12 to 14 days fledging

Finch family (Fringillidae)

PINE GROSBEAK

Pinicola enucleator

Length: 9 inches (23 centimeters)

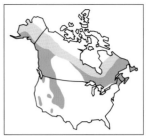

During nesting, the throat develops pouches for carrying food to the young

N OT USUALLY MIGRATORY, preferring to stay in its northern home throughout the year, the pine grosbeak is sometimes forced south by a shortage of seeds, its main food source, and wild fruit. Pine grosbeaks are gregarious birds, living in flocks of up to 100 birds, and they arrive in southern areas in these flocks, seeking coniferous forests, open hillsides, and yards with fruit trees.

PLUMAGE This is the largest of the grosbeaks, with the characteristic heavy conical bill that gives them their name. The male is red, varying from deep rose to bright poppy in color, and has dark wings with two white bars, and a dark, slightly forked tail. It is similar at first glance to the smaller white-winged crossbill *(Loxia*

Favorite food *In winter, pine grosbeaks feed on fruit, especially mountainash.*

leucoptera). The female is grayish overall, with the same dark tail and barred wings as the male.

VOICE The song is a short, clear, musical warble, including *tee-tee-tew* notes.

FEEDING Pine grosbeaks usually forage for seeds in trees, but also feed on fruit, insects, and seeds on the ground, and tree buds, especially maple buds.
 Sunflower seed and grain scattered on the ground will attract pine grosbeaks, as will tree-dried fruit such as crabapples and mountainash and hawthorn berries. They are very approachable at feeders in winter.

NESTING A bulky, loose, open nest of twigs and rootlets, lined with lichens, is built in a spruce, fir, or shrub. Nests in the southern part of the range may be built higher up, because the trees are taller.

Nesting information *May through June • 1 brood • 2 to 6 blue-green or gray-green eggs, speckled with brown and gray • 13 to 14 days incubation by the female • 20 days fledging*

Finch family (FRINGILLIDAE)

PURPLE FINCH

Carpodacus purpureus

Length: 6 inches (15 centimeters)

In courtship displays the wings are beaten rapidly until they become a blur

THE PURPLE FINCH could be described as the "country cousin" of the house finch *(see opposite)*. It spends most of its time in woodlands, but it will come into suburban areas and take advantage of feeders during the winter. Except when they are nesting, purple finches live in nomadic flocks. These descend on a backyard for a short time and then move on, perhaps not to be seen again until the next winter. Because the house finch is so similar in appearance, very careful examination may be needed to confirm that it is a purple finch flock that has arrived.

PLUMAGE The male purple finch is a softer color than the male house finch. He also has more red coloring overall, but this does not develop until the bird is in its second year. He also lacks the heavily streaked flanks of the house finch. The female purple finch is brown above and streaked below. A white stripe over the eye and dark cheeks and ear patches distinguish her from the female house finch. The male Cassin's finch *(Carpodacus cassinii)* has a brown back, and the female lacks the eye stripe.

VOICE The calls are a sharp, metallic *tick,* which is given in flight, and a musical *chur-lee.* The rapid, warbling song resembles that of the house finch, but lacks the harsh final notes.

FEEDING The diet consists mainly of seeds, especially tree seeds, plus buds in the spring and berries in the fall. Some insects are also taken, and nestlings are fed insects.

✿ Purple finches are frequent but erratic visitors to feeders. They come to all kinds of feeders, but prefer those that are quite high off the ground. Sunflower and thistle seeds are the most popular foods, but other seeds, and suet, are also accepted.

NESTING In the breeding season, purple finches retreat from the yard, mainly to coniferous woods. They build in the outer foliage of trees. The nests are cups of tightly woven grasses, fine twigs, and bark strips (cedar is especially favored) lined with mosses, fine grass, and hair.

Nesting information April through July • 1 or 2 broods • 4 or 5 pale-green eggs with brown speckles • 13 days incubation by the female • 14 days fledging

Finch family (FRINGILLIDAE)

HOUSE FINCH

Carpodacus mexicanus

Length: 6 inches (15 centimeters)

Streaked flanks distinguish this from the purple finch

THE HOUSE FINCH has habits similar to those of the house sparrow *(see page 143)*, and thrives around human habitation. It is not as aggressive as the house sparrow and is popular because of its colorful plumage and melodious song. The house finch is native to the west (where it is called the linnet), but in the 1940s pet dealers in New York imported the birds to sell them as "Hollywood finches." When this came to the attention of the authorities, some dealers released the finches to avoid charges. The species prospered and has spread over much of the east. Some birds migrate to Florida and the Gulf for the winter.

PLUMAGE The house finch is brown, with dark streaks below. The forehead, breast, and rump of the male are red or orange, or occasionally yellow. Cassin's finch *(Carpodacus cassinii)* has a red crown, but is paler on the breast, and the male purple finch *(see opposite)* has a red crown, and a brown ear patch.

VOICE The call is a *chirp* or *queet* similar to that of the house sparrow. The song is a hurried, repeated warble, ending with a harsh *chee-ur*.

FEEDING Most of the diet is weed seeds, but buds, insects, and scraps are eaten. ☘ The house finch eats seeds, peanuts, fruit, suet, and kitchen scraps. It competes with hummingbirds at sugar-water feeders.

NESTING The nest of grasses, leaves, twigs, string, wool, and other odds and ends may be built in a tree, cactus, building cavity, or an abandoned nest. ◪ House finches use standard nestboxes and may take over purple martin houses.

Invisible bird These house finches feeding on seeds in winter are excellently camouflaged.

Nesting information March through August • 1 brood • 4 or 5 blue-white eggs, speckled with brown • 12 to 16 days incubation by the female • 11 to 19 days fledging

Finch family (FRINGILLIDAE)

RED CROSSBILL

Loxia curvirostra
Length: 5½–6½ inches
(14–16.5 centimeters)

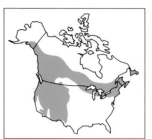

RED CROSSBILLS and the closely related white-winged crossbills *(Loxia leucoptera)* have crossed tips to the bill, for removing seeds from cones. Crossbills nest when and where they find crops; they are nomadic and erratic in their nesting times, because coniferous trees seed at varying times in different areas. Outside forests, crossbills are best known as winter birds. They often go unnoticed unless you listen for calls, or look for opened cones on the ground.

Only two North American birds have a crossed bill

PLUMAGE The male is brick red, darker on the rump, with dark brown wings and tail. The female is mottled buff yellow with dusky wings and tail. Immature males resemble the females but have touches of red on the crown. The male white-winged crossbill is paler, the female less mottled. Both sexes have two white wing bars.

First bite *A crossbill manipulates a hemlock cone to get a good grip on it.*

VOICE Flocks of crossbills utter low twitters to one another when feeding. During courtship, the male whistles and warbles from a perch in a treetop or sings while flying in circles around the female.

FEEDING The cones of pines and spruces are wrenched from branches and held in one foot. The crossed bill is used to hold the scales open while the seeds are extracted with the tongue. The seeds of willows, birches, maples, and other trees are also eaten, as well as some insects. ❀ Crossbills come to sunflower and thistle seed and sometimes to sources of salt.

NESTING The nest is built well out on a branch. It is constructed from twigs, rootlets, and bark, and lined with fine grasses, moss, feathers, and fur. The nestlings hatch with normal bills, and the crossed tips develop slowly.

Nesting information *January through August • 1 brood • 3 to 5 pale blue or green eggs, marked with browns and black • 12 to 14 days incubation by the female • 17 days fledging*

138

Finch family (FRINGILLIDAE)

COMMON REDPOLL
Carduelis flammea
Length: 5–5½ inches (13–14 centimeters)

A BIRD OF NORTHERN tundra and coniferous forests, the common redpoll is best known as a winter visitor. The numbers arriving in southern Canada and the northern United States vary from winter to winter: in some years few appear, in others there is an irruption (*see page 195*). Redpolls often seem oblivious to humans, and can become very tame at feeders. Occasionally, a paler redpoll is seen: this is the hoary redpoll (*Carduelis hornemanni*), which some ornithologists believe belongs to the same species.

The streaked rump distinguishes this from the hoary redpoll

PLUMAGE Common redpolls are streaked gray and brown above, with a red cap, black chin, and pink rump. The underparts are heavily streaked, and some males have a red breast. The hoary redpoll has a shorter bill and is white on the face, rump, and underparts, with a slight pink tinge on the breast.

VOICE The call note is a *swee-e-ee*, coarser than that of the goldfinch. A subdued but constant twitter of lisping notes come from flocks, and males in flocks sing a juncolike song.

FEEDING The diet consists of buds, seeds from cones, weed and grass seeds, and insects in summer.
✿ Redpolls visit hanging feeders and shelves. They take suet, breadcrumbs, and a variety of seeds, especially niger seeds. They cannot open the hulls of sunflower seeds but take hearts or peck the crumbs left by other birds.

NESTING The female builds a loose cup of twigs, rootlets, grass, and moss, sometimes lined with a layer of ptarmigan feathers, in the crotch of a tree. Several nests may be built quite close together.

Invading forces *Redpolls form into flocks in winter and may irrupt into areas with feeders.*

Nesting information *April through August • 1 or 2 broods • 4 to 7 greenish blue eggs with purple spots and lines • 10 to 11 days incubation by the female • 12 days fledging*

Finch family (FRINGILLIDAE)

PINE SISKIN
Carduelis pinus
Length: 5 inches (13 centimeters)

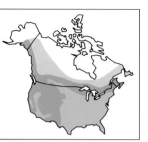

A BOLD BIRD, the pine siskin has no set migration pattern, but wanders the country in flocks of 100 to 200 birds, mixed with other finches. It frequently comes to feeders, where it uses a wings-spread, bill-gaping threat display to chase off other birds.

PLUMAGE The plumage is gray-brown with conspicuous streaking. The yellow patches on the wings and the base of the tail are most conspicuous in flight, or when giving a threat display with the wings spread. The juvenile has a yellow tinge overall. The closely related goldfinch *(see opposite)* is brighter yellow overall.

VOICE The calls include a long *sweee,* a harsh buzzing *zzzzzz,* and a *tit-ti-tit* given in flight. The song is a trilling warble, which includes the *zzzzzz* and *sweee* notes, given in flight or from a perch.

Compared with other finches, pine siskins are swift, high fliers

FEEDING Pine siskins feed mainly on seeds extracted from trees and weeds, or picked from the ground, although they also include insects in their diet, mainly in the summer. They also eat buds and sometimes sip nectar from flowers and sap from sapsucker holes. Ashes and salt put on icy roads and drives in winter are often eaten for their grit and mineral content. ✿ Nuts, rolled oats, and a variety of seeds, especially thistle, are taken from feeders.

NESTING Courtship starts toward the end of winter, while the birds are still in flocks. There is a lot of chasing, and the males present seeds to females or flutter in circles singing, with tails spread. Several pairs usually nest together in a loose colony in trees. The females build shallow nests of twigs, grass, and rootlets, lined with fur and feathers.

Party booking *Pine siskins are frequent visitors to feeders, often arriving in large flocks.*

Nesting information *April through July • 1 or 2 broods • 3 or 4 green-blue eggs spotted with black • 13 days incubation by the female • 15 days fledging*

Finch family (FRINGILLIDAE)

AMERICAN GOLDFINCH

Carduelis tristis

Length: 5 inches (13 centimeters)

The yellow plumage is molted after nesting

THE AMERICAN goldfinch is closely related to the less colorful pine siskin *(see opposite),* and the two species are very alike in their general behavior. This may lead to competition, and it is unusual to see both birds at the feeder at the same time. One remarkable trait of the goldfinch is that it molts its feathers twice a year: in fall after nesting is completed and again in spring. This results in a great difference in the appearance of the males between summer and winter.

PLUMAGE The winter plumage of both sexes is a brownish gray, but the male has yellow on the throat and face. In spring, the male becomes brilliant yellow, with a black cap, wings, and tail, and white at the base of the tail. The female acquires a yellow tinge but is still quite drab.

VOICE The calls include a *per-chick-o-ree* and, in flight, a *see-me, see-me*. The song is a medley of trills and *swee* notes.

FEEDING Tree seeds, thistles, dandelions, evening primrose, sunflowers, goldenrod, lettuce, and other plants that have gone to seed are the main foods. Berries and insects make up a small part of the diet. ♜ Feeders with seeds, especially thistle and sunflower, are popular.

NESTING Loose colonies nest in bushes or trees. The cup nests are sometimes so tightly woven that they can hold water. Nesting is connected with thistles, because the nest is often lined with thistledown.

Solid food *Partly digested thistle seeds are fed to the nestlings.*

Nesting information *June through September • 1 brood • 4 or 5 pale blue eggs • 12 to 14 days incubation by the female • 10 to 16 days fledging*

Finch family (FRINGILLIDAE)

EVENING GROSBEAK

Coccothraustes vespertinus

Length: 8 inches (20 centimeters)

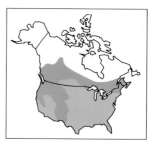

The bill becomes green in spring

IN WINTER THE arrival of a flock of evening grosbeaks in your yard is a magnificent and colorful sight, but they can very quickly empty even the largest feeder. The flocks are nomadic, gathering wherever there are good crops of tree seeds, so you may find plenty of evening grosbeaks in your neighborhood one year and none the next. Once confined to the coniferous forests of the northwest, the evening grosbeak spread eastward to the Atlantic coast in the second half of the nineteenth century, and it visits as far south as the Gulf states in the winter.

PLUMAGE The male has a dark brown and yellow body with black wings and tail, a white patch on the inner wings, and a bright yellow line over the eye. The female is grayish without the yellow eye line, but has two white patches on the wings.

VOICE Evening grosbeaks give a variety of *chip* notes almost constantly. The call is *peeear,* and the song a brief warble.

FEEDING The main food is tree seeds – the bird's bill is strong enough to crack cherry pits. Planting of box elder may have helped the bird's spread; the seeds are a favorite food. Flocks gather at roadsides and on driveways to eat grit and salt.
�п Sunflower seed is popular.

Easy pickings Feeders are popular with evening grosbeaks, although the birds are highly unpredictable visitors.

NESTING The preliminaries to breeding include the male feeding the female and swinging back and forth with wings spread and quivering. Later stages are hard to observe because the nests, shallow cups of twigs and rootlets built by the female, are well hidden in the foliage of trees.

Nesting information *May through July • 1 brood • 3 or 4 blue eggs • 12 to 14 days incubation by the female • 13 to 14 days fledging*

Sparrow family (PASSERIDAE)

HOUSE SPARROW

Passer domesticus

Length 5¾ inches (14.5 centimeters)

*The wings are drooped to the ground
in courtship displays*

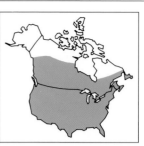

THE HABIT OF nesting near human settlements has enabled house sparrows, also called English sparrows, to spread around the world. They were introduced into New York in the nineteenth century.

PLUMAGE The male is brown streaked with black above, with gray cheeks, crown, underparts, and rump. The throat and bib are black. The female is more uniformly brown, lacking the gray on the rump and crown and the black on the head and throat. Juveniles are like the female. Some native sparrows are similar but have more slender bills.

VOICE There are various *cheep* and *chirp* calls, and the song is a medley of these.

FEEDING The house sparrow is basically a seedeater, but it will eat a wide variety of food, including shoots, flowers, and insects. House sparrows can be pests on farms, where they will steal grain from standing crops, and in warehouses, railroad stations, and other buildings. Urban house sparrows do very well on edible litter and garbage. Spiders and insects are needed for the nestlings.
🐦 House sparrows often come to feeders, being quick to learn new ways of finding food. Many make a good living from food put out for birds in yards and parks.

NESTING In spring, several males will chase each other chirping wildly, and mill about, apparently fighting. The object of the fuss is one female, who fends the suitors off, aided by her chosen mate. The nest may be no more than a lining of feathers brought by both sexes, and is used through the winter. The young birds roost together in evergreens and vines.
🐦 House sparrows readily use enclosed nestboxes *(see page 55)* and may displace native birds.

Close to home *The usual nesting site is a hole or crevice in a building.*

Nesting information *April through September • 2 or 3 broods • 4 or 5 white or pale green eggs with a few brown blotches • 14 days incubation mainly by the female • 15 days fledging*

HOUSE SPARROW

CHAPTER FOUR

BEHAVIOR GUIDE

THE FIRST PRIORITY for a bird, like any animal, is to survive. This means finding enough food to fuel the strenuous exercise of flying, to keep warm through cold nights, and to build up a reserve of fat against bad weather. Successful matings permit the birds to pass their genes to the next generation. The different tactics that each species employs in the struggle for survival are reflected in the variety of behavior that you can observe around the yard. The different ways that birds feed, fly, walk, communicate, nest, and migrate show how they have evolved to make the most of their environment. From the enviable vantage point of the yard, there is plenty of opportunity to observe the lives of many different birds, in particular songbirds, and to increase your knowledge of the motivations behind a broad range of activities.

A killdeer feigns injury to lead a predator from the nest.

· THE LIVES OF BIRDS ·

THE YARD BIRDER enjoys observing birds in conditions of comfort and convenience often denied to the professional ornithologist. You can study birds, often without stepping outdoors, at any hour of the day. We envy birds their freedom, but they also have a routine that, depending on the time of year, may keep them busy from dawn to dusk. In summer, there is the burden of rearing a family, and in winter, searching for food and shelter itself may become a full-time activity.

THE WAY BIRDS BEHAVE

A good reason for making the yard an attractive place for birds is that it provides an unequaled opportunity to look into their private lives. Providing food and nesting sites helps birds survive in an increasingly hostile world, but it also allows you to enjoy their company. The enjoyment is all the greater if you take the time and trouble to observe carefully what the birds are doing and to appreciate why they are doing it.

Appreciation of bird behavior comes in two forms: you can read about a bird's habits and then keep watch in the yard to see them for yourself, or you might observe something new and refer to books for an explanation. Either way you will derive pleasure from discovering something you did not know before.

We are learning about bird behavior all the time. It was once difficult to find out about even the most ordinary behavior of common birds, simply because no one knew the answers. Scientific research shows that a bird's behavior usually has a function or brings the bird some benefit, although the benefits may not always be apparent to the human observer, even after detailed research.

Careful observation can reveal the logic in a bird's feeding pattern. At first sight, it seems that swallows ought to pursue the largest insects that they can find,

Easy prey *A tree swallow hunts small insects rather than larger ones, although it has to catch more of them to make a satisfying meal. Smaller insects are easier to catch, making them a cheaper option in terms of energy used hunting.*

because only a few would be needed to satisfy their hunger. In fact, research has revealed that tree swallows very rarely eat insects larger than ½-inch long, although they sometimes catch dragonflies of up to 2 inches in length.

Their preference is for small flies between ⅒ and ⅖ inch long. These flies are very abundant near the ground, where the swallows fly. They are also easy to catch, so it is more economical in terms of time and energy for the swallows to chase smaller insects than to hunt the larger, faster ones.

Another question answered by some simple science is that of how a robin on the lawn finds worms and grubs buried in the soil. Typically, a hunting robin runs in bursts of about 4 feet, then halts and stands erect for a few seconds, apparently scanning the ground. Every now and then, the robin also cocks its head. Suddenly, it steps back and then lunges forward to seize a worm or insect. Before this behavior pattern was properly investigated, it was thought that the robin was either looking for signs of its prey or was listening for them. The former notion seems to be

Methodical worker *Each bird species, such as this robin, has its own hunting method, which is developed to catch its main food most efficiently.*

correct, since it has been observed that robins catch more worms when the grass is short and the tips of the worms' bodies can be seen protruding from the soil. Hunting is also more successful in wet weather, which brings worms to the surface.

Trying to deduce what advantage a bird gets from a particular type of behavior helps explain much that is going on, but not every puzzle has been solved. There are still many quirks of behavior that are difficult to explain. Some years ago, a birder in North Carolina observed a cardinal that spent several days feeding goldfish. The fish came to the edge of their pond, and the cardinal stuffed worms into their open mouths. We can only guess how this strange association came about. Cardinals and many other birds feed their nestlings by pushing food into their gaping beaks, the brightly colored insides of the mouths acting as a signal to which the parent bird reacts instinctively. Sometimes this instinct leads birds to feed the young of other species, and perhaps this cardinal happened to see a goldfish with its mouth open at the surface of the pond. The goldfish, for their part, must have quickly learned how they could get a free meal.

Feeding instinct *The bright color of a nestling's open mouth as it begs is a signal to which parent birds, like this cardinal, react instinctively.*

THE DAILY ROUND

You will usually notice birds when they are visiting the feeder, singing from a treetop, or flying over to feeding grounds and back to their roosts. The impression is that every moment is busy, but at different times of the year, birds have little to do.

A bird has two main activities during a normal day. It has to feed, which it does in bouts through the day, and it has to maintain its feathers in good condition by preening and bathing. I have noticed that birds visiting my feeder are in no hurry to start feeding in the morning. As it becomes just light enough to see, birds gather in the trees nearby, but they do not begin to feed in earnest until it is fully light. There is some feeding to replenish food stores used up during the night. Some birds start earlier than others. Robins, song sparrows, cardinals, and scarlet tanagers are early risers; warblers, vireos, house wrens, and house sparrows appear later. In the evening, when the birds go to roost, the order is reversed. Roosting may be delayed by a full moon or street-lighting.

The way that a bird fills its day varies throughout the year. During winter, a bird has to spend most of the day feeding, because food is scarce and takes longer to find. Extra rations are also needed to keep

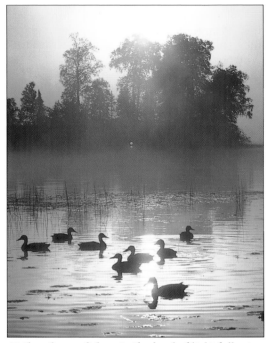

At the close of day As the level of light falls at dusk, mallards gather to roost at their nests along the bank of a pond.

warm. Small birds may have to spend most (if not all) of their daylight hours looking for food. Birds are busy again in summer, when they have families. Food is plentiful at this time, but birds have to feed ever-hungry nestlings and find extra food to sustain themselves on this day-long chore. In spring and fall, many songbirds will spend their days in long migration flights between their breeding and wintering ranges.

Daily chore All birds spend time each day tidying their feathers. Some, like crows, make it a social activity.

THE ANNUAL CYCLE

Three main events in the bird's year require extra energy expenditure: nesting, molting, and, for many birds, migrating. These events do not usually overlap, because a bird clearly needs its plumage to be in the best condition when it is migrating or nesting, to save its energy.

Some birds start serious courtship before the end of winter, but much depends on the weather. Mild winters lead to early courtship, but a cold spell will set the program back and split the couples up again. Nesting generally starts earlier in the south and is nearly one month later for every 25° of latitude farther north, although egg-laying varies by a couple of weeks from year to year in any locality. A bird's calendar centers around finding food for its young. Egg-laying is often timed so that the nestlings grow up when the appropriate food is most plentiful. The screech-owl nests early, because it is easier to hunt mice and voles before the grass grows up and hides them. The cooper's hawk, on the other hand, nests late, so that the offspring are growing rapidly when there are plenty of young, inexperienced songbirds for the parents to catch. Most common plant-eating birds, such as seed-eating finches, feed their young on protein-rich insects, and their nesting coincides with the time when insects are abundant. The red crossbill is unusual, because it lives almost entirely on the seeds of conifer trees and nests when crops of cones are available. This means that it nests at almost any time of year, but most often in late winter. Doves have a very long nesting period because they feed their young on a protein-rich secretion from their throats, which leaves them fairly free of these seasonal constraints.

After nesting, you might notice that birdsong dies down and birds become less visible. This is the molting period, when the birds replace worn feathers. The new feathers ensure that the birds are in peak condition for winter survival or for their long migration flights.

Killing time *The eastern screech-owl starts nesting in March, when the rodent prey on which the young are fed is plentiful and easy to catch.*

· FEEDING ·

A LL ANIMALS NEED fuel for body functions, for powering their
muscles, and for growth. Warm-blooded animals like birds
also need fuel to generate warmth. After finding enough food
to keep healthy, a bird has to collect additional food to rear its
family. The male requires extra food when he is energetically
defending his territory and courting a mate, and the female
needs it while she is manufacturing and incubating the eggs.
Later, both parents must find large quantities of food for
the growing nestlings.

WHAT BIRDS EAT

Feeding is the most important part of any
bird's life. What and how it eats are the
keys to understanding the way it lives. We
should avoid judging birds by our standards,
condemning blue jays or evening grosbeaks
as gluttons for quickly clearing the food we
put out or mockingbirds as bullies for
driving other birds away.These
habits are natural strategies
for obtaining food. A close
look at the feeding habits
of common birds
reveals how each
one finds natural
foods, how it makes the best
use of supplies, and how you can help by
putting out food. Remember that birds are
often adaptable: tree swallows, which
normally chase flying insects, turn to eating
bayberries in cold weather.

Ant-eater *A flicker sits over an anthill and picks
up a meal with its long tongue, which is designed
for removing insects from their hiding places.*

Death grip *An American kestrel holds onto its
prey with one talon, to enable it to tear the food
apart with its beak.*

The size and shape of a bird's bill are good clues to its diet. Starlings, jays, and gulls have general-purpose bills that enable them to exploit a variety of foods. These birds are quick to take advantage of new food sources, a characteristic that has led to their success in towns and other new habitats. Other birds, such as woodpeckers, herons, and shorebirds, have specialized bills that limit the foods they can eat.

A few species use their feet when eating. Crossbills hold cones with their feet as they extract the seeds, and goldfinches hold birch catkins with a foot while pecking at them. Birds of prey, such as kestrels and sharp-shinned hawks, pounce with their talons, and hold their catch when feeding. Chickadees and crows use their feet and even learn to use feet and bill together to pull up a string with food tied to the end.

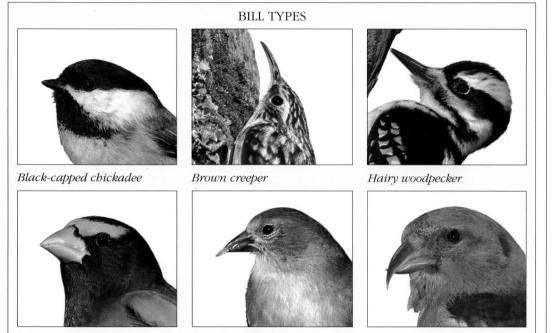

BILL TYPES

Black-capped chickadee   *Brown creeper*   *Hairy woodpecker*

Evening grosbeak   *American goldfinch*   *White-winged crossbill*

Chickadees and wrens have tiny bills for picking insects from their hiding places. Brown creepers have longer, slightly curved bills, also for hunting insects but enabling them to probe deeper. Woodpeckers have chisel-shaped bills for digging deep into wood and long tongues with tiny barbs for extracting insects.

Finches generally have conical bills for cracking and shelling seeds. You can watch cardinals and other finches deftly rolling a sunflower seed until it is held between the grooved upper half of the bill and the sharp-edged lower half. The bill then squeezes like a nutcracker, the seed splits open, and the kernel is removed. The differences in bill sizes and shapes among finches reflect their choice of food. The evening grosbeak has a bill stout enough for splitting cherry pits, while the goldfinch and pine siskin are adept at probing deep into the heads of thistles to extract seeds with their slender bills. Other finches have to tear open the seed heads or wait for the seeds to become loose. The crossbills have the most specialized bill of all the finches. Although the unique crossed-over bill is custom-built for extracting seeds from cones, its design does not restrict the crossbill to a diet of conifer seeds. The bill can be used to split open apples and remove the seeds, or to pry bark off a tree trunk, exposing hidden insects.

ECONOMICAL FEEDING

Putting yourself in the position of a bird that is trying to feed economically is a useful method of understanding the way it behaves. As a rule, birds behave sensibly and get the most food for the least effort. Birds will choose the best food available within the limits of their bill size, toe structure, and other physical characteristics, together with acrobatic and aerobatic abilities. Their objective is clearer if expressed in financial terms. A bird's goal is to make a good living by earning the best income (food) for the least expenditure (energy used getting the food). A healthy surplus, stored as fat, gives it both a reserve for a rainy day and the capital to spend on special activities like nesting and migration. Feeders are popular because they provide an easier living than searching for natural foods, and they are patronized especially when natural foods become hard to find.

A bird selects the food that is easiest to obtain. House and purple finches, mockingbirds, and sparrows feast on the buds of early blooming forsythia, honeysuckle, and fruit trees when the seed crops have finished in late winter. Buds contain very little sustenance, so birds have to consume large quantities of them just to stay alive. This bud-stripping angers gardeners, but the plants usually recover. Some studies have shown that this form of pruning can actually enhance fruit crops.

The flexible rules of bird economics are demonstrated by the effect of weather on the feeding behavior of eastern kingbirds. In fine, warm weather there are plenty of large insects in the air, and the kingbirds spend most of their feeding time hunting them. When the sky clouds over and the temperature drops, the large insects stop flying, and the kingbirds switch to picking smaller insects from foliage. Because these take more time and energy to find, the kingbirds only hunt them when there is no better alternative.

The kingbirds are changing their feeding behavior to make the most of circumstances. They do have a problem if the weather turns bad while they are nesting, and they cannot find enough food to feed their young properly by gleaning insects off foliage. Breeding is therefore less successful in wet summers.

Some birds have found that the quickest and easiest way of getting food is to steal it from another bird. A gull or crow that has found a crust of bread or a donut often cannot swallow it before another bird swoops down to steal it. You may also see starlings and house sparrows stealing earthworms from robins that have spent time and energy hunting them. For sheer boldness, there is little to beat the chickadee that follows a nuthatch and steals the food that it has cached.

Efficiency study Whenever possible, eastern kingbirds will fly out from their perches to hunt large, flying insects, because these are "cheaper" to catch than smaller, creeping insects.

CACHING

One way to guard against going hungry is to save food when there is a surplus. Nuts and sunflower seeds sometimes disappear more quickly than you would expect given the number of birds at the feeder. This is because some birds are carrying them away to hide them. Food is cached mainly in autumn, when it is abundant, or when it is provided at a feeder. Nuts are often stored because they are nutritious and keep well. Food may be left for weeks before the bird returns, apparently remembering the exact location by reference to nearby landmarks.

Chickadees and nuthatches are common hoarders. They wedge food in crevices in rough bark. Chickadees can remember the location of caches for up to four weeks.

Hanging game *A northern shrike has impaled its catch on a thorn, and will return several times to this "larder" to pull meat from it.*

Winter store *Blue jays have been known to recover buried nuts from under a fall of snow.*

Caches are usually an emergency store, but Clark's nutcracker, of the Rocky Mountains, depends on pine kernels for survival throughout the winter, and to begin raising its young in spring.

Hoarder *This acorn woodpecker has established a "grainery" in the wall of a house. It may drill dozens of holes.*

Shrikes impale prey on thorns and barbed wire, and members of the crow family bury scraps. Red-bellied and red-headed woodpeckers are also frequent hoarders. The acorn woodpecker is named for its habit of wedging acorns in holes that it chisels in tree trunks. One was observed pushing acorns through a knothole in a cabin wall. It lost several hundred before giving up.

NEW FOODS

Studies of yard birds have proved valuable in showing how birds learn to take new foods. It is usual for one or two birds to copy others, learning to take food from hanging feeders. It is hard to tell, however, whether they learned by a flash of inspiration or from watching the birds at work. It may be a combination of the two.

Birds normally learn what to eat by trial-and-error. The selection of seeds by different members of the finch family comes about by young birds trying all sorts of seeds, and settling for those that can be dealt with efficiently by their size of bill. They also learn to select high-energy foods, such as the seeds with the most oil. Young thrushes also peck at anything, gradually learning what is edible. The process may be accelerated by watching and imitating parents or other members of a flock.

Sometimes a new habit crops up, and you will see birds behaving in a strange fashion. Red-bellied woodpeckers usually hunt by chiseling wood to expose insects, but they regularly eat grain, and there is a record of a red-bellied woodpecker feeding on the remains of hotdog rolls.

The most amazing example of birds picking up a new trick is that of green herons who have learned to fish using bait. The heron drops a crust of bread or similar bait into the water, then catches the fish that come to nibble it. Once one bird discovered this, others learned to imitate it. One heron has even been seen to retrieve the bait when it floated away and to drive off ducks that tried to eat it. If the habit catches on, it may become a common part of the species' feeding habits.

Skillful hunter *A green heron with its prey. These small, unobtrusive herons have learned to use bait when fishing.*

PELLETS

Owls and other birds of prey are well known for their habit of regurgitating the remains of their prey. Indigestible materials such as bones, fur, and feathers are regularly cast up as pellets. It is not so well known that some other birds also produce pellets. For example, sometimes a robin seems to be suffering from acute indigestion, straining convulsively with its bill open wide. Eventually it will bring up a pellet, which contains seed cases or fragments of the hard bodies of insects. Other yard birds, such as members of the flycatcher and crow families, also produce pellets of similar matter.

Indigestible matter *The young American kestrel on the left is casting up a pellet of fur and bones from a meal brought by its parents.*

BIRDS AND FRUIT

It is easy to get upset when birds strip a carefully nurtured crop of fruit as soon as it begins to ripen, but the birds are actually doing the plants a favor. Encasing its seeds in fruit is a plant's method of getting them distributed. Some plants have seeds that are carried by the wind, like the downy seeds of thistles and the winged seeds of ashes and elms, but fleshy fruits are designed to be eaten. The qualities that attract birds to fruit – bright colors, often red or yellow to contrast with the surrounding green foliage, and a juicy, sweet package of flesh – are the same as those that attract us. After being swallowed, the flesh of the fruit is digested, and the seeds are voided far from the parent plant.

The flesh of fruit is not as nutritious as a diet of insects or seeds, but it has the advantage of being easy to gather. Fruit is an important food for many birds in winter, especially during severe weather. A bird can save a great deal of energy if it gorges at a fruit tree, then perches quietly nearby, feathers fluffed out, until the next meal. Fruit can also be a vital food source during a summer drought.

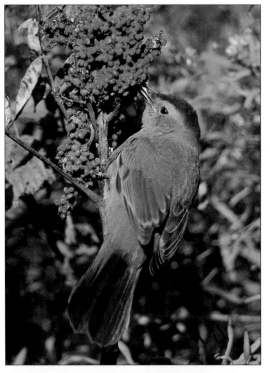

Out of season *Catbirds vary their diet as the availability of different food sources such as insects and fruit changes with the seasons.*

The yard birds that regularly eat fruit and disperse their seeds include mockingbirds, scarlet tanagers, and starlings. Some other birds, such as finches, sparrows, and chickadees, eat seeds that are designed to be wind-dispersed, so upsetting the mutually beneficial relationship between plants and birds.

Fruit eaters often feed in flocks, and one of the delightful sights of winter is a crowd of cedar waxwings or evening grosbeaks at work in bushes or vines. Sometimes a mockingbird attempts to defend its private fruit tree against all comers – a worthwhile effort, because the tree provides a secure food supply. The bird may be overwhelmed if a flock of other fruit-eating birds invades the tree, in which case the erstwhile owner can only join them in stripping the tree of its fruit as fast as possible.

Fruit feast *A Bohemian waxwing feeds on berries, the species' main food. The highly visible bright red color of the fruit attracts the birds.*

· FLIGHT PATTERNS ·

T HE POWER OF FLIGHT gives birds opportunities to move with an ease denied to all other animals except insects and bats. Squirrels can climb trees, and jump from one tree to another, but they cannot flit from tree to tree or from twig to twig like a bird. Mice and deer leave their resting places in search of food, but they do not travel the range of a red-winged blackbird or a heron.

THE COST OF FLIGHT

Birds do have the freedom of the air, and the power of flight allows them to travel far and fast, but there are drawbacks. It is quicker to fly on an airplane than to go by car; but it is more expensive in terms of fuel. The same is true for bird flight. To fly, a bird needs enormous breast muscles that can flap its wings. In one second a kestrel beats its wings 2.4 times, a goldfinch 4.9 times, and a ruby-throated hummingbird 80 times. Flapping flight uses large amounts of energy – about 10 to 15 times as much as walking. Like the human airplane passenger, a bird must sometimes decide whether to forgo speed in the interests of economy.

Energy conservation
Gulls flap when flying from place to place, and glide in energy-saving circles while scanning the ground for food.

When you throw crusts of bread out of the kitchen window, a grackle at the other end of the yard must decide whether to run across the lawn or fly. Its decision will probably depend on whether there are other grackles in the yard: flight is worth the extra effort if the grackle has to beat the other birds to the food.

Some birds, as different from each other as wrens and ducks, have to keep flapping to stay in the air, but many birds reduce the energy cost of flight by gliding as much as possible, making use of gusts of wind billowing around buildings or lines of trees to buoy them up. Swallows and swifts use air turbulence along lines of trees to carry them up and to hunt in flight. The birds gather in the eddies and fly slowly forward into the wind, almost hovering at times, snapping up the rich crop of insects trapped in the spinning air currents.

When flying over long distances, economy can be more important than speed. Hawks soar in thermals, the updrafts of air that rise through the atmosphere when the ground is warming on a sunny day, as an energy-saving means of traveling across country. Swallows, swifts, gulls, and even starlings also use thermals, as they do smaller eddies, both for flying and for hunting. Themals are insects traps, and the birds enjoy an easy meal while they drift upward.

Smaller birds cannot make use of the updrafts provided by thermals in this way, but some, such as finches, chickadees, woodpeckers, and starlings, save energy with a bounding flight in which they alternate between quick bursts of flapping flight and closing their wings. After being carried upward by a burst of flapping, the bird pulls its wings in close to its body and hurtles through the air. This gives the typical bouncing effect seen in a flock of finches or sparrows in flight. They close their wings rather than using them to glide because, for birds of such a small size, the disadvantage of the wind resistance against the outstretched wings would outweigh the advantage of the amount of lift that they could generate.

TAKE-OFF AND LANDING

Like an airplane, a bird has to generate lift in order to become airborne. Instead of speeding along a runway to create an airstream over the wings as an airplane does, the bird sweeps its wings to and fro. It is easier for both airplane and bird to take off and land into the wind, because it gives extra lift.

Most common birds take off by leaping into the air, and hovering just clear of the ground for a split second. This is very strenuous, but the leap gives them an extra shove upward. You might hear doves, which are heavy-bodied birds, take off with a noise like a whipcrack. This is the sound that their wings make when they are flung forward and down to move air over the flight surfaces. Larger birds cannot generate enough power to hover. They simply drop from a perch or nest, spread their wings,

Coming in to land
A cardinal tilts its wings upward to slow down, until, almost hovering, it touches down lightly.

and accelerate under the pull of gravity. When taking off from the ground, they run a few steps to get up speed and generate lift. It is more difficult to leap off water. Some ducks, such as mallards, can manage this, but coots and swans have to run across the surface of the water in order to become airborne.

When landing, the bird has to slow down as much as possible without falling out of the air. Small birds slow down easily until they are virtually hovering on rapidly whirring wings and then gently touch down. Large birds have to be more careful. To land on a perch, they swoop below it and then climb to lose speed before taking a grip. They land on the ground with a thump, followed by a short run to lose their momentum, or hit water with a splash, then slide to a standstill.

In a single bound *Mallards can take off from water with a leap, while ducks with smaller wings have to run along the surface.*

WINGS AND TAILS

The size and shape of a bird's wings determine the way it flies. In essence, broad wings give good lift for the slow flight of a wheeling hawk or for the rapid take-off of a ring-necked pheasant exploding into the sky. Tails give maneuverability: a bird can fly when it has lost its tail feathers, but its range of movement is handicapped. There is no obvious flight function for the excessively long tails of magpies, parakeets, and ring-necked pheasants – courtship and species recognition are likely functions for these.

You can learn a lot about a bird from its wings and tail. A variety of wing shapes has evolved, each of them suited to a specific way of life. A chimney swift hunts for flying insects by driving through the air on its slender, swept-back wings, alternating bursts of flickering wingbeats with short glides. A barn swallow often flies at a lower level and with a less economical flapping flight than the swift. Yet the swallow is the more efficient hunter of the two because its longer tail gives it the maneuverability necessary to catch larger, faster insects. This may be one reason why swallows have a longer breeding season.

Lift-off As this rock dove takes off, the wing feathers separate to act as airfoils, and the tail fans out to provide lift.

Power
Large wings and a round tail give a crow good lift.

Speed A chimney swift's long, slender wings give it fast flight.

Dexterity A swallow's long, forked tail aids its maneuverability.

FLIGHT SPEEDS

Starling	21 mph (34 kmph)	These are the speeds at which a bird will cruise for steady, long-distance flight. A chickadee that is trying to escape a predator, for example, will fly faster, and a peregrine falcon stooping on prey when hunting can exceed 100 mph (160 kmph).
House sparrow	22 mph (35 kmph)	
Mallard	40 mph (65 kmph)	
Herring gull	25 mph (40 kmph)	
Red-winged blackbird	31 mph (50 kmph)	
Crow	29 mph (46 kmph)	

HOVERING

Part of the lift generated by the wings comes from the flow of air over them created by forward motion and part comes from the flapping action. The slower the bird flies, the less lift is generated by air flow and the harder the bird has to flap. When hovering, it relies entirely on lift created by flapping. Some small birds can hover for a few seconds, for instance when investigating a new hanging feeder, but hummingbirds are the only birds that hover for long periods. The hummingbird's wing is specially adapted to allow this. Moving only from the shoulder, the wing is flapped in a figure eight movement. As it moves the wing is turned over, so that the inner side faces down as it moves forward and up as it moves back.

The kingfisher does not hover in the same way as the hummingbird. It pauses on beating wings with its body held almost vertically and its tail feathers depressed and

Invisible speed
A hummingbird beats its wings 80 times in a second in order to hover motionless at a flower or feeder.

spread. A kestrel hovers by flying forward into the wind at the same speed as it is blown back, so it mantains a static position relative to the ground. Other species will hover only when the occasion demands – for example, to pick insects from leaves or to seize fruit.

FORMATION FLYING

It is amazing that more collisions do not occur when a tightly packed flock of red-winged blackbirds or starlings circles in the fading light, or when a gang of sparrows is disturbed and flies up suddenly. The flocks show marvelous coordination, taking off and changing direction as one bird. To all appearances, they respond instantaneously to a hidden signal. In fact, each bird is alert to the slightest movements of its neighbors. As one bird crouches slightly and begins to spread its wings in preparation for take-off, the others quickly follow suit, and they leap into the air almost simultaneously. Similarly, the flock wheels in perfect precision when one or two birds decide to alter course, a wave of movement passing along the birds. Each bird is watching several birds in front, and times its maneuver as the wave of movement reaches it.

This precision allows birds such as geese and swans to fly in the familiar V-formation often seen overhead. In this formation each

bird uses the lift created by turbulence at the wing-tip of the bird in front of it, saving energy on long flights.

Long-haul flight *The V-formation of these snow geese requires precision, but the birds save energy by flying in each others' slipstreams.*

· PERCHING AND WALKING ·

THE BODIES OF birds are superbly designed for flight, but most birds spend only a small part of their lives in the air. You are more likely to see birds perched on a tree or shrub, hopping across a lawn, or climbing among foliage in search of food. The feet of birds, like their wings, vary between different species according to their needs.

PERCHING

Most common birds belong to the large group of species called the perching birds or *passerines,* literally, sparrow-like birds. Many kinds of birds perch, including some seabirds, but the feet of passerines are most suited to grasping slender twigs and wires. Some birds, like the chickadees and warblers, are amazingly acrobatic as they forage for insects.

The feet of most perching birds have four toes, three in front and one behind. The long rear toe is opposable, like a thumb, to enable the bird to take a firm hold on a slender twig. The claws are also long and needle-sharp to give a good grip when the bird lands on a vertical surface. Chickadees demonstrate the effectiveness of this design when they cling to the smooth surfaces of posts and feeders.

Holding tight Long toes curl around a perch, and give this female red-winged blackbird a firm hold on a reed.

Getting a grip Sharp claws enable a chickadee to gain a purchase on almost any vertical surface.

Sleeping on a perch would seem to be a precarious business, but perching birds lock onto their perch, so that their grip will not relax when they doze off. The tendons that flex the toes run around the ankle and knee joints. When a bird's weight settles on landing, and its legs bend, these tendons are pulled tight. This automatically curls the toes around the perch. A second locking device operates on the underside of the tendons in the toes. When the bird perches, hundreds of tiny knobs on the tendon press between ribs on the inside of the surrounding sheath, locking the tendon in place. As the bird takes off, its weight is removed, the legs straighten, the tendons slacken, and the toes uncurl.

CLIMBING

Specialized tree-climbers tend to have short legs with strong toes that make it easy for them to cling to vertical surfaces. Most woodpeckers' feet have two toes in front and two behind, but one or both of the rear-facing toes can be turned to face forward when climbing. Woodpeckers also have specially stiffened tail feathers, which they use to prop themselves against trunks. The brown creeper is similarly equipped, and both of these birds hop up trunks and out along branches in their hunt for food. When they have searched one tree, they fly down to the next and work their way up again. The nuthatches do not use their short tails as props, so they move both up and down trees with equal ease. The use of the tail as a prop is not confined to the woodpeckers and creepers. You can see chickadees and other birds prop themselves in this way when they land on feeders, and birds clinging at the entrance of a nestbox also press their tails against the wood.

Upward spiral
The brown creeper moves in a spiral up a tree trunk, searching for food.

Using a prop *A downy woodpecker supports itself on its tail. The tail feathers are molted only after replacements have been grown.*

Upside-down bird *Because it uses only its feet, the white-breasted nuthatch can climb down as easily as up.*

HOPPING AND WALKING

Birds that spend much of their time in trees, especially smaller species, generally hop when moving around on the ground. The best way of moving through trees seems to be hopping from perch to perch with the feet side by side, and the birds continue to use this action when on the ground.

Birds that spend more time feeding on the ground, like starlings, crows, and blackbirds, either walk or run. This is not an absolute rule: the ground-feeding wood thrush and hermit thrush hop, the robin and song sparrow can hop and run, and the black-billed magpie walks slowly and hops to go faster.

The feet of birds that nest and live on the ground differ from those of perching birds. In the pheasant family, for example, the fourth, rear-facing toe is quite short, and raised off the ground to make running easier. These ground birds are strong runners and may even run from danger rather than flying.

Economy travel *A ground-feeding bird, the starling finds walking or running more economical than hopping in terms of energy.*

WADING AND SWIMMING

Just as the feet of ground-dwelling birds differ from those of perching birds, the feet of wading and swimming birds are adapted to their way of life. Some marsh birds, such as jacanas, have extraordinarily long toes, allowing them to walk over floating plants or, like coots and grebes, fleshy-lobed toes for swimming. Ducks, geese, and swans have webbing between the three forward facing toes, to help them to swim and dive.

The position of the legs on the body is also related to the bird's lifestyle. Geese spend more of their time feeding on land than ducks, and their legs are farther forward on their bodies. This means that they walk more easily and with less of a waddle than ducks. Ducks that dive for their food, such as canvasbacks, scaup, and

Adaptable *The position and length of a teal's legs allow it to move with relative ease on both water and land.*

162

ring-necked ducks, tend to have large feet and short legs positioned close to the rear of their bodies. This arrangement is better for diving and swimming powerfully underwater but makes the ducks clumsy on land. Ducks that live and feed on the surface of water, such as the mallard, teals, and wigeons, have shorter legs placed far apart near the middle of the body.

All birds in the duck family also have a special arrangement of blood vessels in their legs. The arteries that carry blood from the heart down into the feet run alongside the veins coming back, so the cooled returning blood in the veins is warmed by heat transferred from the outgoing blood. This is a highly efficient way of conserving heat, and allows ducks to stand on ice without freezing.

On ice *These mallards are quite comfortable on a frozen lake because of the specialized arrangement of the blood vessels in their legs.*

HEAD-NODDING AND TAIL-BOBBING

Watch a dove in the park or a starling on the lawn, and you will see that it nods its head to and fro as it walks. This is common among birds that walk rather than hop. You might think that a bird would find it hard to see where it was going, let alone find food, when its head is nodding. (Try reading this page while swinging your head from side to side.) If you could see the movement in slow motion the true state of affairs would be revealed.

Steady eye *Because a pigeon's eyes are on the sides of its head, it must nod when it walks, to steady its vision.*

There is a point in every step the bird takes when, although the head is moving relative to the body, it is stationary relative to its surroundings. At this point, the eyes are steady, and the bird can pick out tiny morsels of food or distant predators. (Birds that hop take advantage of the pause between each jump to scrutinize their surroundings.) The evidence that head-nodding is a means of fixing the eyes comes from an experiment in which doves had to walk on a moving conveyor-belt. When the speed of the belt was adjusted so that the doves were stationary relative to their surroundings, they stopped nodding.

The habit of tail-bobbing is less easily explained. Birds normally raise their tails when defecating, to avoid soiling the feathers on the underside of the tail, but some species wag and bob their tails at other times for no obvious reason. Wrens often twitch and jerk their tails when they are excited, and some birds that live near water bob their tails up and down almost constantly. Palm warblers bob their tails when perched, a trait that is helpful in distinguishing them from similar-looking warblers that do not have this habit.

· CARE AND MAINTENANCE ·

FEATHERS ARE USED to regulate a bird's temperature and shed moisture. They also provide the lift and control surfaces for flight. When feathers are damaged or lost, insulation is impaired and flight is more strenuous. This can cost birds their lives in severe weather or if they are pursued by a predator. It is vital for survival that plumage is kept in top condition through daily care and attention, and that worn feathers are replaced once or twice a year by molting.

PREENING

The secret of a feather's strength and flexibility lies in the thousands of barbs that make up the vanes along each side of the central shaft. These are linked together by hooked barbules that work like a zipper. Air trapped between these barbs helps the bird's feathers keep out the wind and repel rain. Some of the barbs become unzipped in the course of daily wear, and must be reconnected to each other by preening. While a little casual preening is done at odd moments, all birds set aside time every day to clean and rearrange their feathers thoroughly and systematically.

Wear and tear
A close-up of the edge of a feather vane shows how two of its barbs develop a split once the interlocking barbules become unhooked. Gentle, precise nibbles with the bill fit the barbs back into position.

Birds preen by gently nibbling or stroking each feather with the bill, zipping up splits between the barbs. You can simulate the effects of preening on any feather. A gentle pull splits the vane, unhooking neighboring rows of barbules. Match the two edges together and run the join firmly between thumb and forefinger to zip it up again.

Preening removes feather parasites and dirt and arranges feathers into position. At intervals, the bird squeezes its bill against the preen gland under the tail to collect preen oil, which it spreads in a thin film over the feathers. This oil apparently kills bacteria and fungi and helps to lubricate the barbules so that they do not become brittle and break. A bird that has been prevented from oiling becomes scruffy. Parts that cannot be reached by the bill, such as the head, are preened by scratching with the feet. Preen oil is transferred either by scratching the oil-laden bill before scratching the head or by rubbing the head against previously oiled feathers.

Keeping in trim *A blue jay takes time out to tidy its tail. The flight feathers must be kept in good condition, or the bird's flying ability will suffer.*

BATHING

Ornithologists are undecided on the exact function of bathing. Cleaning the feathers does not appear to be the main purpose. It is possible that preen oil spreads more easily over damp feathers. Experiments have shown that feathers become more flexible when they are wet, so bathing might also be a means of restoring feathers to their proper shape.

Most common birds bathe, and the importance of a regular bath to keep the plumage in good condition is shown by the way that birds come to the birdbath as soon as you clear the ice after a frosty night. Some birds such as starlings will even break the ice for themselves.

After checking that it is not going to be caught unaware by a lurking cat, the bird enters the water. It ruffles its feathers and wets them by ducking into the water or shaking its head while rolling its body and flicking water with its wings. The bird squats to immerse its belly with tail fanned and scoops water over its back with the wings. Water sprays everywhere. Raising and lowering the feathers helps the water to penetrate between them, but the bird is careful not to get so waterlogged that it cannot escape a sudden attack.

Splashing bird *A killdeer squats down in shallow water to wet its feathers, raising them to allow the water to penetrate to the skin.*

After a thorough dampening, the bedraggled bird flies off to a safe perch to dry. It shakes its wings and tail to throw off much of the water and ruffles the feathers to dry the plumage. A preen provides the final polish and rearrangement.

As an alternative to bathing, doves take showers in the rain. They lean over with one wing lifted and raise the body feathers to let the water in. Warblers, sparrows, and some other birds bathe by flying through rain-soaked foliage, while swallows, swifts, and owls momentarily dip into ponds and rivers while in flight. Hawks sometimes perch with their wings spread in the rain.

Birds also use a form of dry cleaning. The house sparrow dust-bathes, usually after water-bathing. It lands in loose, dry soil or a dusty path, and goes through the same motions as in water-bathing, but filling the plumage with dust. Several other sparrows may join in, and squabbles break out if they interfere with each others' actions. When they fly off to preen, craters are left in the soil. Dust baths might help reduce the numbers of feather parasites.

Bathing on the wing *Tree swallows flying in a flock bathe together in a river with hardly a pause in their flight.*

SUNBATHING

People sunbathe to change color and for the pleasant sensation of the sun on our bare skin. It is not so clear why birds bask in the sun. Sometimes birds simply perch in a sunny place to keep warm on a cool day. They will also sunbathe with their wings spread out on the snow in very cold but clear weather, so they may be trying to absorb the weak rays of the sun. This cannot be the whole explanation because birds also bask in the sun on hot days when they pant with their bills open trying to keep cool.

Birds appear to enter an almost trance-like state when sunbathing. It could be argued that they are simply enjoying themselves, much like human sun addicts, but the function of sunbathing is probably to assist feather maintenance. Vultures' feathers that have become twisted during flight straighten out with a few minutes of exposure to the sun but take several hours to repair in the shade. There could be a similar process at work in the feathers of small birds.

Soaking in the sun *On a hot summer day, a black-billed magpie indulges in sunbathing on a suburban lawn.*

Solar power *A flock of turkey vultures at their roost make use of the rays of the sun to repair their feathers.*

MOLT

Despite the daily maintenance carried out by birds, the plumage eventually becomes worn from the stresses of flight, friction against foliage, and constant rubbing while sitting on the nest. The bird becomes scruffy, and a close look at a feather that has dropped naturally shows the wear. The colors are dull, the vane is thin and threadbare, and the edges are frayed. It is time for a new suit, so the bird sheds its worn plumage and replaces it with a new set of feathers.

Molting usually happens once a year, although for some birds, such as the goldfinch, it occurs twice during the year. The plumage is replaced gradually, minimizing the disruption to the bird's life. Small songbirds take about five weeks to complete their molt, starlings take about three months, and eagles take over a year to change all their feathers. Ducks replace all of their feathers at once, a process that makes them flightless for a period of two weeks to a month.

During the molt, the only clearly visible gaps are in the long feathers of the wings and to a lesser extent in the tail. The old feathers are shed in sequence along the wing or tail, and new ones grow immediately behind them, so that the gap is always kept small. The flight feathers are shed so slowly that the birds are never deprived of too many at once, and are symmetrical to ensure that birds do not become lopsided and lose their flight ability. You may be able to see the gaps in the wings of large birds such as crows and hawks when they fly overhead in winter.

The molt is a time of strain for birds. Not only does a bird with an incomplete plumage have to use more energy for keeping warm and for flying, but it also has to find the energy to manufacture new feathers. Molting birds become retiring; they save their energy by perching quietly and keep out of the way of predators because they could be caught more easily at this time. Most birds molt at

Wearing thin *The rosy color of a purple finch's plumage becomes brighter in the spring as its autumn plumage is gradually worn away.*

the end of the breeding season, but some molt again into a breeding plumage before nesting. Both molts take place when the birds are free of the strain of rearing their families and when food is abundant. The new plumage gives them a better chance of surviving winter weather or the strain of a long migration flight.

Male birds' plumage may be brighter at breeding than at other times. The gradual abrasion of individual feathers causes some males to change color and acquire brilliant breeding plumage. Male house and purple finches look brighter in spring because the new feathers acquired in the fall molt have gray tips. As the feathers wear away during the winter, the gray gradually disappears. A more spectacular example is the dramatic transformation of the male bobolink from its fall plumage of undistinguished brown, similar to the female, to the striking spring pattern of black, white, and buff.

New suit *This starling's fall spangling will be lost through abrasion, accelerated as the bird squeezes in and out of its nest hole in spring.*

· ROOSTING AND SLEEPING ·

BIRDS ARE MOSTLY creatures of the day. Birds of the yard, especially, retire to roost as darkness falls and become active again before it is light enough for you to see them. Roosting times differ between species. Cardinals, juncos, and white-throated sparrows will visit feeders after sunset when house sparrows and pigeons have already retired for the night.

ROOSTING

Regular roosting places must provide birds with both adequate protection from predators and some shelter from the elements. A hole in a tree or a well-placed nestbox is the best place on both counts, but even a bare tree gives birds some protection from the wind. One study has shown that a leafless thicket where cardinals and mockingbirds might roost saves birds a third or more of the energy that they would otherwise have to use to keep warm overnight.

The nest is often used as a roost, especially by the female before laying her eggs. A few birds construct special roosts for the winter. In regions where the winters are severe, house sparrows build winter nests. These are smaller than the breeding nests but are well lined with feathers. Downy and hairy woodpeckers drill out special winter roosting cavities, and nuthatches roost in nestboxes. Roosting sites can often be identified by the accumulation of droppings beneath them.

Evening rush hour *A flock of red-winged blackbirds arrives at the roost.*

The shelter afforded by a roost is improved if the birds huddle together for warmth, as bluebirds do when they pack into nestboxes. Mass roosting is also practiced by many birds, especially outside the breeding season. Enormous flocks of red-winged blackbirds, grackles, and cowbirds retire to communal roosts in trees. It is worth finding one of these roosts to watch the spectacle of streams of birds arriving before sunset. Starlings are also famous for their huge roosts, which can become a nuisance in city centers. The regular evening movements of birds to their roosts, whether they are the strung-out Vs of gulls, the straggling lines of crows, or tight bunches of starlings, are a familiar urban sight. Small parties set out from the feeding grounds and gather together, often at traditional staging posts, to arrive at the roost in a mass.

One function of communal roosts is to give the same safety in numbers as is provided in a daytime flock (*see page 170*). Roosts might also be a means of finding a good place to feed the next day. If a bird is hungry and unable to find a good place to feed, it follows well-fed birds when they leave the roost in the morning, to the place where they had done well.

SLEEP

The precise function of sleep is something of a mystery, even in humans. The best explanation is that sleep is a way of saving energy during a bird's spare time. Because a sleeping bird is quiet and immobile, it also seems likely that sleep helps to make the bird less conspicuous to predators. Whatever the case, sleeping in a safe, sheltered roost is an advantage.

Contrary to the myth, very few birds sleep with their heads "tucked under their wings" – it would be an awkward posture. The bill is tucked under the scapular (shoulder) feathers, or the head is drawn into the breast, and one leg is often tucked up into the feathers. This helps to minimize heat loss.

Birds sleep with their feathers fluffed out to improve insulation and save energy. Some small birds also save energy at night by letting their temperatures drop. In effect, they are turning down their thermostats or banking their fires, as the prudent homeowner does. If a hummingbird is caught by a cold spell, its temperature drops almost to that of the surrounding air and it becomes so torpid that it does not react even when handled. On cold nights, a black-capped chickadee's temperature drops by 50°F (10°C), and its breathing rate falls from 95 to 65 breaths per minute, making an energy saving of 20 percent.

Energy saving
A white-breasted nuthatch reduces the activity of its body functions to conserve valuable energy in the cold.

It is very difficult to creep up unobserved on a sleeping bird. You can see why if you watch a group of sleeping doves or mallards: each bird opens its eyes at intervals. This is a necessary precaution against surprise attacks from predators. If you approach the birds, they open their eyes more frequently to keep watch on you as you get nearer.

• FLOCKS •

SOME BIRDS LIVE IN FLOCKS, especially during winter, while others are never seen in more than ones or twos. A few birds are solitary at some times and sociable at others. There are good reasons why some birds choose to live in flocks while others prefer solitary lives.

THE BENEFITS OF FLOCKS

A bird in a flock gains protection against predators, simply because the predators find it difficult to concentrate their attacks on single targets if there is a large selection. The same effect can be seen if you throw someone one tennis ball or several all at the same time: it is easier to catch a single ball than one out of half a dozen that are bouncing all over the place. For a bird of prey a further complication is that it could injure itself by colliding with one of the flock. Red-winged blackbirds and starlings bunch into a tight formation when a hawk appears, because there is safety in numbers. Each bird is making use of its companions because there is less chance of it being singled out by the hawk if it is in a flock.

Birds in a flock also stand a better chance of escaping in an attack because many pairs of eyes are better than one for keeping watch. Experiments and observations have proved that when danger threatens, flocks of birds take off sooner than do single individuals. The difference is only measured in fractions of a second, but that may be all the time that is needed to make an escape.

Follow the crowd *A flock of grackles descends on a pumpkin patch.*

As a result of these advantages, a bird in a flock does not need to spend as much time scanning its surroundings for danger as it would if it were alone. A bird on your feeder will stop eating at frequent intervals to cock its head and look around. This cuts down the amount of time spent feeding. If it is joined by other birds it can be less vigilant and spend more of its time feeding because it can rely on the others to take a share in the guard duty.

The second major advantage of flocking is that it helps birds to find food. A solitary bird might spend more time than it can afford searching for food, so it will watch other birds to see what they have found. This is why one or two birds arriving at the feeder are often quickly followed by a horde of others: all the birds keep watch on each other's movements and, realizing that a source of food has been found by one bird, the others rush to join.

This behavior indicates to other birds that someone is putting out food, and more birds will flock to your feeder. If the supply dries up, the visitors will look somewhere else, perhaps following other flockmates who know where to go.

Following the example of others also operates at an individual level when birds are feeding. In winter, flocks of chickadees, joined by kinglets, creepers, nuthatches, and downy woodpeckers, feed on the tiny insects and even smaller insect eggs that are to be found lodged among leaves or in crevices in bark. Such food must be hard to find, even for sharp-eyed birds, so time is saved by the birds watching each others' efforts. If one chickadee finds aphids skulking among leaves, the others birds also start to search the leaves. When another bird finds rich pickings of dormant caterpillars or pupae, all of the flock starts to search for this new food.

WHY SOME BIRDS LIVE ALONE

Flocks will generally split up in the breeding season, when males stake out and defend territories, but some birds live alone throughout the year. Why is it that not all birds live in flocks, if they provide these advantages?

A solitary life has its compensations. Predators can be avoided by stealth and camouflage, when it makes more sense to be alone. Feeding in a group is only an advantage when there is plenty of food, as at a feeder. Flocking birds specialize in feeding on large patches of food. These patches of food are spaced out, and the difficult part of feeding is to find a patch, so many eyes make light work. Other kinds of food are thinly but evenly spread, and birds in a flock will get in each other's way. In these circumstances it is better for birds to hunt alone, concentrating on one area, and getting to know where best to search. Birds of prey are solitary for this reason. When necessary, this hunting ground will be defended against rivals, as the winter territories of nuthatches and mockingbirds are.

Lone hunter The red-bellied woodpecker works alone when feeding, chiseling insects from under the bark of trees.

171

· SPACE AND TERRITORY ·

EVERY BIRD KEEPS a personal space around itself. The size of this space depends on the bird's living habits, social position, and circumstances. It is sensible for a bird to keep a distance from its neighbors: it prevents conflicts when feeding and collisions when a flock takes to the air. Birds also defend a fixed area called a territory, which is needed for feeding, breeding, or both.

Arm's reach *Cliff swallows allow enough room between each other for safe take-offs and landings.*

INDIVIDUAL DISTANCE

If two birds come too close to each other, one will give way. The minimum distance at which they will accept one another is called their individual distance. It can be observed when swallows or starlings line up evenly spaced on utility wires. When one bird flies in and lands, another takes off and finds a new place to perch. The size of the individual distance depends on the species: they keep just out of "arm's reach." This is about 1 foot (30 centimeters) for gulls and less for smaller species. Personal space also depends on circumstances: it is close to zero between mates and birds that roost in a huddle. Male birds often maintain greater individual distance than do females.

Maintaining this individual distance makes sense when birds are feeding. Apart from wasting time squabbling over morsels, birds could get in each other's way. Robins will space themselves out when hunting on a lawn so they can creep up on earthworms. The prey would disappear if they were to be disturbed by another robin trampling around nearby.

Squabbles over perches and food are usually settled quickly because each bird knows its place in the pecking order, which is decided by a series of skirmishes. Junior birds always defer to seniors, moving away, and only rarely does a bird change its place in the hierarchy *(see page 175)*.

TERRITORY

A territory is the ground that an animal defends against intruders to preserve some commodity, usually food. The permanence of the arrangement depends on the species and the purpose of the territory. A screech-owl defends a hunting territory through its adult life, but a mockingbird defends a bush only as long as it has berries. Both birds defend their territories because an exclusive food supply provides them with an easy living. If the bush that the mockingbird is guarding is invaded by flocks of ravenous birds, it gives up defense as futile. If there is a glut of fruit in the neighborhood with plenty for all, there is also no point in wasting energy on defending a personal supply. Territories also help space birds for breeding. The male defends the territory, sometimes with the help of the female.

Jealously guarded *Berries are a favorite food of the mockingbird, which will vigorously defend its personal bush.*

Chickadees, thrushes, wood warblers, song sparrows, and wrens defend breeding territories, but some birds, such as goldfinches and starlings, defend only the immediate vicinity of their nests.

As well as providing a haven for rearing the family, the spacing effect of songbirds' territories helps reduce losses through predation. If a crow finds a nest and feeds on the eggs, it will start searching nearby for more nests. Its search will be more successful if nests are close together; if they are spaced widely apart, a predatory bird may give up before it has been rewarded with further finds.

In parceling out space, birds define their use of a neighborhood. Where they are defending food supplies, the size of the territories depends on the supply of food. In times of plenty, each bird can survive in a smaller space, so territories are smaller. Food provided in a yard helps determine how many birds can inhabit it. The weakest will not breed and may starve. Birds constantly watch for a chance to improve their situation. When a territory holder dies, it is replaced almost immediately.

TERRITORIES OF SOME COMMON BIRDS

Black-capped chickadee ......8½ to 17 acres
(3.44 to 6.88 ha)

Downy woodpecker ....5 to 8 acres
(2.02 to 3.24 ha)

Song sparrow ....½ to 1½ acres
(0.2 to 0.6 ha)

House wren ....¼ to 3½ acres
(0.1 to 1.42 ha)

Mockingbird ....¹⁄₁₀ to 1½ acres
(0.04 to 0.6 ha)

Robin ....¹⁄₁₀ to ½ acre
(0.04 to 0.2 ha)

Starling ....1 square yard
(1 square meter)

Chimney swift ....Nest

These figures are approximate: territory sizes and shapes are elastic and depend on the habitat. Larger territories are used for feeding; smaller ones are based around nest sites and tend to shrink after the eggs have been laid.

· DISPLAYS AND FIGHTS ·

BIRDS OFTEN COMMUNICATE by means of displays. These are gestures that are used as signals, in the same way you might shake a fist or beckon. Displays convey information to other birds about the mood and intentions of the signaler and are often used in courtship and disputes over food or territory. If a bird's aggressive displays are not successful in deterring rivals, full-blown fights may occur.

INTENTION MOVEMENTS

The small movements that a bird makes as it prepares to do something, such as a slight crouch before take-off, are the simplest form of communication. These are known as "intention movements" and are often so quick that it is very difficult for us to see them. Intention movements can be used to coordinate the actions of a flock (*see page 170*), or to convey more detailed information. The reaction of a flock of birds to one of their number taking off depends on subtle changes in the behavior of the departing bird. If it shows all of the normal intention movements, it can take off and fly away without disturbing the others in the flock. On the other hand, if it takes off suddenly without showing any intention movements, the others interpret this as an alarm signal, and the entire flock flies off.

Unburried departure *Intention movements have shown that the two turnstones are not taking off in alarm, so the flock is not disturbed.*

DISPLAYS

Displays are signals used to settle disputes and to reduce aggression between potential mates during courtship. The same displays are often used in both, and you cannot always tell what is going on unless the sexes can be distinguished.

When birds are gathered at a feeder, squabbles can break out because the birds are coming closer together than their normal individual distance. Disputes are settled with displays that demonstrate the birds' motivations. Each bird can judge how aggressive another is and decide whether to retreat or stand its ground accordingly.

Formal display *These killdeer have met at the boundary of their territories and are executing a bowing display to reassert their claims.*

THREATS

In a threat display, a bird makes itself appear menacing by showing elements of attack behavior. The bird fluffs its feathers, points its bill at its opponent, or raises its wings. You can observe this sort of behavior especially when there is a crowd at the feeder. A bird signals submission, asking not to be attacked, by sleeking its feathers and crouching.

Displays are often enhanced by a bird's plumage. When male red-winged blackbirds meet at the border of their territories or at the feeder, they stretch forward and spread their wings to expose their red epaulets. Showing off the epaulets enhances the threat of the spread wings and is a clear sign of dominance.

Squaring up
A yellow-headed blackbird raises its wing in a threatening gesture, increasing its apparent size to intimidate its opponent into submission.

FIGHTS

When fighting breaks out, it is most often among strangers that have not learned each other's status, or between near-equals. A dominant bird easily displaces its junior, but a bird of about the same rank will hold its ground, and the two will square up to each other. The displays become stronger, and a fight may break out. A robin may have to do no more than hop toward a trespasser who has strayed into his territory, but if the intruder is another male trying to carve out a new territory, it will hold its ground, and the dispute will escalate. Fights can look very nasty as the feathers fly, but normally there is no serious injury. Fights to the death are very rare among birds. They might happen when one bird is unable to escape, and the other continues the attack.

Rising tempers Two tree swallows *stand up to each other in a dispute that could easily develop into a fight.*

· SONGS AND CALLS ·

THE VOICE IS an important means of communication for birds. Many birds have a vocabulary of calls, used especially when they are living in flocks or mated pairs. Some calls warn against predators or help hold flocks together. Songs are usually more complex and are used for defending territories and attracting mates. Both calls and songs are useful for identifying birds, especially when they cannot be seen.

WHAT ARE BIRDS SAYING?

Some people have the enviable gift of being able to remember and instantly recognize the songs and calls of birds. The rest of us have to spend some time each spring seeking out singing birds, identifying them, and familiarizing ourselves with songs forgotten over the winter. Even then, there are usually a few species that we find difficult to identify, especially when a bird has a varied repertoire or if its song can be confused with another's. It helps if we can put words to the song, like the towhee's *drink-your-tea* or the yellow warbler's *sweet, sweet, sweet, I'm so sweet.*

Singing is most intense during early spring, when birds are staking out their territories. A bird will sing most strongly when a stranger intrudes; once they have settled down, neighbors take little notice of each other. It seems rather a shame that the songs that give us so much pleasure are used by birds as a means of threatening each other. The consolation is that songs are a means of avoiding outright fighting.

Songs are also used by males to advertise for a mate. Ornithologists have found evidence to suggest that the female of some species chooses her mate according to the quality of his songs. A rich and varied song may be equivalent in sound to elaborate plumage such as the peacock's train, designed to dazzle the female into accepting a male. The male mockingbirds with the largest repertoires attract the most females, while the male starlings who have the most elaborate songs, and sing in the longest bouts, attract more females and win

Staking a claim *In spring and summer, marsh wrens sing both by day and by night while clinging to rushes, reeds, or cattails.*

a mate sooner. These starlings are invariably older, more experienced males, and the high quality of their songs indicates to their prospective mates that they are likely to be good fathers.

Some birds, such as towhees, stop singing altogether when they have acquired a mate, but others continue. The song is used as a means of strengthening the pair bond and maintaining the female in breeding condition. The male house wren apparently sings to his mate to show that there are no predators in the area, so she can concentrate on her nesting duties.

SIMPLE AND VARIED SONGS

It is puzzling that some birds have simple songs, consisting of a monotonous phrase that is repeated with hardly any variation maybe hundreds of times, while others have varied outpourings of warbles and trills. A brown thrasher was once recorded singing over 2,000 different songs. Despite this range of phrases, it is not difficult to recognize a thrasher's song, because an overall pattern distinguishes it from the songs of other birds.

If a male thrasher has such a varied repertoire of notes, and a female thrasher recognizes them as coming from a possible mate, how does the thrasher sing the right notes, and how does the female recognize them? In other words, are songs instinctive or learned? In some birds, the song is inherited from the parents, making it completely instinctive, while in others the song is learned, sometimes while still in the nest. Male birds grow up listening to other males of their species and

Vocal styles Eastern and western meadowlarks look almost identical, but their songs differ: the former has a whistle, the latter a flutelike gurgle.

use the memory of those notes to compose their own songs. Similarly, young females learn the songs of their species and, when adult, respond to the correct suitors.

DAWN CHORUS

Birdsong is most intense at dawn. The first notes ring out while it is still dark. As it becomes light, more birds join in, and there is a crescendo of sound. The dawn chorus continues for about half an hour. It starts earlier on moonlit nights, and later in dull weather. Why birds sing so vehemently at dawn has long been a mystery. It would seem that after the long night's fast, their priority should be a good breakfast.

Various explanations have been suggested. Contrary to expectation, a full stomach may not be ideal for small birds, because the increased weight makes flying more strenuous. Another theory is that it is difficult to find food in the dark. The birds delay feeding until the light improves and sing in the meantime. They might also be reminding neighbors not to trespass at the start of the day. But, like birdsong itself, there is probably no one explanation of the dawn chorus. All these factors, and perhaps others, may play a part.

Early morning call A boat-tailed grackle sings out from a treetop perch in the first weak light of the new day.

MIMICRY

The imitation of songs is extended by some birds to mimicking other species. The most famous mimic in North America is the mockingbird. One was noted imitating the songs of 55 other bird species in an hour. Birds of prey and domestic fowl are imitated, as well as songbirds. Mockingbirds have also been heard to mimic complicated human compositions. The starling, catbird, and white-eyed vireo are also good mimics. These birds imitate other birds as well as crickets, the calls of frogs, the mewing of cats, people whistling, and even mechanical sounds. Mimicry is thought to be a way of increasing the repertoire to make the singer more attractive to females.

Champion mimic
Northern mockingbirds have been heard to immitate squeaky wheelbarrows and barking dogs.

Namesakes *The catbird is named for its call, which is not imitative, but can mimic the spitting of a cat.*

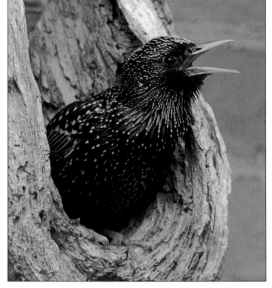

When in Rome *The introduced European starling has been heard to imitate a flicker's tattoo by drumming with its bill as a flicker does.*

CALL NOTES

Birds have a repertoire of calls, with a variety of meanings. These serve a different function from the songs. Red-winged blackbirds have seven calls used in the defense of their nests. The most common is a *check* note, which denotes mild alarm, and at the other end of the scale the female has a loud scream. This not only causes her nestlings to stop begging and lie low to avoid detection, but also brings other redwings to her assistance.

The simplest type of communication is to broadcast one's position to other birds with contact notes. Shrill notes accompany small flocks of chickadees as they make their way from tree to tree. These notes help keep the members of the flock together while they are searching for insects, often out of each other's sight. Birds also have call notes in migration that help to hold the flock together.

When a cat tries to sneak up on birds at a feeder, its attempt is frustrated by alarm calls from a vigilant bird. The call is a

Verbal warning *The red-winged blackbird, a vigorous defender of its territory, uses a range of calls.*

simple harsh note that birds of other species also recognize. As soon as it is uttered, all the birds fly to safety in the nearest trees. The call is also used for mobbing owls. When an owl is discovered on its daytime perch, birds gather around to scold it. Their cries alert other birds, which are drawn to the scene; as a consequence of their actions, the owl often has to abandon its perch for a quieter site.

By drawing attention to a cat or an owl, the birds are destroying the predator's chances of making a catch. A different tactic is used against birds of prey. When a hawk is spotted above, birds withdraw into the foliage and utter thin calls. These calls warn other birds that there is danger overhead. In contrast with the calls made in response to a cat or owl, which are easy to pinpoint, the hawk alarm is hard to locate, at least by human ears. This ensures that the birds giving the alarm are not endangered.

Keeping in touch *Black-capped chickadees in a flock will call to each other almost incessantly while on the move.*

· PAIR FORMATION ·

PAIR FORMATION IS intimately connected with territorial behavior. The songs and displays used to defend a territory often have the dual purpose of attracting mates. Courtship allows birds to choose the best mate. While jealously fending off rivals, male birds help their mates prepare for nesting. The females produce the eggs and undertake most of the work of nesting, but the males of some species help by finding food.

COURTSHIP

As well as giving a bird the chance to choose a suitable mate, courtship reduces the animosity between two individuals that normally results in their keeping their distance *(see page 172)*. The male's instinct is to drive intruders from his territory. A female establishes herself by holding her ground and behaving submissively, and the male starts to court her. Pair formation can be almost instantaneous, but songbirds usually take a week or so to become fully paired, especially the first time.

The female bird does not necesssarily stay with the first male to court her. Birds that pair in autumn do not always breed in spring. Both members of the pair may not survive the winter. Familiarity and experience from the previous year help courtship to proceed rapidly, and nesting to start early. This is an advantage because in some bird species the earliest clutches produce the most young.

Research shows that female birds are somehow able to determine which males will make good mates and fathers, usually the older males. The key to survival is the ability to find food efficiently: an older bird is clearly a survivor. This makes it likely that he will be able to find enough food to sustain a growing family. The female bird must, therefore, be able to recognize an older male. His song will be more elaborate than that of younger birds *(see page 177)*, or he will be more ardent in his advances. Young males do not display so vigorously or pursue unwilling females, while an older male will chase a female across neighboring territories to entice her back.

The thrill of the chase *Four male pintail ducks pursue one female in a courtship flight. The strongest and most determined will succeed.*

Strengthening the bond *A pair of grackles perches together, and the male continues the song that first attracted the female.*

MATE GUARDING

A pair of birds is often inseparable before egg-laying. They roost and feed together, and the male accompanies the female as she collects the nest material. This is not a

Close couple *Male mallards guard their mates jealously to avoid being cuckolded.*

sign of devotion, as some early naturalists believed. A male rock dove, for example, guards his mate to ensure that he will be the father of her offspring. He "drives" her, walking so close behind her that he almost trips over her tail, and if she takes off, he will follow.

On the other hand, a male will take advantage of his neighbor's lapses of vigilance to cuckold him. There is a clear advantage to the male if he can father extra offspring. Male starlings sometimes take a second mate, but they only feed the nestlings from their first union, so this second family is often unsuccessful. Male house wrens regularly build more than one nest but normally only mate with one female. Sometimes, however, a male wren entices a second female into a spare nest if he occupies a territory containing food resources sufficient to rear two families.

COURTSHIP FEEDING

Although in some species the female helps the male to guard the territory, her main concern is to prepare for nesting. This entails building the nest, sometimes with the male's assistance, and developing the eggs in her body. The male often helps by bringing her extra food. Food is still in fairly short supply in spring, but small birds require over one-third more food than normal during this time in order to form their eggs, and this comes courtesy of the male. Courtship feeding continues while the female is incubating, reducing the time that she has to spend off the nest. It ceases when the male switches to feeding the newly hatched nestlings.

Some ornithologists believe that courtship feeding may help strengthen the bond between the pair. This is difficult to prove, but in some bird species the male only goes through the motions of presenting food. It also seems that some females use the male's ability to supply food during courtship as an indication of how well he will provide for the future family.

Bearing gifts *A male blue jay presents his mate with food during courtship in order to prove his ability as a provider.*

· NEST BUILDING ·

THE NEST IS a container designed to keep eggs and nestlings warm and to protect them from enemies. Birds whose young leave the nest shortly after hatching, such as ducks, shorebirds, and quails, build simple nests, often no more than a scrape in the ground. By contrast, the nests of birds whose young remain in the nest until they can fly are quite elaborate. Most common birds make cup-shaped nests, but several kinds nest in holes.

SELECTING A SITE

In late winter and spring, you might see birds hopping from twig to twig through bushes or the branches of trees. Although not searching for food, they are clearly looking for something. The interest shown in the forks of branches indicates that they are prospecting for nest sites. For most songbirds, selecting the site and building the nest are the responsibilities of the female. She may be helped in building by her mate: male robins and mourning doves, for example, bring the nesting material to the female, who incorporates it into the nest. For hole-nesting starlings and chickadees it is the male who chooses the nesting cavity. Male house wrens build the foundation of the nest alone and then attract a female, who lines it.

Solid base *Eastern kingbirds often nest in fenceposts or stumps like this one. In the suburbs, they will sometimes nest in rain gutters.*

Builder's mate *A male robin gathers a beakful of twigs to take back to the female, who will work them into the nest.*

Exactly how the nest site is chosen is something of a mystery to us. Sometimes it seems that a bird has difficulty deciding where to build. Several sites are inspected, and building may start in more than one of these before a final choice is made. Birds appear to look for a suitable configuration of twigs, or some other base that will give a solid foundation. Protection from predators and shelter from the elements are other important considerations. Song sparrows build their first nests of the season in grass or leafy plants near the ground. Later in the season, when the foliage of bushes and trees has sprouted, nests are built higher up. Birds sometimes nest in unsatisfactorily exposed places. This may be because the builder is inexperienced or because there is a shortage of good sites. This is often the case in yards where tangled foliage and undergrowth are discouraged: as a result of such gardening practices birds are forced to make do with less desirable nest sites.

STARTING THE NEST

It is amazing that a vireo's crib, bound with spiders' webs and decorated with lichens, a robin's woven mud-lined nest, and the hanging cradle of an oriole are built mostly with the bill, sometimes assisted by the feet and breast. The robin, for example, starts its nest by wedging together twigs and grasses to make a good foundation. Then, standing in the middle, she pulls grasses in with her bill and shapes the cup, pushing with breast and wings and scrabbling with her feet until the materials mold together into a comfortable fit. Beakfuls of mud are smoothed around the interior with more pushing. Finally, a layer of fine grasses is worked into the wet mud as a lining.

Solid foundation *The robust nests of twigs and mud built by robins survive the winter well enough to be refurbished the following spring.*

Building the nest takes considerable time and energy. A pair of woodpeckers may take more than a month, working several hours a day to chisel out their hole. Most small birds will take less than a week, and sometimes only a day or two, to complete the nest. As a rule, the first nest of the season takes longest to build, and work stops temporarily in cold weather. After it is completed, the nest may remain empty for several days before egg-laying starts. Nest building is a sensitive time for birds: many will desert their half-built nests if they are disturbed and start fresh ones in new sites.

It is surprising how many nests are abandoned after one use. This is in part due to parasites in the nest material (*see page 12*). Most songbirds build fresh nests each year, and sometimes for each clutch hatched in one year. Hole-nesters often build on top of the old nests, however, and barn swallows will also reuse the foundations of old nests. Hawks often use the same nest year after year, adding new material every spring.

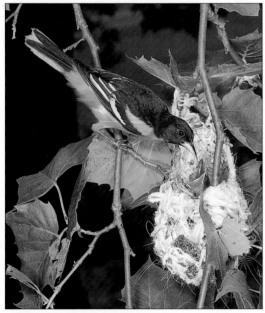

Elaborate construction *Baltimore orioles weave pouches of grasses and stems and will use materials such as yarn left out in your yard.*

· EGGS AND INCUBATION ·

THE SHAPES, COLORS, and textures of birds' eggs have long been admired, but the development of the bird inside and the behavior of the parents while nurturing their eggs are just as worthy of our interest. Egg production is a strain on the female, so it is not surprising that there is often a gap between the building of the nest and egg-laying when she concentrates on feeding. The females of many species also need their mates to help them with extra food at this time.

EGG-LAYING

The formation of an egg starts several days before it is laid. The egg, mainly yolk, moves down the oviduct. Here it is coated in the white and encased in a shell. The shell takes about a day to form and requires so much calcium that the bird's bones are temporarily depleted. Egg production saps energy reserves, and some females become less active.

Most common birds lay their eggs in the morning at 24-hour intervals. Doves, hummingbirds, herons, and owls lay over a longer period. If eggs are lost through predation or the destruction of the nest,

Tiring work *When producing and laying eggs, female birds such as this kingbird may roost in the nest for warmth in order to save their energy.*

most birds can produce another clutch. In most common birds, the size of the clutch is variable, although some birds, such as doves, barn swallows, crows, and gulls, lay a set number. Locality is a factor: northern birds lay more eggs than do those in the south. This may be because longer days allow more time for feeding, but nocturnal northern owls also lay larger clutches.

The number of eggs in a clutch often also depends on how much food the female bird can get, so bad weather often reduces clutch size. Hawks and owls may not even attempt to lay if there is a shortage of prey. Several species of sparrows lay fewer eggs in the first and third clutches, and most in the second, when food is more plentiful.

Small beginnings *Tiny hummingbird eggs, shown here larger than life size, are in fact large in relation to the bodyweight of the bird.*

THE COLOR OF EGGS

White is the basic color of birds' eggs, but most species add pigments as an aid to camouflage. The shell is coated with pigment as it passes down the oviduct. The ground color is added before the layers of the shell are built up, and any pattern is applied to the surface of the completed shell. If the egg is stationary as the pigment is applied, it will have a pattern of spots and splodges; if it is moving, streaks and lines are formed. Some hole-nesting birds, such as woodpeckers and owls, have white eggs – probably so that they show up in the dim recesses of the nest and will not be trampled. Birds that have open nests lay colored and speckled eggs that blend in with the background for camouflage. This is especially important for birds that lay on the ground. There are exceptions to all these rules. Doves and hummingbirds have very conspicuous white eggs, but incubation starts when the first egg is laid, so the clutch is never left uncovered. Ducks cover their similarly vulnerable eggs with vegetation when they leave the nest.

Camouflage by color *The deep blue of a robin's eggs makes them less obvious to predators in the shadowy foliage of a tree.*

Invisible in the open *A killdeer's eggs are so heavily speckled that they are virtually impossible to see, even on open ground.*

Vulnerable *Mourning doves begin incubating as soon as the clutch is started, taking turns to cover the highly visible white eggs.*

INCUBATION

Birds are warm-blooded, and the chicks inside eggs have to be kept warm to develop properly. Heat is provided by the parent sitting on the nest. Shortly before the eggs are laid, the bird sheds feathers from the breast to leave a bare patch of skin called the "brood patch." The brood patch has a rich supply of blood vessels and acts as a heating pad that efficiently transfers body heat to the eggs. Doves, which have a a very long breeding season, have a bare patch all year. Ducks pluck their breast feathers out to use as a nest lining. In the majority of common birds, incubation is carried out by the female parent alone, but when the male shares incubation, as in starlings, doves, and woodpeckers, he also develops a brood patch.

Incubation does not usually start until the clutch is completed. Although the parent bird sits on the nest before this time, it does not apply the brood patch to the eggs. When all the eggs have been laid, the bird ruffles its feathers to expose the brood patch before settling down and tucking the eggs in place.

Regulating temperature *A herring gull moves its eggs around and checks their temperatures before settling down on them again.*

After settling on the eggs, the bird is rather restless unless it senses danger, in which case it will freeze in place. At intervals, the bird gets up and pokes the eggs with its bill, to shuffle them in the nest. This ensures that the eggs are warmed evenly and allows air to diffuse through the shell. Aside from these factors, it appears that the regular motion is also necessary for the proper development of the embryos.

The sitting bird does not remain on the nest continuously during its shift. It takes breaks to feed, preen, and defecate while the eggs are left uncovered for a time. Even when the male brings food to his mate, she will leave the nest.

Incubation is more than sitting on the clutch. The temperature of the eggs must be finely regulated to within a few degrees. The sitting bird has to monitor the nest temperature (which it probably does while shuffling the eggs) and adjust its actions accordingly. The amount of heat needed to keep the eggs warm depends on the weather and the insulating qualities of the nest. Windy weather causes birds to spend more time on the nest, while sunny spells allow them longer breaks. Although the developing chicks are surprisingly resistant to cold, too much exposure will slow development, perhaps fatally.

Nest duty *A female wood thrush undertakes all the incubating duties, remaining on the nest almost constantly for up to 14 days.*

HATCHING

Because incubation usually starts only when the clutch is complete, all the eggs in a clutch hatch together. In owls and other birds of prey, however, incubation starts with the first egg, and the chicks hatch in sequence. In times of scarce food supplies, the oldest chick gets an advantage.

Hatching is a difficult process. It starts a few days before the chick emerges. The young bird changes its position, so that it can push its bill into the airspace in the blunt end of the shell and begin breathing. Then, using its bill, which is protected by the horny, white "eggtooth" that can be seen on recently hatched birds, it hammers a hole in the shell. This is called "pipping" and is the first visible sign that the egg is about to hatch.

Several hours elapse before the final phase, which takes less than an hour. The chick punches a ring of holes in the shell to weaken it, then forces the end off. Once its head is free, it struggles out and lies curled up and exhausted in the bottom of the nest.

Baby clothes *These short-eared owl nestlings hatch with a downy covering, but still have to be fed and cared for by their parents.*

Another mouth to feed *Baby robins hatch blind and helpless and immediately beg for food.*

· CHICK-REARING ·

T HE YOUNG OF MOST common birds – songbirds, doves, hummingbirds, woodpeckers, and birds of prey – hatch in an almost helpless state and stay in the nest until they are ready to fly. They are usually called nestlings. Young birds who leave the nest soon after they hatch are called chicks. Some, like ducklings, feed themselves while their mothers protect them, but others, like young gulls, are fed by their parents.

FEEDING THE YOUNG

When young songbirds hatch out, they are weak, and their bodies are wet with egg fluids. Their parents brood them to keep them warm. As they grow and become stronger, nestlings are left on their own while parents collect food. Brooding resumes at night and in bad weather until the young birds can maintain their own body temperature.

Feeding the family keeps parent birds busy for most of the day. Males that played no part in the nest-building or incubation help to rear their families by bringing food for them. They may take sole charge in the final days before the young become independent, if the female has started another clutch.

Family provider *A male red-winged blackbird with his hungry offspring. The nestlings are dependent on their parents for ten days.*

Most young birds are fed insects and other small creatures, such as spiders, snails, and worms. Even the seed-eating finches give their young this kind of food, because it contains more of the protein, calcium, and other nutrients that are needed for growing bodies. It also contains more fluids, so the young birds do not need to drink.

Collecting insects can be hard work, especially in bad weather. House wrens make as many as 500 trips to the nest with food each day. One was recorded making more than 1,200 trips in one day.

When a parent bird returns with food, the nestlings beg, craning their necks with bills pointing upward and open in a wide gape. When they are very young, before their eyes have opened, they gape when they feel the vibration of the parent landing at the nest. Later, they respond to the sight of the arriving parent and direct their gape toward it. The brightly colored inside of the mouth is a signal for the parent to push food into it. As the chicks reach fledging age, the bright mouth lining fades.

The parent bird feeds the nearest nestling without any attempt to distribute the food equally. This means that the strongest nestling gets the most food. It stops begging when it is full, so that the other nestlings get a share. In this way all the nestlings are satisfied, provided there is enough to go around. If food is scarce, some nestlings go short and may starve, but more young birds will eventually survive if the parents rear a few well-fed individuals rather than many half-starved ones.

CLEANING THE NEST

One of the first chores for the parent bird after the eggs have hatched is removing the empty eggshells. They are a danger because their bright inner surface could catch a predators eye, and they could trap or cut a nestling. If you have birds nesting in the yard, look for the empty shells lying on the lawn. Another chore is to remove the nestlings' droppings, which emerge in a membrane called a "fecal sac." When a nestling has been fed, it presents its rear end to the parent, who removes the dropping and either swallows it or carries it away and drops it a distance from the nest.

The nest would become very messy if droppings were left in it; they could clog the nestlings' feathers and spread disease. It is also important that droppings around the nest not attract predators. This does not matter for birds that nest in safe places, like barn swallows. After the first few days, they do not bother to remove their nestlings' droppings, which gather on the ground below the nest.

When the nestlings are nearly ready to fly, they deposit their droppings on the rim of the nest. An empty but soiled nest is a

Household chores *A male yellow warbler removes the fecal sac of one of the young from the nest for hygiene and safety.*

good indication that the family was raised successfully. Unhatched eggs and nestlings that die are usually removed by the parents or buried in the nest material, so an empty nest does not necessarily indicate successful parenthood.

Clearing up *A parent starling removes a broken shell from the nesting cavity to prevent injury to the nestlings.*

FLEDGING

By the time the young birds have grown feathers, they are so large that they almost burst out of the nest. Resist the temptation to visit them, because they will try to escape by leaping out of the nest, even though they cannot fly properly. This is a defense against predators: although dangerous, it is better than staying in the nest and being eaten. Even without disturbance, young birds leave the nest before their feathers are fully grown. You can recognize these fledglings by their stumpy tails and wings. They also lack the effortless grace of their elders. The advantage to leaving the nest as soon as possible is that it reduces the danger of predation. Birds that grow up in open-cup

Time to leave *These blue jay nestlings have grown so large that they are crowding out the nest, and must soon leave it.*

nests fly at an earlier age than those brought up in the greater safety of nests in holes. Compare the fledging times of hole-nesting birds of the chickadee or titmouse family with those of the cup-nesting finches in the Bird Profiles *(see pages 64 to 143).*

The fledging times of all species vary by a few days because the growth of the nestlings depends both on the abundance of food and on the number of mouths that the parents have to feed. In some species

Halfway there *A young cardinal, still unable to survive alone, has left the nest to perch in a tree but continues to beg.*

Tagging along *Fledgling house sparrows follow their parents when they forage for food, reducing the burden on the parents.*

the family divides at fledging, the young staying with one or other parent. In other species, such as house wrens, the fledglings are cared for by the male, while the female

Slow to go *After leaving the nest, a fledgling mourning dove may return to it to roost for the first two or three nights.*

starts a new clutch. For the first few days after leaving the nest, most fledglings rest quietly in a secluded spot and wait for their parents to bring them food. The whole brood leaves the nest within a few hours, and it can be a dangerous time if the young birds become separated. When young bluebirds leave the nest, the first to go starts to call, and the parents concentrate on it. Unless its nestmates quickly catch up, they may be left behind and abandoned. As feathers grow to full size, the young birds become more confident in the air and start to follow their parents, saving them the effort of flying back and forth between nest and feeding ground with food. Watch for young robins with spotted breasts following their parents as they forage on the lawn. The parents only have to turn and push a worm into a waiting mouth.

LAUNCH INTO INDEPENDENCE

The popular belief that birds teach their young to fly is incorrect. The ability to fly is instinctive. Young chickadees in a cramped nestbox or cliff swallows in their enclosed nests of mud hardly have a chance to spread their wings before launching themselves into the air. It is surprising how capable a young bird is even on its first flight. The complex wing movements and the delicate balance that drive a bird through the air are present and correct from the very start. Some practice is needed, however, to perfect the skills of maneuvering and landing.

Parents sometimes encourage young birds that seem unwilling to fly. Young swifts leave the nest on their own and are independent immediately, but barn swallow parents entice their brood out of the nest by calling to them. They might accompany the youngsters on their first unsteady flight around the neighborhood. Some families, such as American crows, stay together for some time. Young crows may live with their parents for up to four years, helping with territorial defense, nest-building, and the feeding of later broods. It is also not

unusual for the first brood raised by a pair of bluebirds to help with feeding the second brood. In one amazing observation, a male bluebird that was nesting a mile from his parents brought his own offspring to assist in the rearing one of his parents' later broods.

Trying its wings *Before attempting to fly the nest, a young American robin tests the strength and control of its wings.*

· MOVEMENTS AND MIGRATION ·

THROUGHOUT THEIR LIVES, birds are on the move. For much of the year, they move just between their nest or roost and their feeding grounds. There may be seasonal movements within a locality, for example, shifting from woodlands in summer to suburban yards in winter, or finding new feeding grounds as food runs out in a particular area. Many birds migrate over vast distances as they move between different breeding and nonbreeding habitats. More than 300 species found in North America in the summer, including the tiny warblers and hummingbirds, fly to Central and South America for the winter.

WHAT IS MIGRATION?

The notion that some birds are migrants and others are residents is a simplification of the intricate pattern of bird movements. How you classify a bird depends on where you live. Take the ruby-crowned kinglet: it could be a summer visitor, a winter visitor, or a resident throughout the year.

Migration, according to one definition, is any journey that involves a bird changing its home – the area where it carries out its everyday activities of feeding and roosting. A chickadee can be said to be migrating when it leaves its summer home in the woods and settles in a suburban yard for the winter. This change fulfills the main function of migration: it allows the chickadee to exploit two habitats and

To go or not to go *Bohemian waxwings are irregular migrants, flying south one year, staying put in the north the next.*

Homebody *The black-capped chickadee stays in the north for the winter but moves into yards.*

sources of food. To put some order to movements that range from the local travels of chickadees to the huge distances covered by barn swallows traveling between North and South America, it is convenient to speak of the latter as "true" migration. Movements caused by a temporary shortage of food are called local movements. These can occur when a crop of berries has been exhausted or seeds and worms are covered by frost and snow. The most obvious movements are the sudden arrival of flocks of cedar waxwings or the disappearance of ducks from frozen lakes.

TRUE MIGRANTS

The twice-yearly long-distance movement of birds is one of the wonders of the natural world. If we live in a suitable place, we can witness it in the different birds coming to the feeder or passing through the yard. Looking beyond the yard, we may see formations of geese or swans winging overhead and hawks streaming along a ridge or across an estuary. City parks are good places for watching the migration of warblers and other songbirds. Sometimes the bushes are filled with small birds flitting from branch to branch. They are often remarkably tame and, if the leaves have dropped, they are easy to observe.

Each spring brings the return of the migrants from their warmer wintering grounds. We look out for purple martins and swallows darting overhead, for warblers and hummingbirds flitting among the newly opening foliage, and for noisy flocks of red-winged blackbirds. Then at the end of the summer, these birds slip away again and we watch for the heralds of winter – juncos, pine siskins, fox sparrows, snow buntings, and shrikes – escaping even harsher northern winters.

Night flight *Birds on migration can be a magnificent sight, whether in huge flocks or in a graceful formation, like these tundra swans.*

Returning sun *The bright color and rapid song of the yellow warbler are welcome signs of spring.*

Migration is not such a rigid process as it might seem. There are often reports of migrant birds such as swallows and even hummingbirds lingering long after the main body of birds has departed for the south or of individuals that have been swept back up north by contrary winds. Migrant birds seen in their summer ranges as late as early December are late leavers that have somehow managed to find enough food to sustain them until they finally make their departure. (Hummingbirds have been known to remain in New England into the winter by living in greenhouses where there are plenty of flowers.) Others seen in February could be either very early arrivals or birds that have overwintered successfully in the north. Those birds seen around Christmas and the New Year are more likely to be individuals that have lost the migration urge of their species.

PARTIAL MIGRANTS

When the naturalist Carolus Linnaeus gave scientific names to animals and plants (*see page 215*), he called the European chaffinch *Fringilla coelebs*, which is Latin for bachelor finch. The chaffinches remaining for the winter in his native Sweden were nearly all males. Most of the females, as well as some males, moved south to milder climates. The movement of part of a population, which may be one sex or a certain age group, is called partial migration.

Research into the migratory habits of juncos has shown that the females tend to go farther south in the fall flight, and that the winter population in Texas is 75 percent female. Farther north, males outnumber females. Because the sexes have distinctive plumage patterns, you can check the juncos in your own neighborhood. The number of females remaining with the males depends on the temperature – with more females lingering in the north in milder winters – rather than on the level of snowfall.

One reason for this is that female juncos are smaller than males. This means that they are both more susceptible to cold and are less dominant at feeders. The survival chances of the females are therefore better if they move away from the males. Males may stay behind because they will be able to stake out breeding territories earlier if they do not move too far away.

Separatists   When insect food dies off and seeds become scarce, female juncos head south for the winter.

TRANSIENTS

During migration, birds are often seen en route to distant destinations. They may stay a few days to feed or to wait for a fair wind before continuing. These birds are called transients or birds of passage. Many are common birds, but migration seasons are exciting because they offer the chance to spot rare and exotic birds. Anything may turn up, from the Arctic or the Tropics, and even from Europe, Africa, and Asia. These visitors who are outside their normal patterns are called accidentals.

Long-distance traveler
The Arctic tern migrates across the world between the Arctic and the Antarctic.

Because migrating birds can be caught up in storms and swept far off course, they sometimes turn up thousands of miles from their normal migration routes. Lapwings, a species of plover, and fieldfares, a kind of thrush, are European birds that have been known to turn up on the eastern seaboard of North America. When there are severe winter weather conditions in central Europe, these birds fly to the milder climate of the British Isles. They are occasionally swept up by strong easterly winds and carried all the way across the Atlantic, most likely never to return.

IRRUPTIONS

In some winters there is a dramatic invasion of birds, sometimes in such numbers that their arrival is reported in the newspapers. These irruptions are irregular movements on a larger scale than the more usual local movements, both in the number of birds and in the distances involved. They occur when the food supply in the birds' summer home fails. Populations built up in times of plenty suddenly face a famine and are forced to move or perish. This sometimes happens to seed- and fruit-eating birds, whose food sources do not always produce good crops every year: pines, spruces, and other conifers in the north fail to set seed about every two years. One result of this is that flocks of evening grosbeaks, in particular, appear at feeders in yards as far south as the Gulf states in the following winter. The populations of the rodent prey of owls and hawks also fluctuate: lemmings and voles undergo four-year cycles of abundance and scarcity in the north. When prey is scarce, snowy owls and northern shrikes fly south in search of food.

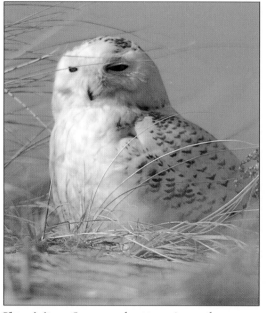

Shy visitor *Snowy owls appear in southern Canada and the United States when lemmings are scarce in their Arctic tundra home.*

Welcome alternative
Sunflower seeds are popular with grosbeaks when seed crops fail in the north.

TIME TO GO

Naturalists realized long ago that birds are not driven to migrate by hunger but escape before their sources of food are exhausted. If birds waited until they were faced with starvation, they would already be losing condition and would perish on the journey. Preparation for migration has to start before departure, and birds fatten up with fuel for the journey. Departure may be earlier in fine weather, contrary to what might be expected, because the birds have been able to feed well. Preparation sometimes involves changes in diet or behavior: insect-eating tree and barn swallows fatten up on carbohydrate-rich berries, and many birds such as barn swallows and waxwings gather in flocks.

In the fall, birds depart for the south in a leisurely way and will wait for fair winds to help them on their journey. Species that rely on a good supply of insects, such as flycatchers and swifts, depart early, while certain swallows stay longer. Tree swallows change to a vegetarian diet, which allows them to take their time. There is no great urgency to leave, and several weeks may pass between the departure of the first individuals of a species and the final disappearance of the last stragglers. Some birds, like orioles, are staying

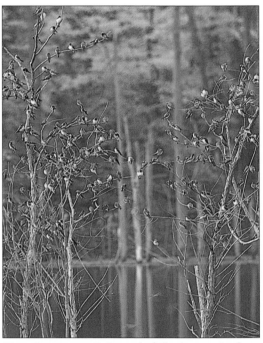

Hanging around *In early fall, changes in the diet of the tree swallows allows them to linger while they gather into flocks for the flight south.*

Changing habits *Migration patterns may change with conditions over long periods of time – Bullock's orioles might one day in the future lose the migration urge completely.*

behind for the winter in increasing numbers because they can take advantage of feeders.

In spring there is less time for delay. The first arrivals claim the best territories, and the birds have to make the most of the breeding season and rear as many offspring as possible. The migrants push north, hard on the heels of the retreating winter. Arrival dates are influenced by the weather: migrants appear earlier in warm, early springs and are late in cold years or if contrary winds have been holding them up. Typically, males arrive first to stake out their territories, and the females arrive a few days later when the food supplies have improved.

LOST MIGRANTS

Rock Creek Park is a forest in Washington, D.C. In 1948, there were ovenbirds, red-eyed and yellow-throated vireos, hooded warblers, black-and-white warblers, and Acadian flycatchers. All have disappeared except the ovenbirds and red-eyed vireos, and these are rare – a pattern repeated over the continent. The vanishing birds are migrants that winter in tropical America, and one reason for their demise is the destruction of the tropical forests.

Populations of songbirds fell dramatically when North American forests were cleared in the nineteenth century. In recent decades, tropical forests have been cleared on a massive scale. There is now a shortage of winter habitat for the birds. Populations of many songbirds have been reduced by three-quarters as a result.

This is not the only problem facing these migrant species. There are also changes in their breeding grounds. The forest habitat of North America is increasingly fragmented by development, and this has a profound effect on the survival of migrant birds. Tropical migrants' eggs are easily found by

Fading fast *A red-eyed vireo feeds two young brown-headed cowbirds. The red-eyed vireo is also threatened by the destruction of its habitat.*

Suburban terrorist *The common grackle not only feeds on the eggs and young of other bird species, but will also kill adults.*

predators because they are typically laid in open nests near the ground. Nest predation may be as low as 2 percent in forests but can rise to 95 percent in suburbia. Blue jays, which have benefited from winter feeding, and cowbirds, which have increased enormously on the spilled grain left by mechanized agriculture, have become overabundant predators. The red-eyed vireo and ovenbird, in particular, are victims of the cowbird (*see page 202*). Other predators, such as raccoons, crows, and grackles, also flourish in the suburban forest-edge habitat that increases as land is developed.

Born survivor *Blue jays are among the most intelligent and opportunistic of North American birds, flourishing at the cost of other species.*

· CURIOUS BEHAVIOR ·

THE PATTERNS OF BEHAVIOR that have been described earlier in this chapter are commonly in evidence around the yard and its surroundings. These tactics have evolved to improve birds' chances of surviving and raising families successfully. From time to time, you may also see birds engaged in some curious forms of behavior that do not seem to serve any particular purpose and that are difficult to explain.

STRETCHING AND YAWNING

Stretching and yawning are known as comfort movements. We often stretch our arms and legs after resting, especially if we have been sleeping or sitting in the same position for a long time. Sometimes you will see birds doing much the same thing. Typically, they open out one wing to its full extent for a second or two before folding it away again. Simultaneously, they extend

Full stretch *A mallard extends leg and wing after sitting for a long time.*

the leg on the same side of the body as the wing and fan out the tail. Some birds, such as ducks, also stretch both their wings at the same time by raising them up over their backs together.

Why humans, birds, and other animals stretch is not known for certain. The action might improve muscle tone or increase the blood circulation in the limbs. Yawning may be a form of stretching, but it could

Open wide
A green heron takes a deep breath at the start of a new day.

also be a means of ensuring a fresh and complete exchange of air in the lungs before becoming fully active.

An action that looks like stretching but that has a different function may be seen in hawks or owls. The bird appears to be stretching both its wings in front of itself, but it is crouching over its prey with tail and wings spread. This is called mantling and is used by birds of prey to prevent other birds from stealing their quarry. It may also trap partially crippled prey.

Hands off *A long-eared owl spreads its wings to guard its catch against other birds.*

ANTING

Anting is a strange form of behavior in which the bird looks as if it is having a fit. It has been observed in many perching birds – in jays and starlings especially, but also in other species, including robins, hummingbirds, flickers, and song sparrows – yet its function remains unknown. The bird half-spreads its wings, twists its tail, and wipes its beak on the wing feathers or else squats with its wings spread out and the tail pressed against the ground, as if it were sunbathing *(see page 166)*.

A closer look reveals that the bird is positioned over an ants' nest or a line of foraging ants. The bird either picks up the ants and rubs their bodies against its feathers or, in the squatting version, allows ants to climb into its plumage. The most plausible explanation of this behavior is that formic acid from the ants' bodies kills parasitic feather lice.

Sometimes birds "ant" with other materials such as citrus fruit, mothballs, pickles, and cigarette ends. They also perch in smoke and go through the motions of anting, even appearing to swallow beakfuls of smoke, which are then placed under their wings. However, if you see birds perching on chimneys or other sources of smoke, it is more likely that they are simply trying to keep themselves warm.

Strange antics *A blue jay picks ants from a nest to wipe through its feathers. The ants are not eaten afterward but are discarded.*

ATTACKING WINDOWS

Birds often accidentally crash into windows (*see page 211*), but deliberate attacks on windows are a different phenomenon. The habit is most often seen in robins, cardinals, grackles, and other birds nesting in yards. Sometimes the chrome hubcap or side mirror of a car is attacked. The bird sees its reflection, mistakes it for a rival on its territory, and tries to drive it away. One ornithologist worked out the boundaries of a cardinal's territory by moving a mirror around the area of its nest until the bird ceased attacking it. The attacks may go on for days or even weeks, and can be so ferocious that the glass becomes marked with the attacker's blood. The problem can be cured by placing a screen over the window or by coating the affected zone with an opaque fluid or spray until the bird has forgotten about it.

No trespassers *A rufous-crowned sparrow attacks its own reflection in a mirror placed within its territory by an ornithologist.*

Own worst enemy *Mockingbirds are highly aggressive and take on all comers – even themselves.*

ACTS OF DESTRUCTION

While we can accept that birds attack the blossom and fruit on our trees because they need to eat, it is hard to forgive apparently wanton destruction. Mockingbirds and house sparrows sometimes attack flowers without eating them, and the only explanation for this seems to be sheer vandalism. This was once thought to be the case with starlings that pluck leaves and carry them back to the nest, but tests have shown that the leaves starlings choose have insecticidal properties and appear to be a way of controlling blood-sucking mites in the nest. One nest in Indiana contained the leaves of catnip, parsley, spearmint, bee balm, and lemon balm.

A greater nuisance is caused by birds that attack houses. The worst offenders are flickers, but red-bellied, acorn, and pileated woodpeckers are also responsible. These woodpeckers not only drill cavities in search of insects, but also drum on gutters, stove pipes, and television antennas. Apart from the damage caused by these activities, the noise can be a considerable nuisance. One solution is to hang galvanized mesh or a taut plastic sheet over the affected area. Another is to get up early and wait for the woodpecker with a hose, ready to squirt it.

Housebreaker *Wooden walls can prove an irresistable temptation to flickers, as both possible sources of food and sounding boards for tattoos.*

MOBBING

Hunting birds such as owls and hawks, as well as other predators such as snakes, may be mobbed by groups of smaller birds.

Mobbing has been observed in birds of all kinds, from titmice and kinglets to crows. The birds gather in gangs, often of several different species, and harass their target. Songbirds sometimes gather around a perched owl and give alarm calls *(see page 179)*, which warn other birds of the danger and tell them where the predator is.

Hunting birds are also often followed as they fly, which makes it difficult for them to hunt properly. Mobbing can drive a larger bird from its roost, and occasionally the mobbing birds will attack the predator and may even kill it.

Tailgating *Two crows follow a barn owl, preventing it from hunting.*

PARASITIC HABITS

The cowbird is notorious as a brood parasite, a bird that lays its eggs in the nests of other birds, but it is not as well known that other bird species occasionally lay eggs in host nests.

Ring-necked pheasants and brown thrashers sometimes lay eggs in the nests of other birds, but without much chance of success. More often, birds such as eastern bluebirds or barn swallows lay eggs in the nests of other birds of their own species.

Eggs found on the ground near the nest were once believed to have been laid by females that had been "caught short." While some birds such as ring-necked pheasants do lay surplus eggs in "dump nests" or on open ground, these are more likely to be eggs laid by one female in another's nest that have been detected and removed by the owner of the nest. A female starling that has started to lay, however, does not discriminate against interloping eggs and incubates them as her own.

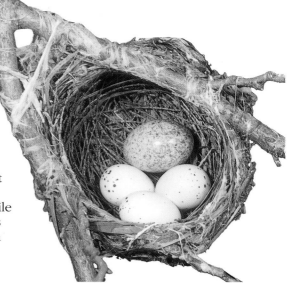

Obvious interloper *A brown-headed cowbird's egg in a red-eyed vireo's nest. In spite of the difference in appearance, the host bird will incubate this egg and raise the chick.*

Easily fooled *This brown-headed cowbird is being raised by a western flycatcher, a common host.*

FOSTER FEEDING

It is instinctive for a parent bird to push food into a brightly colored opening. Normally this is the mouth of one of its own offspring, but occasionally something goes wrong and the young of another bird – even of another species – benefit. There was a case of a Carolina wren that adopted a family of house wrens. He first fed the female while she was incubating and then fed the nestlings. Young birds continue to beg after they have left the nest, and sometimes an adult that may have recently lost its own young starts to feed a strange youngster that has been pestering it for food. Occasionally, the foster parent will even enter another bird's nest with food. One of the strangest cases of foster feeding on record is that of a cardinal that fed goldfish in a pond (*see page 147*).

Colorful language *A clutch of nestling crows open their mouths in a wide gape, a clear signal to their parents.*

Irresistable urge *The feeding instinct is powerful enough to make this brown thrasher feed a cowbird fledgling.*

Creche system *If young Canada geese, seeking safety in numbers, form into a group like this, parent birds can recognize their own offspring.*

CHAPTER FIVE

BIRD SURVIVAL

THE HAZARDS IN A bird's life mean that it will be lucky to live beyond a couple of years. The unfortunate majority die before they are a year old. There is very little you can do to alter these sad facts or to remove the many natural and manmade dangers. Providing extra food and protecting nest-sites will help some birds to survive, and improve their chances of breeding, but you should be prepared to accept that most birds die young, and that being killed by a predator is a quicker death than starving. It is often hard to ignore a bird that is wounded, exhausted, or orphaned, but most such birds are beyond saving. For many good reasons, help can be given only by licensed persons.

This baby blue jay may not live to see a second summer.

• SURVIVAL AND MORTALITY •

THE LIVES OF MOST common birds are surprisingly short. There are records of individuals living for many years, but these cases are unusual. Very few of the eggs laid each year produce chicks that survive into adulthood. In general it is the healthiest birds that survive the hazards of the first months of life and that continue the species.

LIFE EXPECTANCY

It is tempting to believe that the mockingbird that appears in the yard, and the phoebe that nests among the vines, are the same birds every year. Unless they have some uniquely identifiable features, however, it is impossible to be sure that your favorite birds have not died in the course of the year and been replaced by exact lookalikes.

We have become used to the idea that most people live to a ripe old age, so it is not always easy to accept that common birds suffer very heavy losses of eggs and nestlings each year. If young birds survive the hazardous first few weeks, their life expectancy improves slightly. As a general rule, larger birds live longer than smaller ones and the longer-lived birds have a lower breeding rate. Even so, an average of half to three-quarters of the total population of adult small birds dies each year, and the average life expectancy of an adult songbird is only one or two years.

This high mortality rate ensures that the population remains stable. For numbers of a species to remain constant, each pair of

Safety in numbers *Phoebes produce two or three clutches in a year, but only a few young survive.*

206

birds needs to rear only two offspring to grow up and replace them. Since a pair of song sparrows may lay two or three clutches of three to six eggs in a summer, the country would soon be swarming with song sparrows if all of these offspring lived. In practice, the population at the end of winter is the same as it was in the previous spring.

The lost eggs and young birds are a doomed surplus, but their short lives are not pointless. The high number of eggs laid enables birds to recover their population levels rapidly after a catastrophe such as a hard winter, or the failure of an important food supply. The survivors breed well, raising more young to restore numbers quickly.

Not all wild songbirds die young, however, and a small proportion survives into old age. A cardinal in the wild has been recorded living to the grand old age of 13 years, and a captive one has reached 28 years.

Senior citizens *In banding studies* (see page 213), *northern cardinals have been recorded among the longest-lived songbirds.*

Prepared for the worst *Song sparrows' nests are among those vulnerable to predators, so a large number of eggs are laid in each season.*

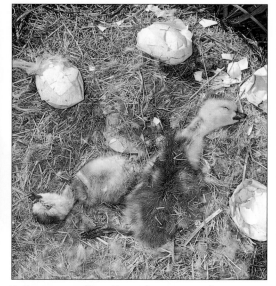

Infant mortality *From the moment the eggs are laid they are vulnerable, like these young Canada geese, which were lost to predators.*

CAUSES OF DEATH

As many as one-third of all eggs fail to hatch. Some are infertile, and others become chilled, perhaps because a cold spell has forced the parent to spend too much time off the nest in search of food. Entire clutches are lost when nests are robbed by predators, or if the nest is smashed by torrential rain or high winds. It is not pleasant to think that we may contribute to some of these deaths. How often have we continued to work or to relax next to nests in the yard, while parent birds scolded us, without our realizing what the fuss is about? The eggs become chilled as a result of the parent's absence from the nest, and inquisitive predators are attracted to the disturbance.

To offset the enormous loss of eggs, a bereaved pair quickly starts a new clutch. It may take two or three attempts for them to rear a family, but breeding is more successful than the egg losses suggest. The loss rate drops once the eggs have hatched: the most vulnerable nests have already been lost, and birds are also less likely to desert nestlings than eggs. Nonetheless, some nestlings do die, through starvation, being squashed by the parent, or falling from the nest.

Death by starvation is probably more common in yards than in the wild, because natural food may be scarce *(see page 15)*. To make things worse, pesticides can harm birds that feed on insects. The solution to this problem is to use one of the less toxic insecticides, such as pyrethrum, on your plants, or to try the traditional treatment of a strong soap solution.

Food chain *Too often, gardening practices do not take wildlife into account, destroying or poisoning natural foods.*

GARDEN DANGERS

The depredations of nest robbers, although they are distressing to witness, are probably not as serious as the largely unnoticed losses from other natural causes (which are all too often exacerbated by our gardening practices). It appears that predators tend to find the nests that are going to fail anyway: the continual begging calls of the starving nestlings serve to alert and attract predators.

Of all the nest robbers in the garden, cats are the worst. Rats can also be a serious problem, together with squirrels, raccoons, opossums, and even mice. Some bird

Picked clean *The remains of a hawk's prey show that in nature, little is wasted – all flesh has been torn off and eaten.*

Unfriendly neighbors *While raccoons are fascinating animals in their own right, they can be a menace to birds nesting in your yard.*

Breaking in *As well as stealing food from feeders, squirrels will take any opportunity to feed on nourishing birds' eggs.*

species, such as jays, crows, and occasionally owls, rob nests. Birds nesting in holes are safer than those in exposed cup nests, but nestboxes are vulnerable to predatory mammals and birds if these can reach in to the eggs through the entrance or gnaw through the walls.

Once the young birds are out of the nest, starvation and exposure to cold are still the main causes of death, but accidental death through collisions with windows and motor vehicles must be added to these, as well as rarer problems, such as becoming tangled in netting or strands of string and thread. Among the live dangers, cats are still a major problem, and they are joined by birds of prey. A pair of hawks and their offspring, for instance, need to kill about 2,000 small birds in a year in order to survive.

Red in tooth and claw *Great horned owls will prey on songbirds such as this unfortunate robin, as well as on small mammals.*

Systematic hunters *It seems that magpies raid nests where there is a high density of songbirds, as is the case in many yards.*

REDUCING PREDATION

While it is good to know that the yard environment can support a range of wildlife that includes hawks and owls, one feels a twinge of conscience when birds attracted into an exposed position on the feeder are swept away by a winged predator. It is not easy to protect birds from predators, but there are a few measures that may help against persistent attacks.

Advocates of aversion therapy keep buckets of water for dousing cats. A direct hit is not necessary: the shock of a near miss is usually sufficient to discourage stalking. A dog should also provide a deterrent against visiting neighborhood cats, especially if it is let out in the early morning. You can lay chickenwire on the ground around a feeder, to slow a cat's approach and give the birds time to escape. You can also take care over the positioning of your feeders *(see page 34)*.

Losses of nests are higher early in the breeding season, when new foliage on trees and shrubs is still sparse. Dense evergreens provide safer nesting places, and clipped hedges produce more impenetrable growth, which will deter both cats and hunting

Home safe *The foliage around this yellow warbler's nest makes it harder for a predator to find or get to it.*

birds. The disadvantage of trimming hedges to create dense foliage is that later in the year they will bear smaller berry crops for fruit-eating birds.

If a nest appears to be in a vulnerable position, try protecting it by spreading netting over the top of the bush. This will keep predators out, but allow the nesting birds to enter the nest underneath. You can also use 2-inch (5-centimeter) wire netting, which small birds can get through. It is best to put it in place after the clutch is complete, when the bird has started to incubate. Remember to keep your activity around the nest to a minimum, since any disturbance may cause the birds to desert the nest, and you could also be providing a trail for any inquisitive predators.

A screen of chickenwire will keep cats and other predators out of a nestbox. Reinforcing the edges of the box with metal strips, and fixing a metal plate around the entrance hole *(see page 55)*, will prevent woodpeckers and squirrels from gaining entrance.

Bad planning *A badly placed nestbox can become a home to predators.*

STRIKING WINDOWS

As more houses are fitted with picture windows, so the toll of birds injured and killed by collision with the glass increases. Sometimes a bird will bounce off the glass and fly to a perch where it can sit and recover. Other birds drop, stunned, to the ground beneath, where they are easy prey for cats. Move these birds to a place where they will be safe until they become fully active and can fly away.

It seems that the birds either see open sky and foliage through a farther window, and do not notice the glass in the way, or mistake reflections for the real thing, and are convinced that they are flying toward an open space. One solution is to stick the silhouette of a hawk, or some other pattern, onto the panes. Another is to hang curtains that destroy reflections.

Sudden death *Many birds, like this robin, die in collisions with windows – accidents that could easily have been prevented.*

· RESCUE ·

IT IS A MISTAKE to think that a bird that appears helpless needs your help. It is also illegal to keep almost any kind of bird captive. If you find a bird that is injured or is otherwise truly incapable of fending for itself, you should notify a licensed carer. You can find the nearest carer by contacting your Audubon Society, game department, or SPCA.

ORPHANS

Late spring onward is the season of "orphan birds." It is often assumed, by children especially, that fledglings found hopping across the lawn or sitting quietly under a bush have lost their parents and need to be rescued. They look helpless and often call plaintively, so it is easy to think that they have been abandoned. In fact, a parent is either collecting food for them or is nearby, waiting for you to go away. The most common "orphans" are birds that leave the nest before they can fly well and struggle to follow their parents while they search for food. They are only orphaned after they have been picked up and carried off.

Leave these fledglings alone, and if one has been "rescued" take it back to where it was found. If you are worried that it is in danger, keep watch from a distance, or return in a couple of hours to see how it is doing. If the bird is in a very dangerous place, put it on a safe perch, but some young birds are mobile enough to try to escape and may get into worse trouble if you try to help them. Some fledglings leave the nest before they can fly, and some nestlings fall out accidentally. The latter can be recognized by their partly formed wing and tail feathers. It can be dangerous to try to return these birds to the nest, because the other nestlings may jump out if disturbed. Leave the bird alone, or put it on a nearby perch, and the parents will continue to feed it.

False impression
These fledglings look lost, but they have not been deserted.

BANDED BIRDS

One to two million birds are captured and banded every year in North America, by people who have undergone a training program qualifying them to hold an official license. Banding is the only method that enables researchers to identify individuals. Many of the details of birds' habits in this book have come from studies of banded birds. The information obtained from banded migratory birds revealed their movement patterns, and no one appreciated just how short the life expectancy of small birds was *(see page 206)* until the results of banding were analyzed. If you find an injured or dead bird with a metal band, and sometimes one or more plastic ones, on its leg, you can make a contribution to our understanding of birdlife.

With this ring . . . *Birds like this rufous-sided towhee are caught in nets during migration and banded by trained researchers.*

Life story *These leg bands, sized for different types of bird, will tell researchers when and where a bird has been in its life.*

Most birds are found within a short distance of where they were first caught, but there is always a chance of finding one with a foreign band that has come from some exotic place. Carefully record the number stamped on the metal band, and look for the address in tiny letters. If the bird is dead, remove the band and flatten it. If there are plastic bands, record the colors, which leg they are on, and their order, reading from the top to the bottom of the leg. It is vital to double-check the number and color sequence. Write out this information (taping the flattened metal band to your letter) together with the date of discovery, the location and approximate mileage to the nearest town, how you found the bird, and its condition (dead, alive, whether released). Send it to Bird Banding Laboratory, U.S. Fish and Wildlife Service, Washington, D.C. (no zip code needed) and you will receive a Certificate of Appreciation.

Radio contact *These Canada geese carry neck bands and radio transmitters.*

· GLOSSARY ·

altricial Term used to describe nestlings that are born naked, blind, and helpless. The opposite of *precocial.*

asynchronous hatching The hatching of a clutch in sequence, rather than simultaneously.

avian snowshoes Fringes of scales along each toe, acquired in winter by grouse to increase the surface area of the foot and facilitate walking on snow.

Blue List The National Audubon Society's annual list of bird species in decline.

call A vocalization that is generally shorter and simpler than a song.

coloniality The tendency of birds such as cliff swallows to nest in close colonies, governed by some of the factors that affect flocking.

commensal feeding Association of species in feeding, neither competing nor deliberately cooperating, as the brown-headed cowbird feeds on the insects stirred up by cattle.

cooperative breeding Non-breeding birds assisting with the raising of other birds' young, as when the young from one season remain with the parents into the following year.

crop A thin-walled food-storage sac located in the throat of some birds, such as pigeons.

dabbling A feeding method of waterbirds. The bird floats on shallow water and tips the head down and tail up to reach submerged plants.

disruptive coloration Plumage patterns designed to camouflage a bird, for instance, the mottled back of a brown creeper against a tree, or the stripes of a shorebird on pebbles.

distraction display An act put on by a bird to make itself as conspicuous as possible when its nest is threatened. A killdeer, for example, will feign a broken wing to lead away predators.

feral birds Birds that have escaped from captivity or domestication and become established in the wild. There are several feral species of parrot in the southern United States.

filter feeding A feeding method found in waterbirds such as mallards. Water is sucked into the bill, and fragments of food are filtered from it as it is pumped back out.

gizzard A muscular section of the stomach lined with horny plates or ridges, for crushing grains, nuts, and other hard-shelled foods.

interspecific Describes the behavior of one species toward another.

intraspecific Describes the behavior of members of a species toward one another.

iridescence Interference of light giving shimmering, metallic colors to plumage. The effect is known as *structural color.*

irruptives Species whose numbers in an area fluctuate widely from winter to winter, such as pine siskins, redpolls, and evening grosbeaks.

lek A traditional site for courtship displays, mostly of open-country birds such as grouse.

monogamous A pair bond of one male with one female for a single nesting, a season, several seasons, or life. The vast majority of bird species are monogamous. See also *polygynous* and *polyandrous.*

palmate Webbed, describing the feet of birds such as ducks.

piracy One bird harassing another in order to force it to give up food.

polyandrous Describes the mating of one female with more than one male. See also *monogamous* and *polygynous.*

polygynous Describes the mating of one male with more than one female. See also *monogamous* and *polyandrous.*

precocial Term used to describe young that are born in a developed state, with feathers and open eyes. The opposite of *altricial.*

promiscuous Uniting only for mating, as hummingbirds do, without forming pair bonds.

range The areas where a species is usually found each year, either throughout the year or for breeding or overwintering.

raptors Birds of prey.

sexual dimorphism Physical differences between the sexes in a species, as in many bird species in which the females are duller in color than the males.

site tenacity The tendency of birds to return to the same territory or nest site each year.

stoop The steep dive of a *raptor* from its vantage point onto its prey.

structural colors Colors in a bird's plumage produced not by pigments, but by tiny particles in the feathers (blue is produced this way), or by *iridescence* (as in some hummingbirds).

· BIRD CLASSIFICATION ·

When you start observing birds, it is not always easy to sort out the different kinds. What are they, and how are they related to each other? It is easy to tell that the house finch must be a close relative of the purple finch, but what about the relationship among swallows, martins, and swifts?

Early naturalists gave plants and animals scientific names and classified them according to their relationships. The modern system of naming and classifying was devised by Carolus Linnaeus. Each recognizable type of bird (or any animal or plant) is known as a species, and closely related species are grouped into a genus. A subspecies is a variant of a species, as in the northern flicker (*see page 84*). The genus and species of any living thing are shown by its two-word scientific name. This is given in Latin or ancient Greek, the international languages of Linnaeus's time. The first word identifies the genus and the second the species. A species name may be derived from a bird's appearance or habitat, or from the naturalist who discovered or classified it. For example, *Anas* is the Latin for duck. The mallard is *Anas platyrhynchos,* "flat-billed duck," and the American wigeon is *Anas americanus,* for its homeland. These names tell us more than common names. The European goldfinch, *Carduelis carduelis,* and the American goldfinch, *Carduelis tristis,* are of the same genus, closely related. This is reflected in the common names, but the pine siskin, *Carduelis pinus,* is also a close relative, which is not apparent from its common name. Birds with different genus names are not as closely related, even if they have similar common names. The evening grosbeak is *Coccothraustes vespertinus,* but the rose-breasted grosbeak is *Pheucticus ludovicianus*, so they are not close relatives. Genera with similar characteristics are grouped into families, and families that have points of resemblance are arranged into orders. Warblers, tanagers, and buntings are in the family Emberizidae. Swallows and martins are in the family Hirundinidae, but swifts, despite apparent similarities, are in the family Apodidae. The Emberizidae and Hirundinidae, along with others, such as the Fringillidae (finch family), are in the order Passeriformes, the sparrowlike birds. This order includes all the perching birds and songbirds. Hummingbirds and swifts are in the order Apodiformes.

The table on the following pages shows the families of the birds in this book, showing how appearances may be deceptive. You can see, for example, that the house sparrow imported from Europe differs from native sparrows.

Founding father *Swedish naturalist Carolus Linnaeus originated the classification system still used today in his* Systema Natura *in 1758.*

BIRDS IN THEIR FAMILIES AND ORDERS

The names used are taken from the current American Ornithologists' Union Checklist
of North American Birds, 6th edition plus supplements.

ORDER	FAMILY	COMMON AND SCIENTIFIC NAMES
Anseriformes	Anatidae	Canada goose *Branta canadensis*
		Mallard *Anas platyrhynchos*
		Hooded merganser *Lophodytes cucullatus*
Falconiformes	Cathartidae	Turkey vulture *Cathartes aura*
	Accipitridae	Sharp-shinned hawk *Accipiter striatus*
	Falconidae	American kestrel *Falco sparverius*
Galliformes	Phasianidae	Ring-necked pheasant *Phasianus colchicus*
		Northern bobwhite *Colinus virginianus*
		California quail *Callipepla californica*
Charadriformes	Charadriidae	Killdeer *Charadrius vociferus*
	Scolopacidae	Ruddy turnstone *Arenaria interpres*
Columbiformes	Columbidae	Rock dove *Columba livia*
		Mourning dove *Zenaida macroura*
Strigiformes	Strigidae	Eastern screech-owl *Otus asio*
		Great horned owl *Bubo virginianus*
		Snowy owl *Nyctea scandiaca*
		Burrowing owl *Speotyto cunicularia*
Apodiformes	Apodidae	Chimney swift *Chaetura pelagica*
	Trochilidae	Broad-billed hummingbird *Cynanthus latirostris*
		Ruby-throated hummingbird *Archilochus colubris*
		Anna's hummingbird *Calypte anna*
		Rufous hummingbird *Selasphorus rufus*
Coraciiformes	Alcedinidae	Belted kingfisher *Ceryle alcyon*
Piciformes	Picidae	Acorn woodpecker *Melanerpes formicivorus*
		Red-bellied woodpecker *Melanerpes carolinus*
		Yellow-bellied sapsucker *Sphyrapicus varius*
		Downy woodpecker *Picoides pubescens*
		Hairy woodpecker *Picoides villosus*
		Northern flicker *Colaptes auratus*
		Pileated woodpecker *Dryocopus pileatus*
Passeriformes	Tyrannidae	Black phoebe *Sayornis nigricans*
		Eastern phoebe *Sayornis phoebe*
		Eastern kingbird *Tyrannus tyrannus*
	Hirundinidae	Purple martin *Progne subis*
		Tree swallow *Tachycineta bicolor*
		Cliff swallow *Hirundo pyrrhonota*
		Barn swallow *Hirundo rustica*
	Corvidae	Steller's jay *Cyanocitta stelleri*
		Blue jay *Cyanocitta cristata*
		Black-billed magpie *Pica pica*
		American crow *Corvus brachyrhynchos*
	Paridae	Black-capped chickadee *Parus atricapillus*
		Tufted titmouse *Parus bicolor*
	Aegithalidae	Bushtit *Psaltriparus minimus*
	Sittidae	White-breasted nuthatch *Sitta carolinensis*

ORDER	FAMILY	COMMON AND SCIENTIFIC NAMES
Passeriformes *continued*	Certhiidae	Brown creeper *Certhia americana*
	Troglodytidae	House wren *Troglodytes aedon*
	Muscicapidae	Golden-crowned kinglet *Regulus satrapa*
		Ruby-crowned kinglet *Regulus calendula*
		Eastern bluebird *Sialia sialis*
		Mountain bluebird *Sialia currucoides*
		Wood thrush *Hylocichla mustelina*
		American robin *Turdus migratorius*
	Mimidae	Gray catbird *Dumetella carolinensis*
		Northern mockingbird *Mimus polyglottos*
		Brown thrasher *Toxostoma rufum*
	Bombycillidae	Bohemian waxwing *Bombycilla garrulus*
		Cedar waxwing *Bombycilla cedrorum*
	Laniidae	Northern shrike *Lanius excubitor*
	Sturnidae	European starling *Sturnus vulgaris*
	Vireonidae	White-eyed vireo *Vireo griseus*
		Red-eyed vireo *Vireo olivaceus*
	Emberizidae	Yellow warbler *Dendroica petechia*
		Yellow-breasted chat *Icteria virens*
		Scarlet tanager *Piranga olivacea*
		Western tanager *Piranga ludoviciana*
		Northern cardinal *Cardinalis cardinalis*
		Rose-breasted grosbeak *Pheuctictus ludovicianus*
		Blue grosbeak *Guiraca caerulea*
		Indigo bunting *Passerina cyanea*
		Painted bunting *Passerina ciris*
		Rufous-sided towhee *Pipilo erythrophthalmus*
		American tree sparrow *Spizella arborea*
		Chipping sparrow *Spizella passerina*
		Song sparrow *Melospiza melodia*
		White-throated sparrow *Zonotrichia albicollis*
		Dark-eyed junco *Junco hyemalis*
		Bobolink *Dolichonyx oryzivorus*
		Red-winged blackbird *Agelaius phoeniceus*
		Western meadowlark *Sturnella neglecta*
		Common grackle *Quiscalus quiscula*
		Brown-headed cowbird *Molothrus ater*
		Baltimore oriole *Icterus galbula*
		Bullock's oriole *Icterus bullockii*
	Fringillidae	Pine grosbeak *Pinicola enucleator*
		Purple finch *Carpodacus purpureus*
		House finch *Carpodacus mexicanus*
		Red crossbill *Loxia curvirostra*
		Common redpoll *Carduelis flammea*
		Pine siskin *Carduelis pinus*
		American goldfinch *Carduelis tristis*
		Evening grosbeak *Coccothraustes vespertinus*
	Passeridae	House sparrow *Passer domesticus*

· FURTHER READING ·

ATTRACTING BIRDS

George Adams, *Birdscaping Your Garden,* Rodale Press, 1994

Bill Adler and Heidi Hughes, *The Expert's Guide to Backyard Birdfeeding,* Crown, 1990

John V. Dennis, *A Complete Guide to Birdfeeding,* Rev. ed., Alfred A. Knopf, 1994

John V. Dennis, *Summer Bird Feeding,* Audubon Workshop, 1989

George Harrison, *The Backyard Birdwatcher,* Fireside, 1983

Kit and George Harrison, *The Birds of Winter,* Random House, 1990

Stephen W. Kress, *The Bird Garden,* Dorling Kindersley, 1995

Noble Proctor, *Garden Birds,* Rodale Press, 1986

Sara Stein, *Noah's Garden,* Houghton Mifflin, 1993

Donald and Lillian Stokes, *The Bird Feeder Book,* Little, Brown and Company, 1987

John Terres, *Songbirds in Your Garden,* Algonquin Books of Chapel Hill, Rev. ed., 1994

Connie Toops, *Bluebirds Forever,* Voyager Press, 1994

BIRD BEHAVIOR

Stephen W. Kress, *Bird Life,* Golden Press/ Western Publishing Company, 1991

Alice Mace (editor), *The Birds Around Us,* Ortho Books, 1986

Lester L. Short, *The Lives of Birds: Birds of the World and Their Behaviour,* Henry Holt, 1993

Calvin Simonds, *Private Lives of Garden Birds,* The Globe Pequot Press, 1991

FIELD GUIDES

John Bull and John Farrand, Jr., *National Audubon Society Field Guide to North American Birds: Eastern Region,* Rev. ed., Alfred A. Knopf, 1994

National Audubon Society Pocket Guide to Songbirds and Familiar Backyard Birds: Eastern Region, text by Wayne R. Peterson, Alfred A. Knopf, 1994

National Audubon Society Pocket Guide to Songbirds and Familiar Backyard Birds: Western Region, text by Richard K. Walton, Alfred A. Knopf, 1994

National Geographic Society Field Guide to the Birds of North America, Rev. ed., National Geographic Society, 1987

Roger Tory Peterson, *A Field Guide to Eastern Birds,* Houghton Mifflin, 1980

Roger Tory Peterson, *A Field Guide to Western Birds,* Houghton Mifflin, 1990

Chandler S. Robbins, Bertel Bruun, Herbert S. Zim, and Arthur Singer, *Birds of North America,* Golden Press/Western Region, 1986

Miklos D.F. Udvardy, *The Audubon Society Field Guide to North American Birds: Western Region,* Rev. ed., Alfred A. Knopf, 1994

OTHER MATERIALS

Eyewitness Virtual Museum: Bird CD–ROM, Dorling Kindersley Multimedia, 1995

Godfrey-Stadin Productions, *The Audubon Society Videoguides to Birds of North America, Volumes 1–5,* distributed by MasterVision

National Audubon Society Interactive CD–ROM Guide to North American Birds, Alfred A. Knopf, 1995

· NATIONAL AUDUBON SOCIETY ·

The mission of the NATIONAL AUDUBON SOCIETY is to conserve and restore natural ecosystems, focusing on birds and other wildlife for the benefit of humanity and the earth's biological diversity. In the vanguard of the environmental movement, it has 560,000 members, 14 regional and state offices, and an extensive chapter network in the United States and Latin America, plus a professional staff of scientists, lobbyists, lawyers, policy analysts, and educators. Through our nationwide sanctuary system we manage 150,000 acres of critical wildlife habitat and unique natural areas for birds, wild animals, and rare plant life.

Our award-winning *Audubon* magazine, published six times a year and sent to all members, carries outstanding articles and color photography on wildlife and nature, and presents in–depth reports on critical environmental issues, as well as conservation news and commentary.

We also publish the newsjournal, *Audubon Activist; Audubon Field Notes,* a journal reporting seasonal bird sightings continent-wide; and *Audubon Adventures,* a bimonthly children's nature newsletter reaching 600,000 elementary school students.

Our acclaimed *World of Audubon* television specials, airing on the Turner Broadcasting System, deal with a variety of environmental themes; companion books and educational computer software give viewers an opportunity for further in-depth study of the subjects covered by the television series. Audubon's travel program sponsors many exciting trips every year to exotic places like Alaska, Antarctica, Indonesia, Baja California, Galapagos, Japan, and Patagonia.

For information about how you can become a member, please write or call: National Audubon Society, 700 Broadway, New York, New York 10003, 212-979-3000.

OTHER ORGANIZATIONS

Publications are given in *italics*.

American Birding Association P.O. Box 6599, Colorado Springs, CO 80934 *(Birding)*

American Ornithologists' Union, National Museum of Natural History, Smithsonian Institute, Washington, DC 20560 *(The Auk)*

Bird Feeders Society, P.O. Box 225, Mystic, CT 06355 *(Around the Bird Feeder)*

Bird Watcher's Digest, P.O. Box 110, Marietta, OH 45750-0110

Birder's World, 720 East 8th Street, Holland, MI 49423

Canadian Nature Federation, 46 Elgin Street, Ottawa, Ontario K1P 5K6 *(Nature Canada)*

Canadian Wildlife Federation, 2740 Queensvue Drive, Ottawa, Ontario, K2B 1A2 *(Wildlife Report, International Wildlife)*

Center for Conservation Biology, Department of Biological Sciences, Stanford University, Stanford, CA 94305

Friends of the Earth, 530 Seventh Street, SE, Washington, DC 20003

Laboratory of Ornithology at Cornell University, 159 Sapsucker Woods Road, Ithaca, NY 14850 *(The Living Bird Quarterly, Project FeederWatch)*

Long Point Bird Observatory, Box 160, Port Rowan, Ontario, Canada N0E 1M0

National Audubon Society, 700 Broadway, New York, NY 10003 *(Audubon, Audubon Field Notes, Migratory Songbird Action Kit)*

National Wildlife Federation (Backyard Wildlife Habitat Program), 1400 Sixteenth Street, NW, Washington, DC 20036-2266 *(National Wildlife, International Wildlife, Ranger Rick)*

Nature Society News, Purple Martin Junction, Griggsville, IL 62340

Sierra Club, 730 Polk Street, San Francisco, CA 94109 *(Sierra)*

World Wildlife Fund, 1250 Twenty-fourth Street, NW, Suite 200, Washington, DC 20037

· INDEX ·

A

Accipiter striatus, 66
Agelaius phoeniceus, 130
Anas platyrhynchos, 65
annual cycle, 149
anting, 199
antisocial behavior, 201
antisquirrel devices, 41
Archilochus colubris, 77

B

banded birds, 213
bathing, 165
bill types, 151
bird shelf, 58
birdwatching
  urban birdwatching, 23
  watching yard birds, 10–13
birdbaths, 50
birds of prey
  annual cycle, 149
  caching prey, 153
  preying on songbirds, 209
  see also American kestrel,
    eastern screech-owl, great
    horned owl, sharp-
    shinned hawk
blackbird
  red-winged, 17, 130, 160, 168,
    179, 188
  yellow-headed, 175
bluebird
  eastern, 28, 53, 103, 208
  mountain, 104
bobolink, 129
bobwhite, northern, 69
Bombycilla cedrorum, 110
bowl feeder, 39
bowl nest, 58
Branta canadensis, 64
brood parasites, 202
brood patch, 186
Bubo virginianus, 75
budgerigar, 21
bunting
  indigo, 121
  painted, 24, 122
  snow, 20
bushtit, 97

C

caching, 153
call notes, 179
Callipepla californica, 70
Calypte anna, 78
cardinal, northern, 118
Cardinalis cardinalis, 19, 118,
  146, 157, 190, 207
Carduelis
  flammea, 139
  pinus, 140
  tristis, 141
Carpodacus mexicanus, 137
Carpodacus purpureus, 136
catbird, gray, 51, 107, 155, 178
Certhia americana, 99
Ceryle alcyon, 80
Chaetura pelagica, 76
Charadrius vociferus, 71
chat, yellow-breasted, 115
chick-rearing, 188-91
  cleaning the nest, 189
  feeding the young, 188
  fledging, 190–91
  see also foster feeding, parasitic
    habits
chickadee, black-capped, 11, 16,
  19, 95, 151, 160, 179, 192
city birds, 22
cleaning the nest, 189
climbing, 161
Coccothraustes vespertinus, 142
Colaptes auratus, 84
Colinus virginianus, 69
Columba livia, 72
common visitors, 19
conservation
  banded birds, 213
  do birdfeeders help birds, 16
  lost migrants, 197
  the march of the suburbs, 14
  rescue, 212
  survival and mortality, 206–11
Corvus brachyrhynchos, 94
courtship, 180
courtship feeding, 181
cowbird, brown-headed, 133,
  202, 203
creeper, brown, 99, 151, 161
crossbill
  red, 138

white-winged, 151
crow, American, 94
curious behavior, 198–203
  acts of destruction, 201
  anting, 199
  attacking windows, 200
  foster feeding, 203
  mobbing, 201
  parasitic habits, 202
  stretching and yawning, 198
Cyanocitta
  cristata, 92
  stelleri, 91

D

dark-eyed junco, 18, 128, 194
dawn chorus, 177
Dendroica petechia, 114
destructive behavior, 201
displays, 174
Dolichonyx oryzivorus, 129
dove
  mourning, 73, 191
  rock, 72, 158
ducks, *see* mallard, sleep, urban
  bird-watching, wading and
  swimming
Dumetella carolinensis, 107

E

economical feeding, 152
eggs and incubation
  the color of eggs, 185
  egg-laying, 184
  hatching, 187
  incubation, 186
enclosed nestbox, 55

F

Falco sparverius, 67
feathers
  anting, 199
  bathing, 165
  molt, 167
  preening, 164
  sunbathing, 166
feeder fare, 42–49
  fruit, 46
  grains and seeds, 42–43

ACKNOWLEDGMENTS

Author's acknowledgments
I would like to thank, in particular, Gerry Bertrand and Simon Perkins of Massachusetts Audubon Society for their unstinting advice on the habits of backyard birds, and Arthur Brown for information on birdfeeder equipment. I am also very grateful to the following for hospitality: Doug and Barbara Flack, Don Hill, Cathy Yandell, the Schieffelin family, Gerry and Faith Bertrand, Joel Rosenbaum and Connie Drysdale, and Flo McBride. Everyone helped to make my stay in the United States extremely memorable.

Dorling Kindersley Ltd. would like to thank the following people for their help during the preparation of this book: Alison Anholt-White for coordinating the North American photography, Gerry Bertrand of Massachusetts Audubon Society for advice, and all who worked on the RSPB Birdfeeder Handbook.

Dorling Kindersley Inc. would like to thank the following people for all their help and advice: Dr. Susan R. Drennan, Dr. Stephen W. Kress, and Katherine Santone of the National Audubon Society, Deslie Lawrence, and Dr. Henri Ouellet, National Museum of Natural Sciences, Ottawa, Canada.

PHOTOGRAPHY

Abbreviations: t=top, c=center, b=bottom, l=left, r=right

Dorling Kindersley
Alison Anholt-White 8, 14bl, 91br **Martin Brigdale** 46tr **Jane Burton** 41tr, 72b **Peter Chadwick** 9, 61 **Alan Duns** 46tc **Steve Gorton** 34, 39, 40, 41cl, 41br, 42tr, 42cr, 42br, 43bl, 43tr, 43cr, 44br, 47bl, 49cl, 51br **Dave King** 25 **Maslowski Photo** 6bl, 7tr, 56bl, 67t, 69t, 69b, 73t, 76, 77b, 80b, 83t, 84b, 86t, 87t, 88t, 94tl, 97b, 99b, 100b, 101t, 101b, 102t, 102b, 103, 104b, 106b, 109b, 112b, 115t, 116t, 118t, 118b, 120t, 121t, 126t, 127t, 127b, 128t, 129t, 131b, 132t, 133b, 134t, 138t, 138b, 139t, 141l, 149, 151c, 154tr, 157tr, 161bl, 164bl, 171, 179bl, 195b, 197tr, 209b, 212 **Trevor Melton** 42bl **Graham Miller** 46cr **Kim Taylor** 4, 14br, 21br, 23tr, 27bl, 29tr, 29bl, 33br, 35, 36, 37, 38, 43tl, 43cl, 44cl, 44c, 44cr, 44bl, 45, 46tl, 46bl, 46bc, 46br, 47tl, 47c, 47bc, 47br, 50cr, 50bl, 51cl, 54cr, 55, 57, 58, 65t, 72r, 93tr, 100t; 110, 143tr, 145; 158bl, 178br,181tl, 205, 208br, 210t

Agencies and photographers
Allstock Kim Heacox 81t; Tim Fitzharris 129b **Animals, Animals** Margot Conte 11tr; Richard Kolnar 26; C.C. Lockwood 168; Leonard Lee Rue 191tl **Dr. Alan Beaumont** 12tr **Robert Burton** 31tr, 52tl **Bruce Coleman Inc.** Laura Riley 204 **Bruce Coleman Ltd.** B. and C. Calhoun 11tr; Robert Carr 33bl, 165bl; Jack Dermid 105b; Jeff Foott 17b, 49tr, 187b; Stephen Krasemann 160cr; Wayne Lankinen 18br, 20tr, 79t, 167tr, 175tr, 184cr, 196bl, 208tl; Scott Nielsen 23br, 167cl, 185tr; Charlie Ott 20cl; Andy Purcell 154br; Leonard Lee Rue 52br, 53tr, 134b; John Shaw 33tr, 160bl; Jeff Simon 180br; Kim Taylor 189b; Joseph Van Wormer 21tr, 172; Gunter Ziesler 153tr **Sharon Cummings** 68, 89t, 130t, 148b, 178tr, 178bl, 194cl, 209tl **Richard Day** 13, 19tr, 24, 109t, 130b, 185bl, 187tr **Clayton Fogle** 159tl **Frank Lane Picture Agency** Ron Austing 112t, 114b, 142t, 184bl; Ray F. Bird 190br; Hans Dieter Brand 83b; A. Christianssen 157b; Desmond Dugan 18bl; A.R. Hamblin 162tr; Peggy Heard 93b, 166cl; Daphne Kinzler 51bl; Karl Maslowski 151tr; Steve Maslowski 137b, 201tr; Roger Tidman 110b; B.S. Turner 143b; L. West 147bl; B.R. Young 199br **J.C. Fuller** 86b, 97t, 194br, 195cr **Russell C. Hansen** 78t, 82t, 92t, 95, 106t, 107t, 108t, 113t, **George Harrison** 2, 51cr, 60, 67b, 74bl **Imagery** Scott Nielsen 19bl, 53br, 64t, 71b, 75, 80t, 135t, 139b, 148tr, 151cl, 151cr, 151bl, 155bl, 183tr **Arthur Morris** 12br, 65b, 71t, 84t, 152, 155tr, 156, 161tr, 163bl, 172, 174tr, 177tr, 179tr, 201br **Natural History Photographic Agency** L. Campbell 163tr; R. J. Erwin 31br, 66b, 137t, 151bc, 188; Steve Krasemann 15bl, 16cr, 22, 89b, 193bl, 211t; W.S. Paton 94b; John Shaw 15tr, 161br, 162br; David Tomlinson 28tr; Helio Van Ingen 29tr **Oxford Scientific Films** Scott Camazine 203tr; Jack Dermid 19br, 81b, 197bl; Mark Hamblin 12cl; Leonard Lee Rue 192cr; Zig Leszczynski 199t; Colin Milkins 27tr; Stan Osolinski 88b, 144, 108b, 177br, 190bl, 191br, 198cl, 203bl; James H. Robinson 117b; Robert A. Tyrrell 48, 77t; Tom Ulrich 122t, 122b **Photo Researchers Inc.** Ron Austing 74r, 183bl; L. Bachman 125b; Nick Bergkessel 206; John Bova 82b, 185br. Ken Brate 73b, 126b; Scott Camazine 207br, 211br; Robert Carlyle 124b; Stephen Collins 150bl; Tim Davis 7br, 176; Joe DiStefano 78b, 213tr; Phil Dotson 117t; Bill Dyer 116b, 119b, 175b; R.J. Erwin 150br; Jan Robert Factor 186tr; James R. Fisher 196br; Sam Fried 165tr; Richard R. Hansen 202b; Hal Harrison 90b; Harold W. Hoffman 133t; Dr. William J. Jahoda 213cl; Steve Krasemann 142b; Leonard Lee Rue 56tr, 90t; Jeff Lepore 123b, 170; Charles W. Mann 124t; Thomas W. Martin 125t; Maslowski 115b, 147tr, 200b, 209tr; Tom McHugh 200tr; Anthony Mercieca 85b, 91t, 104t, 114t, 120b, 123t, 207bl, 141b; William H. Mullins 131t; Patti Murray 202tr; O. S. Pettingill 113b; William Ray 96b; Greg Scott 87b; Alvin E. Staffan 105t; Dan Sudia 99t; Joseph Van Wormer 128b; L. West 207tr **Leonard Lee Rue Jr.** 66tr **Ron Sanford** 32, 64b, 140b, 153br, 159br, 166cr, 180bl, 193cr **Greg Scott** 1, 10, 16bl, 17t, 23bl, 28tl, 30cr, 30bl, 52cl, 53tl, 92d, 98t, 98b, 107b, 121b, 135b, 140t, 146, 153cl, 169, 174br, 181br, 182cr, 182bl, 186bl, 189tr, 190tr, 192bl, 197 cr, 198cr, 203bl, 210br, 213bl **Hugh P. Smith** 3, 70t, 70b, 79b, 85t, 96t **D.C. Twichell** 119t **Vireo** S.J. Lang 49br; J.R. Woodward 136t